M000048659

GOD'S KINGDOM

GOD'S KINGDOM

FULFILLING GOD'S PLAN
FOR VICTORY

STEPHEN EVERETT

Destiny Image₀ Publishers, Inc.
P.O. Box 310
Shippensburg, PA 17257-0310

*"Speaking to the Purposes of God for This Generation
and for the Generations to Come"*

ISBN 0-7684-2274-4

For Worldwide Distribution
Printed in the U.S.A.

This book and all other Destiny Image, Revival Press, MercyPlace,
Fresh Bread, Destiny Image Fiction, and Treasure House books are available
at Christian bookstores and distributors worldwide.

1 2 3 4 5 6 7 8 9 10 / 09 08 07 06 05

For a U.S. bookstore nearest you, call
1-800-722-6774.

For more information on foreign distributors, call
717-532-3040.

Or reach us on the Internet:
www.destinyimage.com

Dedication

Dedicated to every minister, male and female, who heard the call and with courage ministered the word and life of the Kingdom of God as a present reality along with its wonderful future. I salute you for your boldness and passion to teach with clarity the message that Jesus Christ preached, taught, and demonstrated.

Acknowledgments

Of the three projects I have worked on thus far, this one has taken the longest to write. There are concepts in this book that will change all of us if followed carefully. Since 1975, God has been forging a Kingdom understanding in me. This book is the result of some of those endeavors. I have tried to harness a number of relevant experiences in order to speak a seasoned word to the current generation. It is with a prophetic mandate upon my life that I entrust these treasures to you.

To the Holy Spirit, my Teacher, who has carefully guided and instructed me in Kingdom understanding.

To Dr. Daniel Williams and the Present Truth Ministries family. May your prophetic encouragement and support be doubly rewarded.

A big thank you to Lisa Ott, and the editorial staff, who made very meaningful editorial suggestions in order for this project to become the product it is.

Endorsements

There is not a more vital subject to the understanding of the serious believer than that of the Kingdom of God. Stephen Everett, with eloquence and clarity, has taken what is often taught as "spooky" and "spiritual" and has made it both relevant and revelatory. From his opening statements in Chapter one that makes *"The Case for Man Being Special"* to the final chapter on *"Death to Disenfranchisement"*, Everett historically and scripturally explains with definition the current and future operation of the Kingdom of God, and thereby exposes the reader to an alternate society. It is my honor to recommend this book to every student of the purposes of God. I know your life and vision will be expanded.

Bishop David R. Huskins
Cedar Lake Christian Center
Fellowship of Vineyard Harvester Churches
Cedartown, Georgia

I consider Dr. Stephen Everett to be an exceptional prophet/apostle, author and friend. I have known Stephen and his wife and children since 1992. This is significant because I believe a person imparts who they are, not just what they write and preach. It has been my experience since knowing the Everetts that they walk the walk that they talk. Dr. Everett has exceptional prophetic revelation and insight into apostolic reformation and kingdom authority. He has the ability to skillfully reduce difficult information so the ordinary folks can comprehend extraordinary truth.

This new book has a steady rhythm that makes me think of the heartbeat of our Lord. It is lucid yet challenging to traditional religious concepts. Please open your spirit and your mind to the biblical truth Dr. Everett carefully develops line upon line and precept upon precept. I hear a clarion call on every page urging the church to grow up, embrace change and the Kingdom of God as a gallant new world.

Dr. Clarice Fluitt
CoPastor & CoFounder of Eagle's Nest World Prayer Center
Founder & President of Christian Evangelistic Outreach
& Lighthouse Mentoring School

God's Kingdom addresses the most important message of the Bible and provides a unique perspective of the value of man and God's great purpose and plan for him in His Kingdom. I believe this work by Stephen will inspire many to seek first the Kingdom again.

Dr. Myles Munroe
Bahamas Faith Ministries

Apostle Steve Everett's new book *God's Kingdom* captures the importance of one of the most significant subjects in the Bible. In his writings, Apostle Everett takes you on a journey back to God's original intent for mankind. He offers revelatory insights, concepts and strategies for Kingdom impact in our society. I highly recommend this book as an invaluable resource for leaders, churches, and all those who have a relentless passion to see God's Kingdom at work in the world today.

Bishop Levy H. Knox
Living Word Christian Center
Mobile, Alabama

Table of Contents

Preface

Father God is animated about a daring, adventurous plan conceived in the council of the Godhead many eons ago! It's an all-inclusive plan spanning the creation of all things unto the restoration of all things spoken by the prophets. Meticulously this plan is unfolding just as it was prearranged before the foundation of the cosmos. At the heart of it is liberation—liberation for all in the universe. If there's one thought that discernibly captures this plan in its entirety, it's called the Kingdom of God—a kingdom as real as David's, Solomon's, and the current United Kingdom. The Kingdom is a glorious vision of comprehensive transformation of individual lives, communities, and nations. God designed this Kingdom with the intent of producing a gallant new world.

Consider this: The Kingdom is *now manifest* but not fully *yet*. Jesus told stories that made it present, and yet, with a future materialization. Note these scriptural paradoxes about the Kingdom:

- The Kingdom is come (see Luke 11:20), yet shall come (see 2 Tim. 4:1).

- We have been translated into the Kingdom (see Col. 1:13), yet we shall enter into it through struggle (see Acts 14:22).

- We are heirs of the Kingdom (see James 2:5), yet it is the Father's good pleasure to give us the Kingdom (see Luke 12:32).

- We must seek the Kingdom (see Matt. 6:33), and if we continue to sin, we shall never inherit it, though it was given to us (see 1 Cor. 6:10; Gal. 5:21; Eph. 5:5).

- Though the Kingdom is within us (see Luke 17:21), we must strive to enter in (see Luke 13:24).

- Some are in the Kingdom now but will be cast out because of a life of disobedience (see Luke 13:28).

- We receive the Kingdom by faith, the faith of a simple child (see Mark 10:15).

- We enter the Kingdom through much tribulation (see Acts 14:22), which makes us worthy of the Kingdom (see 2 Thess. 1:4-5).[1]

After reading through these seeming inconsistencies, you may be scratching your head and saying, "What is the truth?" My reply: *All of the above!* Right now, the Kingdom doesn't have boundaries, specific countries, capital cities, and certain cultures—it's in the hearts of men. Like a stealthy, advancing army, it dispossesses one heart at a time of evil, resulting in ungodliness being overtaken. The Kingdom is a transcendent power that works its way like yeast into all the fabric of society. Before you know it, just as God planned, it will fill the whole lump called planet Earth.

God is currently in the transformation business, which will cause the Kingdom to fully come in the earth. His children are being transformed in their thinking and conformed to the image of Christ, who is the image of God. They're special to His heart, and they help to form the embassy of God in the earth. Looking at them in their current state wouldn't seem to indicate this. However incomprehensible this may seem, our frail, fragile human condition doesn't tarnish God's bona fide plan for His children. We may look upon ourselves as rustic, while He views us as royalty; we think human, He sees holy; we see identity crisis, He sees total acceptance in Christ. By calling us *kings* and *priests,* He consolidates the secular and the sacred.

The concept for this book entered my heart shortly after I completed my previous book, *The Sound That Changed Everything.* Coupled with that, Dr. Kelley Varner requested that I minister as the plenary speaker during the annual summer convention, June 2003. With the theme being *Awake O'Zion,* I sought the Lord for fresh revelation. The Holy Spirit prompted me to study the Book of Exodus. I agreed this was a reasonable request since Moses did beseech God to show him His glory. It didn't take long before I recognized why the Holy Spirit had drawn my attention to this Book. Exodus became a new Book to me with fresh insights. It was quite inspiring to see the nation of Israel delivered from slavery and prepared to become a Kingdom nation. If I could summarize my findings in one statement, it would read as thus: *Beyond all the corruption, complaining, chaos, and challenges, Father God built a people and a house for His glory*! Our Lord demonstrated what He could accomplish through His indescribable, matchless grace. Taking an inorganic, unorganized mass of slaves, He turned them into a people for His name's sake.

Can you imagine a world with no covetousness, no violence, no theft, no prejudice or injustice—just one of agape love? It would be a world in which human beings understand their original purpose. If I look down the prophetic tunnel of divine purposes, it's not so difficult to envision! At the end of the tunnel lies a dream almost beyond human perception, something so strange and illogical to the natural mind. Even Dr. Martin Luther King Jr., a modern prophet, envisioned such a world in his historical *I Have A Dream* speech, given in 1963. In this book, such a world is *an alternate society,* a gallant new world. Alternates are replacements selected just in case the originals don't necessarily pan out. Adam, God's original idea, missed the mark (see Gen. 3). Father God immediately spoke of His alternate idea called the *seed of the woman,* which became the chief prophetic asset throughout all Old Covenant history. No matter the time frame, one must notice how assiduous God was in birthing this idea. This thought finds its highest ideal in the person of Jesus Christ.

In both the Old and New Testaments, Father God develops an alternate society using this principle. The Old Testament is a painstaking precursor to the lavish outpouring of the rhythms of God's grace in the New Testament. It is a panorama of an individual and a corporate story; it's a journey, a learning process. It's the development of God's people from divine conception into an orderly society. It's my story; it's your story; it's every believer's story! Consistently, it's the parallel account of both the nation of Israel and the Church—one of achievements and failures, times of celebration and times of deep consternation of the soul. It comprises the human experience as we seek to manifest our true identity as a holy nation, a kingdom of priests, and a peculiar people.

The apostle Paul stated: "[Jesus] *gave Himself for our sins that He might deliver us from this present evil age, according to the will of our God and Father*" (Gal. 1:4). Although we live in this world, we are not of this world system. We have been delivered by His grace! That makes us an alternate society, a new creation in the midst of society at large. Webster II defines *alternate* as "in place of another."[2] Jesus Christ opened the door for God to have this type of community in His death, burial, and resurrection. Prior to His appearing, all that men could offer God was carnal strivings, moral efforts, and scrupulous keeping of commands. Human behavior was controlled by divine impositions that prevented men from obliterating themselves. Unfortunately, from time to time, rebellious tyrants arose, nearly bringing humanity to the brink of disaster. Father God, however, had a secure plan regardless of their evil plots. His plan also surpassed the best of all humanitarian efforts attempting to offset diabolical dreams of tyrants. Jesus Christ, as the last Adam, took all that every man had done and will do, and with one stroke of grace nullified the old and validated a new order. He ended the fleshly labor, the frenzied attempts to find God, and paved a fresh path for us to discover the undisclosed side of God.

Each chapter deals with a specific aspect of our journey. It all begins with a recognition that Father God, before time and ages, decided to create and form a vast family in the earth. This family would consist of men in His image, totally endeared to His heart—a special people. As far as the initial development of this family from a messianic standpoint, it began as God apprehended Abraham. Out of his call and loins, the nation of Israel evolved as the legal messianic line. After giving them an inheritance, God prearranged for his family to be a priestly/agrarian society, teaching them principles of sacrifice, seed, and harvest. They observed three annual feasts to instruct them in these principles. However, I have discovered that the Old Covenant could not totally produce this family; in fact, it provided only a vine and a seed man. From the revelation of God's Word, the ultimate seed man is Jesus Christ (see Rom. 10:4; John 12:24). Father God planted Him into the soil of human experience and reaped a brand-new man.

We are yet to understand all the truths associated with the new man. In God's mind, the new man, who is the in-Christ man, is unique. Though corporate, he is the original intention of Father God's heart. Man, created in the image of God and re-created in the image of Christ, is the by-product of the sufficiency of grace. The new man is a blessed man! The apostle Paul said, "[Father God] *predestined us to the adoption as sons by Jesus Christ to Himself, according to the good pleasure of His will*" (Eph. 1:5). It is God's perfect will for us to be His children. Sons reflect their father and aren't devoid of the family's DNA, destiny, or inheritance. The Message says, "It's in Christ that we find out who we are and what we are living for. Long before we first heard of Christ and got our hopes up, He had his eye on us, had designs on us for glorious living, part of the overall purpose He is working out in everything on planet earth" (Eph. 1:9-10). Grace, who is a teacher, must instruct us concerning this purpose and legacy. The administration of the law gave us mixture, and essentially short-circuited any opportunity to enter fully into our inheritance in Christ. If this book accomplishes nothing else, it is my hope that each son will discover the revelation concerning God's view of him; and cast off any rust of false convictions denying the sanctity of truth in God's Word.

Because we are special, God has no intentions of hoodwinking us or dangling some carrot of opportunity before us with no possible fulfillment. Though omnipotent, He distances Himself from such methodology. With pristine clarity, the Scriptures reveal the

God-ordained purpose of the human race, which is one of dominion on earth and participating in His life. It actually pleases the Lord to deal kindly with us—to woo us—to refresh and reform His sons and daughters because of this purpose. The nation of Israel is one of the first recipients nationally of such amazing grace. Israel's deliverance from Egyptian bondage occurred during a time of refreshing; more perfectly, it was a time when God's dream reformed itself in Abraham's seed. God sent an old man, Moses, with a message of grace and authority that said, *"It's time to rediscover My purpose for you!"* They eventually rallied around the message. God's grace propelled them into seasons of new beginnings. God was now actively delivering His son from a covenantal standpoint.

The heavenly Father trumpets the same message in the Church today. We must awaken out of our incorrigible, hopeless patterns of religious practices sterile of Kingdom effectiveness. God's times of refreshing are upon us, purposed to unlock, reposition, and reset us. Let's breathe deeply the freshness of God's presence, ingest His life, and live again. Refreshing is a reprieve, an antecedent to full freedom. Now, beware of something: There's a great and terrible process that's implemented once we are refreshed. I call it Kingdom education—a school for sovereign subjects. It's great when we read the seasons of God accurately—terrible when we don't. God's sovereignty and grace are the reasons we prevail. His intentions aren't to clobber us into submission; they're only to bring us into a place of transformation. If we attempt to duck the process, we'll miss the enormous provision of God's grace that delivers us, converts us, and conforms us into the image of Jesus Christ.

This book will remind you of the school of the Holy Spirit you've been in since the time of your new birth. Grace delivered us from our bondage, grace keeps us, and grace instructs us. The apostle Paul said, *"For the grace of God that brings salvation has appeared to all men, teaching us that, denying ungodliness and worldly lusts, we should live soberly, righteously, and godly in the present age, looking for the blessed hope and glorious appearing of our great God and Savior Jesus Christ"* (Titus 2:11-13). Grace radiates the light of God and floods our souls with the warmth of unconditional love. There's also a practical, prophetic edge to the sword grace wields: We live out of the life of God, which over-comes the mortality of Adam's death-riddled flesh. Grace accentuates God's optimism about mankind, thus de-emphasizing and swallow-ing human propensity for weakness. The powerful message of grace, when we clearly perceive it, magnifies divine strength in the midst of human fallibility. Grace provides everything we need to reconnect with Almighty God without feelings of apprehension or guilt. Grace says, *"God can, even when we can't!"*

The best way to use this book is to study and meditate on one chapter at a time. Chew and re-chew these potent truths by the spirit of revelation. Don't read it too quickly! Catch all the sayings behind what is said, all the different nuances of truth. It's not a new message necessarily; it's the same Bible message spoken in a 21st-century para-digm for people who were born for such a time as this. Journey with me as we proceed from the joy of initial deliverance to the vibrancy of citizenship in an alternate society. Sandwiched in between are all the divine ideals and experiences constructing us into a rich, exciting soci-ety of Kingdom citizens. With great foresight, Father God provides purpose, vision, foundations, and a crystal-clear justice system based upon precepts of truth. In the New Covenant, justice finds its true identity in the person of Jesus and the things He taught. Jesus pro-vides a purview of an order that supersedes anything the Old Covenant had postulated.

It took an iron will of manufactured love to meet the stringent demands of the law—especially, when a man's nature hadn't been converted. The children of Israel placed themselves into a rigid, inflexible position by saying they would keep the Lord's commands. Of course an omniscient God knew they wouldn't! I thank God over and over that what He's doing today isn't predicated entirely upon the Church possessing an iron will of obedience with sterling success stories. It's high time to completely leave the massacre of Genesis 3 and zealously pursue the naked, simple fellowship of God's grace. Humanity's musty, moldy ways can't twist God's intentions. His pru-dent purposes advance methodically from one generation to the next. Grace is the rudder that guides this ship; and love is the engine that powers it. Apart from God's grace, we can be or do nothing. May we move beyond our human stumbling, mollycoddling our weaknesses, and enter into the ubiquitous conquest of God's grace. Let's behold the action of vigorous love and infinite grace in developing *a gallant new world.*

Stephen Everett, Ph. D.

ENDNOTES

1. These thoughts were drawn from *Theological Dictionary of the New Testament,* by Geoffrey W. Bromiley, (Grand Rapids, MI: William B. Eerdmans Publishing Company, 1985), 101.

2. Webster's II New College Dictionary, Riverside University Dictionary (New York: Houghton Mifflin Company, 1995), 33.

Foreword

I have known Stephen Everett for over 20 years and have had the privilege of watching him grow into maturity in relationship to God and the Body of Christ. Now, with the voice of an apostolic father, he calls out to the Church with clarity and wisdom for a realignment of vision and a reformation of character that the principles of the Kingdom of God might be manifested in the earth.

God's Kingdom is one of the most profound and balanced writings of the move and expression of God that I have read within the last 25 years. Its boldness to deal with the issues of the individual believer as well as the Church as they grow up into Him offers us a clear perspective on the struggles as well as the gems of our faith. It is rare to encounter a book with such depth of compassion and insight into the issues of practical growth and understanding. It is a seasoned manual just in time to instruct the Body of Christ about the growing revelation of the Kingdom of God that is sweeping the world's consciousness.

Drawing from rich personal experience, Stephen Everett moves beyond the hype that often clouds the gospel's message in this time and places us solidly on the foundation of spiritual truth. Seeking to know the will and face of God, Stephen constantly taps into Christ's immeasurable grace as he teaches us of a God-centered rather than man-centered gospel. He encourages and inspires us to move beyond a self-centered culture so prevalent in the world and into a culture that sacrificially embodies the Christ, having as its center the will and purpose of God, so that as believers, we can live an alternate way of life that produces a gallant new world.

Dr. Everett exposes the inner and hidden instability of a Christian consciousness filled with issues of duality that have frozen the Church in time and caused Christianity to appear weak and immature and redirects us to accept and believe our true identity in Christ. He explodes the myth of satan's continuing power and equality and sheds light through Scripture and experience on the path of maturity with balance, grace, and love. He moves us beyond the showers of refreshing and revival and awakens us to true reformation, challenging us to receive the full inheritance available to us as sons in the Kingdom of God as a present and *now* opportunity to be clothed in glory.

Through Holy Spirit inspiration, Dr. Everett shakes our church model and calls us to live in the truth and reality of Kingdom principles even as Jesus walked them. In the world, torn by violence, injustice, social, economic and racial inequalities, *God's Kingdom* stands as a beacon of hope and agape love to all who have an ear to hear. Truth is layered within its sentences, pearls of wisdom within its observations, and humility in its conclusions. A must-read for those who seek a deeper walk and a deeper life with God, and who desire to embrace their full inheritance in God.

Pastor Kathy O'Keefe, Th.D.
Kingdom Life Ministries
Roanoke, Virginia

sTArt Here

1

The Case for a Special People

One of the foremost distinctions in all of Bible history is that the nation of Israel was called God's special people. What made them so special? It could be summed up in one word—grace!

This prolific story begins with one of the indisputable calls of God recorded in the Scriptures. The Lord called Abram out of Ur, which would be some place in modern southern Iraq. Known as the land of Shinar and the land of the Chaldeans, it was one of the great civilizations of the ancient world. Some writers in antiquity called Babylon the breadbasket of the world and the cradle of civilization. It was a culture polluted with idolatry and a state of limitless indulgences in human vices. The New Testament presents it as a model of pantheism formed from the synthesis of diverse religious beliefs. Babylon was the ultimate contrast to what the Kingdom of God represents.

Comparing other biblical accounts of God calling men, Abram's call was the first time the Lord chose to dislodge a man from his homeland in order to work out His purposes in his life. For example, Enoch, Methuselah, and Noah were very important to the generational purposes of God, but not one of them was asked to leave his home. Concerning Abram, the Lord took someone of no distinction, with no descendants, and turned him into a holy nation. It would be speculative and improbable to think he would have ever changed apart from the call of God. The grace of God created a new man, Abraham, out of the man called from the darkness of Ur, of the Chaldees, into the glorious light of fresh beginnings. This light did not stop shining until Abraham's descendants became a nation—the nation of Israel. Creation's Messiah would come out of this nation.

Many centuries later, the apostle Paul, a descendant of Abraham, in a moment of reflection, described Israel's uniqueness in this fashion: "*Who are Israelites, to whom pertain the adoption, the glory, the covenants, the giving of the law, the service of God, and the promises; of whom are the fathers and from whom, according to the flesh, Christ came, who is over all, the eternally blessed God. Amen*" (Rom. 9:4-5). This is a very thrilling, captivating narrative as it unfolds in the Old Testament. One cannot read it without becoming impressed with the sovereign power of Almighty God. God developed and preserved them with one miracle after another. Spiritually, morally, and socially, Israel was unlike any other nation. Their illustrious, unsurpassed legacy includes these couplets: the patriarchs and the prophets, the Tabernacle and the Temple, the priesthood and the Feasts of the Lord, their royalty and their covenants, etc. No one in the beginning could have imagined this kind of heritage. Israel, as a nation, wasn't favored because of merit; the Lord's acceptance of her was by divine predetermination. Ultimately, after being incarcerated by a divine plan, God took a group of disorganized slaves and turned them into the toast of nations. Listen to the words of Moses, the great shepherd and statesman:

> *For you are a holy people to the Lord your God; the Lord your God has chosen you to be a people for Himself, a special treasure above all the peoples on the face of the earth. The Lord did not set His love on you nor choose you because you were more in number than any other people, for you were the least of all peoples; but because the Lord loves you, and because He would keep the oath which He swore to your fathers, the Lord has brought you out with a mighty hand, and redeemed you from the house of bondage, from the hand of Pharaoh king of Egypt* (Deuteronomy 7:6-8).

His message is quite evident: You are special because someone else had a special relationship with your heavenly Father. Abraham,

Isaac, and Jacob secured the future of their people through their obedience and proper responses to God's heart.

Other writers in the New Testament often compared Israel and the Church. In his zest for apostolic accuracy, the apostle Peter applied something God had stated about the nation of Israel to the new Israel of God —the Church.

> *But you are the ones chosen by God, chosen for the high calling of priestly work, chosen to be a holy people, God's instruments to do His work and speak out for Him, to tell others of the night-and-day difference He made for you—from nothing to something, from rejected to accepted* (1 Peter 2:9-10 The Message). *Sfore*

starts → Because of Kingdom advancement, the Church has become Abraham's seed (see Gal. 3–4), spiritual Israel (see Rom. 2:28-29), the true circumcision (see Phil. 3:3), the holy nation (see Matt. 21:42-43), and the New Jerusalem (see Heb. 12:22-24; Rev. 21:9-11). Through the means of His cross, Jesus laid the axe to the old tree and chopped it down to its foundation. Including branches of the old tree, and grafting in new branches, He formed a new tree with a different covenant.

The Church, based upon apostolic understanding, is a special, called-out people. She boasts a rich, and at times, dramatic history. Although she tallies hundreds of millions today, it wasn't always that way. Her beginning, like the nation of Israel's, originated with a very small number of ordinary people with an extraordinary call. In stark contrast to other nations, the Church probably appeared to be insignificant because of a lack of sophistication. She didn't fit into the current culture, and lacked its specific tastes. Her education was one by the Holy Spirit, rather than the sages of the times.

God's love, grace, and purpose are the reasons for her existence. The Church's spiritual account consists of the adoption, acceptance, redemption, forgiveness, wisdom, inheritance, the seal of the Holy Spirit, life, grace, and citizenship—briefly, every spiritual blessing. (See Ephesians 1:3-14.) From this list, the Church and natural Israel are in many ways alike; there's continuity, although they are not coterminous. Natural Israel is Abraham's seed that speaks to the sands of the seashore—an earthly seed; whereas spiritual Israel, the Church, speaks to the stars of Heaven—a spiritual seed. (See Genesis 22:17.) The natural is always first, and then the spiritual by divine principle. *"Physical life comes first, then spiritual—a firm base shaped from the earth, a final completion coming out of heaven"* (see 1 Corinthians 15:46 The Message). God has created something very new in the Church. Now, she is the standard of what it means to be called a chosen people.

MAN IS SPECIAL

If we travel completely back into antiquity, the fundamental argument for a special people begins with one man, who was the seed of all men. That man was Adam, the genesis man. Created in the image of God, he was the visibility and the original intention of the Creator's heart. He distorted the image through disobedience and eventually gave way to Noah, who became the preserved seed of the old generation, and the new seed of a new genesis. Abraham succeeded Noah in becoming the seed man and progenitor of the Messiah. Finally, the Messiah called Himself a seed corn, out of which came an abundant harvest—a new creation. In each case, the heavenly Father's purpose was to communicate the seed principle. Although every other part of the material creation had its seed principle, nothing was quite like the man. God stamped the man with His image and likeness, and allowed him to become the specific amalgamation of the human and the divine.

Man is special! There is no doubt about it! Grace, mercy, and God's loving-kindness affirm this wonderful truth. Great thinkers have dialogued, disputed, defended, and debated this thought for centuries. The pondering psalmist in a moment of prophetic wonder asked, *"What is man that You are mindful of him, and the son of man that You visit him?"* (Ps. 8:4), indicating, perhaps, there is something special about man. Conversely, the words of Ecclesiastes' wise sage do not suggest anything special about man. In fact, King Solomon gave us a contrary view of man by saying, "All is vanity" (Eccles. 1:2)! "All" includes man. Is man just vanity, or emptiness? On another occasion, the psalmist said, "*Certainly every man at his best state is but vapor*" (Ps. 39:5 KJV). Is man just vapor, or something insubstantial and fleeting?

Bildad, in the Book of Job, during a scathing attack on Job's character, had some less than flattering remarks about man. His position and state of mind made it impossible for him to discern correctly. It is most difficult to get a proper perspective when you're on the ash heap of despair, attempting to persuade someone of their spiritual ineptitude, and yet blinded by your own. He compared man to a "*a maggot and a worm*" (see Job 25:5-6). What would lead any person to believe man is just some soft-bodied larva found in decaying matter? Others in the Old Covenant adopted this same point of view on various occasions (see Ps. 22:6; Isa. 41:14). This very idea has served as a parasitic anomaly. Using man as a host, it has hijacked him from his rich nobility and elevated position in the scheme of God's purposes.

Perhaps most logical people on this planet today will say, "I will tell you who man is! Man is who I am, or who I think I am!" This reply sounds reasonable. The psalmist said man is wonderfully made, which contradicts the theories of evolution (see Ps. 139:13-16). A basic course in biology, especially since the discovery of DNA in 1953, reveals how complex man really is. It required a master strategist to build him. Now, 50 years later, we have the human genome, which is composed of about three billion pairs of DNA chemicals within 24 chromosomes. There are over ten trillion cells within the human body. Each cell is filled with intelligence and has the ability to communicate with each other. They have memory and can transfer information in sequences that can cause the body and mind to manifest in various manners. Obviously, there was a mastermind involved in the creation of man. If we will go back and examine the truth inside the crust of the original question, something in us will be emancipated. Somewhere buried within the spirit of man is the answer to "*What is man?*" There is a hidden ladder, a template of information untapped that only the Spirit of God can make real to us.

Various academic disciplines have taken a shot at answering this question, "*What is man?*" Sociology says man is society and institutions. Anthropology will tell you man is defined by behaviors resulting from physical, social, and cultural developments. Biology attempts to define man from the processes of structure, functioning, growth, origin, evolution, and distribution of living organisms. Psychology approaches man from the realm of mind and emotions. After reading these approaches, have you settled on a definition? Alternatively, is the answer any clearer? *"What is man?"* After their probing analyses, scholars decipher information only about the natural man and his soul without subsidizing it with a God-consciousness and a Christ-centered relationship. Natural reasoning is tenuous, leaving academia in a state of wonder and confusion.

In his musings, the renowned evangelist C.H. Spurgeon said, "Well might the psalmist wonder at the singular exaltation of man in the scale of being, when he marked his utter nothingness in comparison with the starry universe."[1] Considering all the old and newly discovered galaxies, constellations, and solar systems in the universe, some of them having much larger stars than our sun, *"What is man?"* When the universe has been expanding at the speed of light since God spoke it into existence, *"What is man?"* If we used the largeness of the universe as our point of reference, the light years it requires to go from one star to another, man is like the atom that can't be seen with the naked eye.

Although this probing question was asked centuries before Christ first appeared in the flesh, the answer is not so complex. Place your ear to the open door of the heavens and listen intently to the whisper of infinity. With bated breath, God lovingly responds, *"Man, male and female, is My visible image—the seen form of Me the Unseen—the one chosen to localize Me everywhere—the object of My unconditional love!"* Wow! When the mind of an omniscient God first conceived man, when there existed nothing, His thoughts were fixed immediately and became nonnegotiable. Man is specifically created to be God's tangible image, the one who would commune with Him and participate in His life! Man would provide God an earth-suit as God manifested the powers and characteristics of His invisible Kingdom on earth.

Athanasius, the fourth-century apologist, made critical statements about man being in the image of God. Eastern Christianity apparently grasped certain understandings that Western Christianity politely tiptoed around. A very important quotation from his writings substantiates that men of God in every century understood the importance of man's identity and purpose. He writes:

> We are made in the likeness of God. But in course of time that image has become obscured, like a face on a very old portrait, dimmed with dust and dirt.
>
> When a portrait is spoiled, the only way to renew it is for the subject to come back to the studio and sit for the artist all over again. That is why Christ came—to make it possible for the divine image in man to be recreated. We were made in God's likeness; we are remade in the likeness of his Son.
>
> To bring about this re-creation, Christ still comes to men and lives among them. In a special way he comes to his Church, his body, to show us what the image of God is really like.
>
> What a responsibility the Church has, to be Christ's body, showing him to those who are unwilling or unable to see him in providence, or in creation! Through the Word of God lived out in the Body of Christ they can come to the Father, and themselves be made again in the likeness of God.[2]

It appears Athanasius received knowledge few men grasped. Also, from other writings, several scholars and authors held the same view of man's participation in the life of God. Men such as St. Irenaeus of Lyons, St. Augustine, St. Maximos the Confessor, and C.S. Lewis believed this was the natural culmination of our life in Christ. This must be understood and practiced by men who have had the death-blow of the cross, selfless humility, worked into their lives; otherwise, men will rise up and pervert this truth just as Adam did in the beginning. Note this quote from G.I. Mantzaridis of the University of Thessaloniki concerning the work of elevation as God's greatest gift to man and the ultimate goal of true sons of God:

> It is that which from the beginning has constituted the innermost longing of man's existence. Adam, in attempting to appropriate it by transgressing God's command, failed, and in

place of deification, met with corruption and death. The love of God, however, through His Son's incarnation, restored to man the possibility of deification: Adam of old was deceived: wanting to be God he failed to be God. God becomes man, so that He may make Adam god.[3]

It is very important to understand the reasoning behind such seemingly strong language. Some brethren would consider such a statement blasphemous and shameful because the created is attempting equality with the Creator. It is exactly the opposite: God, the Creator, initiated the joining of the human and the divine. His theanthropic actions allow men to have this great anticipation of transformation. God's great heart of love motivated Him to share Himself with man in this manner. Being neither misguided nor heretical, there is great truth in this statement when understood from the premise of divine perspective or original intention. If we look at this from the vantage point of God's heart, it is possible, whereas, from a human, selfish view, it becomes corrupt. Father God established a law in Genesis that says that every seed will reproduce after its own kind (see Gen. 1:11-12). Our natural birth was because of the seed carried by our natural fathers. Why weren't we born monkeys, elephants, or dogs? Because we are of human seed. Human beings can only beget human beings! Therefore, when the apostle Peter said that we were born again of incorruptible seed, the Word of God, he was stating that God was producing His own kind. Only the seed of God can reproduce the offspring of God. There are several witnesses in the Scriptures that confirm this truth.

Having been born again, not of corruptible seed but incorruptible, through the word of God which lives and abides forever (1 Peter 1:23).

Of His own will He brought us forth by the word of truth, that we might be a kind of firstfruits of His creatures (James 1:18).

For both He who sanctifies and those who are being sanctified are all of one, for which reason He is not ashamed to call them brethren (Hebrews 2:11).

*Since the One who saves and those who are saved have a common origin, Jesus doesn't hesitate to treat them as family (*Hebrews 2:11 The Message*).*

*For in Him we live and move and have our being, as also some of your own poets have said, "For we are also His offspring." Therefore, since we are the offspring of God, we ought not to think that the Divine Nature is like gold or silver or stone, something shaped by art and man's devising (*Acts 17:28-29*).*

Regardless to whether one would use language this strong or not, there's much in Mantzaridis' quote to ponder. Just think for a moment: Mankind, and no other created being, is God's identifiable image in the earth. Man is the image-bearer, just as the coin has been an image-bearer of emperors, kings, presidents, and other historical figures! God is mindful of man, or holds him constantly in His remembrance. In a beautiful thought about memory, Samuel Johnson said: "The true art of memory is the art of attention."[4] God's vast, infinite mind is full of thoughts about man—His attention is on us! If God remotely had a weakness, this would be it (see 1 Cor. 1:25). Nothing God has created has the potential to excite Him, hold His attention, or disappoint Him like man. This doesn't mean God has any illusions about man because you can't be eternally sovereign and surprised at the same time. Man was crowned with glory and honor and given dominion over the works of God's hands. This assignment and subsequent responsibility qualifies him to be special beyond all other created beings or things.

Theology, philosophy, and history leave the psalmist's query unanswered until the appearing of our Lord Jesus Christ. The writer of the epistle to the Hebrews, prompted by apostolic accuracy and the preponderance of undeniable evidence, puts all things in proper perspective. He said, "'*What is man that You are mindful of him, or the son of man that You take care of him?... You have put all things in subjection under his feet.' For in that He put all in subjection under him, He left nothing that is not put under him. But now we do not yet see all things put under him. **But we see Jesus**, who was made a little lower than the angels, for the suffering of death crowned with glory and honor, that He, by the* *grace of God, might taste death for everyone"* (Hebrews 2:6,8-9, emphasis added). When we see man, we must see Jesus! He was the last Adam, therefore the end of that order, actually the end of a nightmare.

David Huskins, a colleague, did an extraordinary job illustrating this truth at his summer convention in July 2002. If there were a prevailing theme in those meetings, it would have been this: *We'd better take another long look at the grace of God.* In a dramatization of the grace of God, Jesus Christ, the last Adam was cast as every man— MR. ALLMEN! Jesus withstood a host of accusers and was able to satisfy every legal claim they presented. His obedience made our heavenly Father a happy Daddy, a blessed God (see 1 Tim. 1:11). He reinstated mankind's uniqueness and resurrected God's image out of the rubble of human deprivation. Man's consciousness of being special, his moment to recover his true self, was rightfully renewed in Christ. In this recovery, man would fulfill the ultimate intention of Almighty God.

Twenty-six years ago I experienced one of the most exhilarating delights a man could experience—my wife gave birth. I took my place among the fraternity of proud first-time fathers. Shortly afterward, one of the nurses held my firstborn child in the nursery window so I could get my first glimpse of her. After so much anticipation, it was difficult to pinpoint any one of the vast arrays of emotions I felt at that moment; however, it seems I felt all of them at once. I could have wept and laughed in tandem, probably danced and pondered simultaneously. I was standing there mesmerized in absolute astonishment. Temporarily forgotten was the long, arduous labor my wife had just endured only to be shortly reminded of it by the clamps and stitches of a caesarean section. We now had a healthy, crying baby girl, whom I thought mirrored me exactly. (Of course, all proud fathers think this way.) For the first time, I really knew experientially the true exuberance of parenthood. Secondly, the gateway opened to comprehend what it must have meant to our Father God to have a son in His image.

God has granted the privilege of seeing my own image as a father uniquely expressed twice. Our children, Natalie and Stephen, answered an extraordinary yearning to extend my life into another generation, thus having a multigenerational effect. Their birth meant that the good intentions of God had provided our family a future and a hope. I desperately hanker for them to know just how special they were and are. My personal way to endear them, because words are of particular weight in the formative years, was by calling Natalie, "Daddy's baby," and Stephen, "Daddy's boy." We also gave them a foundation by providing shelter, safety, security, significance, and a sense of self-worth. These validated their significance to our family.

Although our children are now young adults, my heart still pulsates with enthusiasm about their uniqueness and thrilling future in the Kingdom of God. I love them unconditionally and sacrificially. These qualities came directly from the fatherhood of God, who loves the entire creation that way. Not even challenging teen years, requiring the firmness of parental discipline at times, diminished my love. The reason they are special is not based on their performance—it is because of who they are! They are a part of who I am. They will continue to be special and the joy of life, even after their children are born. If I can feel this way about two children, one may easily discern God's position for His entire creation. Red men, yellow men, black men and white men are all precious in His sight.

The crux of the matter is that one of the two great dynamics in man's statement of purpose is to produce descendants like him. The other is to *have dominion,* which is more fully expressed with an abundance of descendants. God will always take a man and produce a nation. If we look deep enough, one acorn always has a grove of oak trees inside it. With that as a principle, our children constitute the immediate extensions of the Everett grove. The Bible establishes this principle repeatedly. God chose Abraham to be the legal line of the messianic purpose. He became many through a process of time. In the New Covenant, Abraham's seed, Christ, became many from the germ of life that was in Him—beginning on the Day of Pentecost. Each man became a special people. Special people are called to make manifest the Lord of glory and the difference He makes.

DEFINITION OF *SPECIAL*

Prior to our discussion of the technical definitions of *special*, it will be important to forsake some of the modern, trendy definitions that have evolved through time. They almost cast a disapproving tone. The King James translators called the word *special* "peculiar." This is not "peculiar" as though we are some strange phenomenon with alien tendencies from another world. Nor does it imply the believer has a monopoly on being different, unique, eccentric, unusual, or exclusive. All of these are words synonymous with the modern concepts of "peculiar." It is better understood by the original meaning of the word.

A word history reveals that the sense of *odd* for "peculiar" has developed since the word was borrowed into the English language, and it is possible to reconstruct its original meaning. Peculiar is derived from the Latin *peculiaris*, which originally meant, "pertaining to private property" but developed the extended sense of "belonging to oneself alone."[5] It carried the idea that the chosen one for the married man was more than enough. The Middle English word was used with the sense of the Latin *peculiaris*. During the 17th century, when the King James translation occurred, *peculiar* applied to private personal property as distinguished from what is owned in common.[6]

When the heavenly Father labeled believers as "peculiar," He was speaking of *His* ownership rights. The Hebrew and Greek definitions used in the Strong's Concordance both testify to this truth. They maintain that we have been placed into a superlative position in Christ. In the Old Testament, *peculiar* carries the meaning "wealth as closely shut up, a jewel, peculiar treasure, proper good and special."[7] It varies little in the New Testament, meaning, "*being beyond usual.*" God spoke of the Old Covenant nation Israel in this distinct manner on five different occasions (see Exod. 19:5; Deut. 7:6; Deut. 14:2; Deut. 26:18; Ps. 135:4). Please note that three of these were in the Book of Deuteronomy. The Exodus generation primarily had the wrong attitude and missed God's desire completely. With much at stake, God reinforced this message in their progeny. The Scripture says, "By the mouth of two or three witnesses every word shall be established" (2 Cor. 13:1; see also Deut. 19:15; Matt. 18:16).

The Church is called "special" on two occasions (see Titus 2:14; 1 Pet. 2:9). Having a pure revelation of God's grace, Paul, the apostle, concluded the reason we are special is that God redeemed us from every lawless deed and purified us unto Himself. Not only through creation, but also through redemption we are God's personal property. The price paid at the redemptive moment insures the redeemer the rights of purchase.

Webster defines *property* as "something tangible or intangible to which the owner holds legal title."[8] As much as we value individual freedom and human rights in the Western world, it's amazing that in the Kingdom of God you legally get one right: the right to be wholly the Lord's. Church leaders must emphasize to the modern church the same apostolic sentiment of Paul: *We are bought at a price* (see 1 Cor. 6:20; 7:23). While our ex-taskmasters, sin and death, unmercifully paraded us on the open market of this slavish, worldly system, a wonderful thing happened. Jesus divested Himself of glory, walked as one of us, and then became the highest bidder for our lives. He fulfilled the role of creation's kinsman-redeemer, meaning He was one of us, and yet, He was able to become the necessary price to purchase us. Now we must not bite the hand of the One who gave His life to redeem us.

ISRAEL AND THE CHURCH'S FAILURE

The nation of Israel did not grasp what God was saying to her in this thought: *You are a special treasure*; and the Church has not fully either. Anytime humans fail to grasp God's idea about a thing, the outcome of our expectation will not be what God intended. In many ways, we still practice ownership of ourselves and have failed in our responsibility to totally submit to God's idea. Both have played the harlot with many idolatrous lovers and have produced Ishmaels aplenty, which are unacceptable for the purposes of God. In many ways, the nation of Israel and the Church are micro pictures of the whole creation. The plausibility of being special has not plugged the empty expanse in creation's accumulative heart. This has led to much bondage rather than freedom—a freedom that comes from the revelation of knowing you are God's featured attraction.

The immediate impact of this is many of God's children have wounded spirits, toxic psyches, and ravaged physical bodies. Many are robbed of their health with continuous anxiety attacks, fretfulness, no peace, and manipulated by the spirit of fear. The whole man is affected—spirit, soul, and body. Preachers, psychologists, and physicians alike are constantly in search of new methods to deal with the conundrum of difficult issues that seemingly possess elusive powers. What is needed is not just one more inspirational sermon, clinical diagnosis, or therapeutic fix that comforts temporarily but does not radically change us internally. A true permanent, biblical identity fix is needed—a fix that brings us into compliance with God's eternal view about us. Most believer's can stand a strong dose of identity therapy.

I have sat in the counseling chambers many times trying to fix people who had lost their victory because of erroneous ideas, and a failure to have dominion in their circumstances. Sometimes it lasted a few months, a few days, or just a few minutes. One particular parishioner was so absorbed in feelings and self-deception, it was impossible to penetrate the emotional fortress she had built. Her self-worth was judged based on *what she felt that particular day*. I finally understood, after a few unproductive attempts, something more was needed than just a few comforting, sympathetic words. Although this person had received the gift of salvation, the victory of Jesus at Calvary had very little impact in her personal circumstances. A true revelation of Jesus, that would turn her inside out, was greatly needed.

We are in need of a revelation that will affect us night and day, and will remove every objectionable concept that is inconsistent with who we really are. In other words, something must change in our subconscious world before it reflects in our conscious awareness. If the inside doesn't change—the outside won't. We must converge with that truth which is divine—a truth that delivers first and then frees us finally. Jesus said that true disciples would know the truth, and the same truth would *make* them *free*. God said that we are highly favored, accepted, and cannot be impeached from our position in Him. Grace is speaking! In addition, that alone qualifies us to be special! This was true of Israel in the Old Covenant, and true of the Church in the New Covenant. We will develop this idea later in the book.

DELIBERATE MISINFORMATION

Because mankind has been hijacked from his identity, misinformation has been his constant assailant. Misinformation is half-truths, propaganda, and an incorrect impression. The acceptance of inaccurate information plunges man into a downward spiral. A misinformation campaign has canvassed every nation since the original fall of mankind. Consequently, many people groups are spiritually, cognitively, and culturally deprived of their true value. Very few people or nations consider themselves special from God's perspective. Any idea of being special seems to carry with it a need to feel superior to other people rather than considering them of equal value in God's purposes. The vast array of idols created to appease empty souls is living proof this is factual.

If we each had the time to go on a worldwide tour, we could prove this conclusion true. It would become obvious that some nations more than others are totally wrapped and enveloped in misinformation. Then others, such as the United States, a relatively young nation in comparison to some of the African, Asian, and European nations, have had great success in most endeavors, thus establishing a strong sense of independence and self-worth. Such nations aren't ravaged by cognitive and cultural misinformation. However, they become vulnerable to self-deception and a lack of true spirituality. High standards economically, technologically, and militarily are very telling in these nations. However, did you notice morals and ethics are conspicuously absent from this list?

When it seems a few nations have such advantages, others depreciate their own uniqueness when they compare themselves. The apostle Paul stated that when people compare themselves to others, it is not wise. America's wealth and seemingly privileged status have served as a source of jealousy for many. (Please remember the United States is the confluence of many other cultures.) If the truth is known, much of modern America can be likened to the Laodicean Age of the church. (See Revelation 3:14-22.) What appears to be privileged status has gone amuck—we possess more idols and culturally violent trappings than we can afford. Of course, other nations before America considered themselves the privileged apex of all nations. Their pride created a twisted superiority mentality—a myopic kind of nationalism that made other nations subservient to themselves. In this operation, there exists the powerful and the powerless without an understanding that power is to be transferred into empowerment in the less fortunate.

The 20th century seemed to be packed with those who held these tendencies: colonialists, communists, and fascists, just to name a few. It was once suggested that the sun didn't go down on the British colonial empire. The Japanese empire flexed their muscles in Southeast Asia with colonial desires during the first half of the 20th century. Adolph Hitler thought the Third Reich was destined to rule the world, thus creating a perfect society for Aryan people. Marxist philosophers thought socialism would rid the world of inequality and capitalistic delusions with an ultimate society. Part of their motivation was global domination. President Franklin D. Roosevelt, valiantly attempting to convince a skeptical nation, argued for a program that would support freedom fighters against fascists. Our president understood the lurking dangers behind the masks of fascism and communism. He spoke of the secret spreading of poisonous propaganda by those who sought to promote discord among the nations.

In the words of Mr. Roosevelt, these assailants were masters at misinformation. Because individual freedom was suppressed and puppetry imposed, inspired resisters would immediately launch a kind of national resistance until these ideas were capitulated and disengaged. Vietnam, Afghanistan, and South Africa are other examples of this point. France, the United States, the Soviet Union, and the apartheid regime failed miserably although they managed a brief moment of successful occupation. As the hypocrisy behind occupation began to unravel, it infuriated freedom fighters and stirred them to action. The desire for freedom is much stronger than the clutches of any captivity. Committed men and women will make the ultimate sacrifice in order that their children can hug the bells of freedom. No person, nation, or continent will continue to abide quietly under a concept that deprives them of the freedom God intended—the right of divine uniqueness, and the freedom of expression in that uniqueness, as well as dominion in their environments.

NATURAL ISRAEL'S SIGNIFICANCE

The story of Israel as a model will have great significance to us. They were God's jewels and a nation pregnant with hope. This hope was an anchor of the nation's soul, and had its roots in a promise God made to the patriarch Abraham during the event of covenant-cutting in Genesis 15. The fourth major division of the Book of Genesis illustrates how divine strategy created a special people out of Abraham's seed. This is the storyline: From Abraham to Joseph, God's promises began to come to fruition in a great nation possessing a great land.

Abraham begat Isaac, who illustrated the truth of biblical sonship—a lifestyle of total trust. He is one of the most poignant illustrations of the death and resurrection of Jesus Christ in the Old Covenant. Isaac begat Jacob. In him, God took a son and transformed him into a new man. Jacob begat Joseph. His story is extremely relevant to the modern church! In Joseph, God processed a man in 13 years of obscurity, and brought him to a place of rulership and authority. At the end of Genesis, God had a small remnant harvest of less than one hundred souls to continue His purposes. They had become a special people.

Many years were sandwiched between those primal years with Abraham and the Exodus. Before their deliverance from Egyptian bondage, they suffered the impenetrable grasp of bondsmen inspired by a four hundred-year sentence Heaven determined before their birth. They could not exercise self-determinism because it was not the right season for it, and besides, the sovereign hand of God had a grasp around the neck of their destiny. They were pilgrims in another man's country. Israel was under the tight wraps of divine sequestration unable to break the grip of sovereignty. If someone was to resist the taskmasters, a whip and a rebuke were the immediate responses with jeers and snickers perhaps following.

As they moved from one generation to the next, the cry in some to connect with their identity resonated louder and louder. I am sure everyone hadn't forgotten God's promise. Godly intercessors, like prophetic midwives, bombarded Heaven night and day. The carnal simply loathed the shackles of slavery without any sense of responsibility to freedom's fortune. How can anyone enjoy slavery when the patriarch of the nation, along with his seed, carried a prophetic purpose antithetical to slavery? As E.H. Chapin said, "Israel had to learn that tribulation will not hurt you unless it hardens you—makes you sour, narrow and skeptical."[9] Finally, in the fullness of times, God sent a deliverer by the name of Moses. He had a special message from a loving God and heavenly Father:

> *Therefore say to the children of Israel: "I am the Lord; I will bring you out from under the burdens of the Egyptians, I will rescue you from their bondage, and I will redeem you with an outstretched arm and with great judgments. I will take you as My people, and I will be your God. Then you shall know that I am the Lord your God who brings you out from under the burdens of the Egyptians. And I will bring you into the land which I swore to give to Abraham, Isaac, and Jacob; and I will give it to you as a heritage: I am the Lord" (Exodus 6:6-8).*

Moses would reconnect the nation with a true sense of their national destiny. What had been their everyday, ordinary experiences would be no more. True deliverance always produces a radical, revolutionary change. A delivered person or nation initially experiences the event of change with the process of transition to follow. The delivered nation faced two initial crises which we will now discuss. First, would they be able to think outside of a slavish, narrow-minded box defining their past? Second, did this box place a toxic, bitter taste in their spirits preventing them from receiving the Lord's corporate grace and refreshing?

THINKING BEYOND THE FORMER BOX

In one beginning psychology course, I recall an experiment conducted by scientists in which flies were sealed in a ventilated jar and left for a prolonged period. This was a study on conditioned behavior. The flies initially would bang against the lid trying to escape. When this did not happen, they settled for the limited environment they had come to know. Finally the lid was removed; but well-conditioned by now, the flies did not try to escape anymore. They stayed within the perimeters of the jar, going on in the familiar patterned behavior they had established. Their reality was the tight confines of that jar and no more. It had become their only world. To leave this safe place was not something they were necessarily ready for.

The Exodus generation faced the same peril as every first generation of emancipated people. They had to transfer from the overt controls of physical and mental slavery to a culture of freedom. They had to shift from a conditioned world to a free world. This would require a crystal-clear navigation process that included hearing the voice of God, which is our transportation from cyclical bondage to freedom's frontier. Attitudinally, they had to be ready to color outside of the previous lines. How do you suddenly cancel 430 years of servitude and the destruction it has caused to the national psyche? This question is very important because an incorrect response will postpone your date indefinitely for an optimistic future. At this point, attitude is everything. What we will experience from this point forward is dependent upon the environment in our own minds. Are we just circling around the perimeter or taking steps outside the jar? A man of God ministered many years ago: Our altitude will be affected by our attitude. We will not go very far with a deplorable attitude continually seized by the circumstances of the past.

Since the first generation of Israelites refused God's message, their attitudes and mind-sets were never adjusted. God's idea for them never became their general concept. Full of soulish, venomous waste, they entered a long period of transition, enduring 40 years without much progress. Moving from camp to camp in that great and terrible wilderness made Egypt seem less objectionable with each horrendous day. God purposed to shake the very last vestiges of Egypt off them. They did not remain faithful to their Deliverer, and never quite managed to mix faith with the hearing of God's Word. In fact, they flirted with death and took counsel from the chambers of hell every day. The result was a muddled understanding that was cluttered with fear, rebellion, and unbelief. They did not align with the purposes of God and failed to seize the moment to initiate something fresh in the earth. The Scripture says of them:

> *For who, having heard, rebelled? Indeed, was it not all who came out of Egypt, led by Moses? Now with whom was He angry forty years? Was it not with those who sinned, whose corpses fell in the wilderness? And to whom did He swear that they would not enter His rest, but to those who did not obey?* (Hebrews 3:16-18)

Now, the next generation had to read the spiritual signposts and learn quickly. They had to think beyond the carnal box that the previous generation stuffed with failures and left to them for an inheritance. When anyone "thinks beyond the box," it allows the Lord to impregnate him or her with His thoughts with the final analysis being the birth of His dream. Conversely, choosing to think within the box of the last generation, and its diabolical confinements, limits our potential tremendously. That box narrows our worldview and imprisons us to a way of life and thought that is far beneath the truth of bona fide freedom.

This is very relevant because, as the administration of Pentecost came to Jacksonville, North Carolina, many became second-generation modern Pentecostals. We faced many boxes in our spiritual adolescence. The first 50 to 60 years of neo-Pentecostalism had produced a variety of boxes, from water baptism formulas to what constitutes being saved and being baptized in the Holy Spirit. A number of them were also attitudinal, such as our unscriptural legalisms about women's attire. Very insecure men also maintained control of almost every move women made. Eventually, the Holy Spirit challenged us to vacate those positions and go beyond the fruit of mixture in modern Pentecostalism. That wasn't easy because it required an acknowledgment of our limitations and carnal impositions. One will not change what cannot be acknowledged and voiced. As difficult as it may be, an honest confession, in this instance, is good for the soul.

Thinking beyond the box necessitates movement—movement from what is static, stagnant, and immobile. The spirit of inertia, which paralyzes the Church and is incongruous with the dynamics of change, tumbles into its rightful abyss as we choose to move. Borrowing an Old Covenant thought, God desires to bring us into a land *flowing* with *milk and honey*! "Flowing" signifies movement—no stagnation. The Hebrew terminology means "to flow freely as water; also to overflow."[10] Prophetically, I see a place in God that will not only satisfy us but will also saturate us through and through. There will be no place untouched by God in our spirit, soul, and body as the Spirit of God freely moves.

"Milk and honey" foretold God's *double portion benefit*. God custom-made an inheritance for His redeemed children and tailored everything for their refreshment. I cannot imagine any greater picture of what it means to be in Christ. Milk is a perfect food for the immature—the babe (see 1 Pet. 2:2); and honey is the enlightenment essential for the mature—those engaged in enforcing the total triumph of Calvary (see 1 Sam. 14:25-29). Together, they give a compelling and inclusive view of the *finished work* of Jesus. However, one thing God did not say about the new inheritance: It will take some effort in procuring the milk and honey. Someone must become imaginative and execute a strategy. The cattle and the goats must be raised, domesticated, and milked. Someone must, also, search out the beehives, risk being stung, or possibly suffer death from honey-loving bears, to collect the honey. My father in ministry taught us many years ago that with every blessing comes responsibility.

The land of the Old Covenant is the Kingdom of the New Covenant. God employed the principle of contrast to expand their thinking. Israel was moving from despicable limitations to a roomy new homeland. They were trampled upon and culturally conditioned to an Egyptian environment of lack. Their limited mind-set was called nothing more than a garden of herbs (see Deut. 11:9-10

KJV). What should we, the modern Church, call our limited mind-set? Maybe Premillennial Dispensationalism? Just a thought.

However, *garden* means, "something hedged or fenced in."[11] It is an enclosure that requires heavenly seismic activity to shake us free. Frankly, whether we're in a garden or a box, neither lends to free, liberated thinking. South African freedom fighter, Stephen Bantu Biko once said, "The most potent weapon in the hands of the oppressor is the mind of the oppressed![12] An oppressed mind is a box, a vegetable garden at best. Boxes prevent us from seeing the overall picture. We are restricted to investigating our own little corner, creating theologies of exclusivity and repetitiveness. Thank God, He rescues us from our corners and delivers us over to the trusteeship of the Holy Spirit, who hands us over to the headship of Jesus. Christ acquaints us with the Father's fuller divine view.

WE MUST LEARN!

The Word of God commands us to do two very important things with Israel's historical significance: We must learn from them, and second, not repeat their mistakes. How easy it is to fail to read the signposts God gives us! They are there to steady us as we move into a new frontier in the economy of God.

> *Even if it was written in Scripture long ago, you can be sure it's written for us. God wants the combination of His steady, constant calling and warm, personal counsel in Scripture to come to characterize us, keeping us alert for whatever He will do next* (Romans 15:4 The Message).

> *These are all warning markers—DANGER!—in our history books, written down so that we don't repeat their mistakes. Our positions in the story are parallel—they at the beginning, we at the end—and we are just as capable of messing it up as they were* (1 Corinthians 10:11 The Message).

What was written and what happened were for us. We are parallel stories—Israel being the former under the Dispensation of Law, and we the latter under the Dispensation of Grace. Israel was God's alternate society in their day just as we are today. *Parallel* comes from the Greek word, *parallelos*, which comes from the Latin, *parallelus*, meaning "beside one another."[13] Our stories contain recognized similarities and comparable parts. If we do not listen carefully to God's instructions, we will temporarily obscure our place in history too. God took special care in preparing them before He announced their corporate purpose through Moses in Exodus 19. They were delivered by the blood of the Passover lamb; and they were baptized into Moses under the glory cloud even as they passed through the Red Sea. This cloud radiated the presence of the Eternal One, and was probably visible for miles as it hovered over all Israel.

For the New Testament believer, we are baptized into Christ. Somehow, we must translate this thought into a language that the postmodern *non-believer* can understand. We have also experienced water baptism as well as the baptism of the Holy Spirit. Just as Israel disconnected from their past, so have we. Baptism is the official public statement of belief mixed with actions. The best thing we could do is give our past the burial it deserves and get on with the resurrection life we have in Christ. Because of Christ, a New Covenant has been activated with better privileges and promises, and our standard of living has significantly improved. If we added nothing else to this, this alone would qualify us to be a special people, a kind of peculiar treasure to our heavenly Father.

A REFRESHED PEOPLE

Before God commenced working with a people who were peculiar, yet sterile to Kingdom purpose, He had to awaken a new sense of freshness in them. They were living dead men because the only real kingdom to Israel was Pharaoh's, which was built by the resourcefulness of their free labor and backbreaking tasks. That certainly did not refresh them; it only sucked the life out of them. Through the Lord's Passover, a new vision with a different set of objectives was set in motion for them. They had to become preoccupied with another idea other than the discomforts of slavery and its internal barbed wires. Perhaps this is a bit difficult when you have only known a continuous, low-lying black cloud of disenfranchisement—an insidious taskmaster railing you every day, hurling insults, and daring resistance. When Moses arrived, things changed. Deferred hope became joyful anticipation. The former silence of disappointment had now become the shouts of birth pangs as they considered victory over the imperialistic power of Egypt.

Egypt would eventually go too far. Their cup of iniquity and insults finally overflowed. They would challenge Almighty God one time too many with demigod aspirations, and a plethora of idols. The cries of God's children ascended as prayerful vapors precipitating a time of release. Pharaoh, and all his cohorts, would be judged in the impending judgment. Never again would they be the lethal hammers of bondage they once were.

The prophets would later liken this to the operation of the Day of the Lord. Israel was delivered with an opportunity for the truth of God's Word through His servant Moses to free them. The Day of the Lord was the blight of night for Egypt, and the blithe of day for Israel. A nation would be born in a day. God would be magnified and verified to be the covenant-keeper He is.

God never breaks a promise! He remembered faithful Abraham. Israel wasn't delivered because of impeccable integrity, or some staggering acts of righteousness. They did not deserve their deliverance. It was all the grace of God just as our deliverance is predicated on God's grace. The gods of Egypt fell into oblivion just as the gods of the Canaanites would fall in the future. Israel was now living in a time of visitation and refreshing from the presence of the Lord.

1990s REFRESHINGS

The 20th century ended with the Lord refreshing the Church many different times, and in many different places. This was only a glimpse of things to come. Religion and religious behavior had sucked the life out of many believers. Much religion had just about made the Church mad—she had become a lame woman with many structural defects. After becoming a conduit of healing to the lame man, while preaching in Solomon's Portico, the apostle Peter said "times of refreshing" would come from the presence of the Lord accompanying repentance and conversion (see Acts 3:19). Times dictate many opportunities with various approaches. God is diverse and creative enough that He doesn't have to become stereotypical in His visitations or movements. Sometimes groups and networks are so interested in spiritual cloning, they fail to understand how much God desires variety. There certainly is great leeway in the way God chooses to express Himself.

Our local church personally witnessed the effectiveness of this promise in the mid-1990s. God sent an Australian evangelist, Chris Harvey, to our region in which we served as one of the host churches. He ministered very simply, but powerfully. Thirsty members of our assembly and other local churches were touched by the power of God. People laughed; they cried; they were slain in the Holy Spirit; some stood frozen by the Spirit in different positions, which was very bizarre to say the least. Each night seemed to present different manifestations. At first, I had some doubts about some things that were going on.

Though very much amazed and appreciative, those with many years of the Lord's dealings clearly understood the temporary nature of such things. They were less affected by most of the manifestations because they had learned to enter the Lord's rest, which is the best place to be. The move of God touched children and adults alike. It was an equal opportunity of refreshing for all. Unfortunately, there were mockers and cynics—those who thought Chris moved too much by the power of suggestion rather than the anointing, which would suggest psychic, paranormal activity rather than Holy Spirit-endorsed activity. However, the move of God in certain lives was enough to silence the critics. God will meet hungry people even if the vessel He uses is imperfect.

Arnaldo Perez, a spiritual son, was such an example. He is a faithful supporter of the ministry, and often very quiet in temperament. People could easily misjudge the depth of Arnaldo's relationship with Christ because of his quietness. Many watched him glued to the back wall in our local church building for several days laughing until he was without strength. Knowing he is no hypocrite, this aided in removing skepticism. This even affected Arnaldo on his job. God used the life in him to give life and laughter to someone suffering a life-threatening situation. At this point, I was like Simon Peter at Cornelius's house, when he asked the penetrating question to his Jewish brethren: *"Can anyone forbid water, that these should not be baptized who have received the Holy Spirit just as we have?"* (Acts 10:47) The apostle Peter knew the real deal when he saw it. The things happening made it more than evident that God was present. What happened to Arnaldo was too convincing to deny any longer the authenticity of God's involvement.

After enduring much prodding and choosing to think beyond my box, my safe haven, I was reminded by the Father of a beautiful truth about Himself: He can move without our permission or initial agreement any time He chooses. Because I'm very analytical, my head, at times, attempts to overthrow the convictions of my heart. Trying to hold the moving of the Holy Spirit into a certain paradigm may be nothing more than a religious spirit. The Scripture later revealed how baseless my skepticism really was. People of God have laughed, cried, jumped, shouted, and prostrated themselves before God in most generations. This visitation was nothing new—just new to this generation. If one is overly concerned about these manifestations, just search the annals of Church history. Leaders cannot control the methods by which God will refresh His Church. After all, it is His Church, and He may choose to confound or perplex our narrow thinking in the way He moves in her. I am just thankful God gave us the grace to host these gatherings. Although it was a school of unsolicited new discoveries about Kingdom operations, God taught most of us anyway.

As this gate opened, it became very therapeutic to our congregation. Refreshing through laughter took on a new meaning to our local church in the Spring of 1999. Although we had gone through many challenges as a local church, this year was the most challenging. A dear friend had come for a series of meetings that eventually led to a nasty church split. Many used those powerful messages as a scapegoat just to camouflage their real intentions. He taught on being under the Lord's command, which exposed the independent spirits in many. What can be so wrong with Kingdom people being under the command of King Jesus and His delegated authority, provided men's hearts are pure and their motives proper? The Lord's plumb line comes to us through apostolic and prophetic vessels. Obviously, our heavenly Father knew what we would face after these meetings. The Lord baptized us in the spirit of laughter the last service to the point of overwhelming us and removing our physical strength. We would need more than physical strength to carry us through the year. Laughter prepared and strengthened us for the coming weeks. The joy of the Lord was our strength, and we survived what the enemy intended for much evil.

Many of our Christian brethren must discern the heart of God more perfectly in these special seasons. They do not last forever, nor do they change your specific purpose in God. God's objective is to refresh a people who have been in a subnormal Kingdom condition for some time, and subsequently have been worn out. We move from the current level of operation to a new dimension. Just to change levels would be to improve the same things we're already doing. A dimension change is far different! We discover something God has never done in our lives before and participate in it. A level change is a knowledge change, whereas a dimension change requires a heart change. For example, a person may change levels because of growth in prophetic expressions. Dimension change occurs by leaving Pentecostal paradigms and going on to the Feast of Tabernacles, going from one dimension to the next.

Once refreshed it is time to get back to business—the King's business, not regular church business. Refreshing acts will rebuff the damage we may have incurred along certain segments of our journey. It is God's way of saying, "The past is history—forget it and go on!" Although it may not be spoken this sternly, this is clearly the message. God declassifies us from all the stuff and reclassifies us in His own purposes during refreshing. Christians must accept nothing will improve or undo the past. Even reliving the memory day after day doesn't change anything!

Adopt the apostle Paul's attitude: "*Brethren, I do not count myself to have apprehended; but one thing I do, forgetting those things which are behind and reaching forward to those things which are ahead, I press toward the goal for the prize of the upward call of God in Christ Jesus"* (Phil. 3:13-14). The Message expresses this passage beautifully: *"I'm not saying that I have this all together, that I have it made. But I am well on my way, reaching out for Christ, who has so wondrously reached out for me. Friends, don't get me wrong: By no means do I count myself an expert in all of this, but I've got my eye on the goal, where God is beckoning us onward—to Jesus. I'm off and running, and I'm not turning back."* We are God's chosen and special people, off and running toward Him. Have we apprehended all that He has made available in Christ yet? Not hardly! However, we do press on with intensity and a sense of urgency as we develop in the reality of who we have become in Christ. Our goal is not all the distractions along the way, only the prearranged prize of the high call of God in Christ.

WE REALLY ARE HISTORY MAKERS

We are history makers, sky walkers, and special people. God's redemptive purposes are greatly maturing in this generation and creating havoc in the fleshly passageway of men's kingdoms. A long, difficult road of struggle is reaching its climatic end as each century passes. The vitriolic taunts of the adversary haven't discouraged us. God is compelling us to consciously make manifest the glory of God that is within us. If this is to be true, we must follow the apostle John's admonition:*"Dear children, be on guard against all clever facsimiles"* (1 John. 5:21 The Message). In good ole King James lingo, "Keep yourselves from idols!" Idols desensitize and numb people to the things of the Spirit, distracting them specifically from their generational purpose. We must model the brilliancy of Christ and frustrate our deepest fears and inadequacies. Our children are watching us. Shall we mark them with the signet of their importance to God, or leave them vulnerable to the modern slave traders of misinformation, the taskmasters of insecurity and superiority, and the cultural butchers of this world's system? I beseech each of us to adopt The Message's rendering of Romans 12:1-3:

So here's what I want you to do, God helping you: Take your everyday, ordinary life—your sleeping, eating, going-to-work, and walk-

ing-around life—and place it before God as an offering. Embracing what God does for you is the best thing you can do for Him. Don't become so well adjusted to your culture that you fit into it without even thinking. Instead, fix your attention on God. You'll be changed from the inside out. Readily recognize what He wants from you, and quickly respond to it. Unlike the culture around you, always dragging you down to its level of immaturity, God brings the best out of you, develops well-formed maturity in you.

May we recognize what God wants from us, and quickly respond to it. Let us begin an adventurous journey into the culture of a special people. Let us step beyond our ordinary life—our sleeping, eating, and going-to-church, going-to-work, and walking-around life into the economy of God's freshness. Life in the Kingdom is not cut-and-dried. However, a divine blueprint, the disciplines, and the provision are well documented in the Scriptures about this journey.

But now, God's message, the God who made you in the first place, Jacob, the One who got you started, Israel: Don't be afraid, I've redeemed you. I've called your name. You're Mine. When you're in over your head, I'll be there with you. When you're in rough waters, you will not go down. When you're between a rock and a hard place, it won't be a dead end— because I am God, your personal God, the Holy of Israel, your Savior. I paid a huge price for you: all of Egypt, with rich Cush and Seba thrown in! That's how much you mean to Me! That's how much I love you! I'd sell off the whole world to get you back, trade the creation just for you" (Isaiah 43:1-4 The Message).

Just think, our heavenly Father would sell the whole world, all its political and circumstantial systems, just for His children. The world system will fade and pass away; the Word of God guarantees us of that. It cannot respond to the love of God, or reciprocate love to God as man can. Even though we may face many dilemmas, yet God's love never tarnishes. Our Father has no ability to discolor Himself with anger forever as most religions teach. He is a personal God, a fabulous Father, and a precious Savior who exercises the prerogative to love His children with unblemished love. What was true for Old Covenant Israel is equally true for the Israel of God (see Gal. 6:16) in the New Covenant.

ENDNOTES

1. Charles H. Spurgeon, *The Treasury of David, Volume One* (Peabody, MA: Hendrickson Publishers), 83.

2. Athanasius, Bishop of Alexandria, Theologian, Doctor (www.elvis.rowan.edu/~kilroy/JEK/05/02.html), 2-3.

3. Robert Rakestraw, *Becoming Like God: An Evangelical Doctrine of Theosis* (www.bethel.edu/ ~ rakrob/files, June, 1997), 4.

4. Virginia Ely, *I Quote* (New York: George W. Stewart Publishers, Inc., 1947), 224.

5. Martin H. Manser, *King James Bible Word Book* (Nashville: Thomas Nelson Publishers, 2002), 280.

6. Ibid.

7. James Strong, *"Hebrew and Chaldee Dictionary,"* Strong's Exhaustive Concordance of the Bible (Nashville: Abingdon, 1976), #5459.

8. Webster's II New College Dictionary, Riverside University dictionary (New York: Houghton Mifflin Company, 1995), 887.

9. Virginia Ely, 227.

10. James Strong, #2100.

11. Ibid., #1588, #1598.

12. Stephen Biko — Famous Quotes and Quotations (www.brainyquote.com).

13. Webster's II, 796.

2

Times of Refreshing

*Repent therefore and be converted, that your sins may be blotted
out, so that times of refreshing may come from the presence of the
Lord, and that He may send Jesus Christ, who was preached to you
before, whom heaven must receive until the times of restoration of
all things, which God has spoken by the mouth of all His holy
prophets since the world began* (Acts 3:19-21).

Since the Church and Israel are parallel stories, we share many
things. One of them happens to be our need for refreshing before
God implements a fresh awareness of His dream in our lives. It seems
that we're always on the cutting edge of greatness but must be constantly reminded of our true identity. I believe that's the purpose of
refreshing. Refreshing has a way of reviving hope and destroying the
debilitating spirit of inertia, which causes Kingdom activities to be
sluggish or dead. In this chapter, we will approach scriptural refreshing from two of its three levels of intensity: showers and regular rains.
This will differentiate the types of visitation the Heavens release. The
early reformers had *showers*; the Pentecostals had *rains*; and the 21st-
century Church will encounter the "Day of the Lord," which is a violent storm against secular and religious control mechanisms. (The
Day of the Lord will be dealt with in the next chapter.) There is no
time in the history of mankind that one of these three levels was not
affecting some nation or individual.

I submit that Adam, the first Kingdom man on earth, experienced the first true refreshing presence of God. After having blown the breath of life into him, God walked with him in the Spirit each day until his disobedience. Because God is Spirit, that is the only way He can walk with man. Think of it: man experiencing and getting to personally know God each and every day without someone having to explain Him! I would say that alone qualifies as Bible refreshing. The foundation of everything else in God's interaction with men finds its footing in God's desire to have fellowship with human beings. It is also the reason God preserved Noah and his family out of the old dispensation. This leads to the importance of the call of Abraham, and the selection of his natural and spiritual seed. God promised Abraham a time of corporate visitation with financial remuneration (see Gen. 15:12-14). As the Genesis era closed, Joseph on his deathbed reminded Israel, "I am dying; but God will surely visit you, and bring you out of this land to the land of which He swore to Abraham, to Isaac, and to Jacob" (Gen. 50:24). Israel finally left Egypt, the house of bondage, after unrivaled judgments on Pharaoh's kingdom. God affirmed the hour of their visitation by His presence in the glory cloud. "He did not take away the pillar of cloud by day or the pillar of fire by night from before the people" (Exod. 13:22).

Can you imagine waking up every single day with the glory cloud as a canopy over your life? Even if your attitude was indifferent, resistant, or downright rotten, the cloud remained. No other nation on the face of the earth had such a protective covering. Israel had the comfort of God's manifest presence and still without rhyme or reason missed the purpose of their hour of visitation. There is an imminent danger in this: An attitude of familiarity with divine things breeds contempt. When the nearness of God becomes common in our thinking, we fail to revere His holiness. Men begin to disdain the proper attitude essential to maintaining a progressive relationship with Him. It proves that one may be in the tangible presence of the Lord and fundamentally not change internally. Change in your physical geography does not denote change in your mental and spiritual geography, which is real change.

Once they crossed the Jordan River, there is no more evidence of the glorious cloud. Our heavenly Father will spoon-feed us in our infancy but wean us without hesitation when it's time to mature. Any sane parent will be wise enough to do the same, and so will any understanding leader. God conceded to lead His people by a different set of principles in the Promised Land versus the wilderness. Where did the cloud go? It ascended back into the heavens until the construction and completion of the Temple (see 1 Kings 8:10-11). Prophetically, God was telling us it would require a temple (something permanent) rather than a tent (something temporary and transient) for the abiding presence of the Lord. This is why the Church is called a "temple" in the New Covenant (see 1 Cor. 3:16; 2 Cor. 6:16; Eph. 2:20-22). New seasons demand new things in God!

The very moment the new generation submitted to Joshua's command of circumcision at Gilgal, a new order became effective. Their new birth into the Promised Land required cutting off all association with the previous life. This procedure was an edit of closure and God's divine order for covenantal participation; it was more than a hygienic measure. As God excised their physical foreskins, He also expunged the reproach of Egypt off their collective consciousness. He disinfected the new generation from the toxic, irresponsible attitudes of their parents. In the words of apostle G.C. McCurry, they celebrated the Passover of Conquest and began a brand-new diet. Their previous food supply and the outward signs of a visitation far spent were history. Insanity could have propelled them to search behind every rock in the new administration for what once was. Get a revelation! You won't find it! What God used to sustain us within our infancy and adolescence will not survive adult environments.

Earlier, God had spoken of a new type of visitation as Moses mentored the new generation concerning living in Canaan. God's endorsement of them as an agrarian society would come in the rains—the early rain and the latter rain. Rain became representative of refreshing and a stipulation to prepare the soil and reap the harvest sown. The whole order in the Kingdom of God at that time had drastically changed. Does this sound familiar? Let's draw upon this metaphor of rain to explain the current need of the Church in the realm of refreshing. The apostle Peter said our rain, or refreshing presence, has a name: Jesus Christ (see Acts 3:20). A new, unadulterated revelation of the presence of Jesus Christ will reinvigorate the Church from her juvenile delinquency. He will come from no place other than the carnal tomb of unimportant things we have used to smother Him within our spirits. Christ is in you, not someplace else (see Col. 1:26-27). The same one who abides in the presence of the Father now lives in us! It's as if Christ has a dual residence.

DISTINCTIVENESS OF RAIN

Refreshing has been called "showers of blessings from the presence of the Lord." Webster defines *showers* as "a brief fall of precipitation, as rain, sleet, or hail; a brief or sudden downpour."[1] The Hebrew word for showers speaks to "rain (as an accumulation of drops)," coming from a base word meaning "increase from casting together."[2] Combining Webster's definition and the Hebrew definition, showers are something brief, not permanent, and intense. Showers are the least intense in God's panorama of refreshing.

Jesus Christ apprehended me in a season of regional refreshing in eastern North Carolina. Refreshing was a glorious event and a glorious season for about a decade. Almost every week we would experience a different kind of shower. Nothing was stereotypical. The Spirit of God invaded many local communities and apprehended many lives that are still bearing fruit today. Nevertheless, the rains eventually stopped because showers aren't intended to be permanent. I trust this isn't too shocking! God knew believers would camp out at revivals if the fountains weren't shut off. Enjoying revival certainly makes more carnal sense to immature believers than growing up in Christ.

Since moving to Southwest Florida in 1986, we have experienced showers and rains in a way like never before. Naturally, it rains every day during the rainy season, which begins late May and continues until early November. Because of the weather patterns, one can expect a shower between 2:00 and 5:00 pm daily. They are a welcomed relief from the sweltering heat and humidity blanketing most of Florida during the summer months. Because Florida is a peninsula, the rains come in from either the Gulf of Mexico or the Atlantic Ocean, making a booming splash. They are very intense, loaded with an awesome display of lightning, and may instantly create dangerous conditions. The showers and rains scurry just as quickly as they come. Finally, the sun peaks through the remnant clouds as the system passes by. As it heats the atmosphere once again, it creates a sauna effect. It's as though there was never a soaking rain at all. As autumn approaches, the pattern shifts more to mornings. The point is: If not for these rains, Florida would be unbearable in the summer months. Refreshing from the presence of the Lord equally makes the spiritual process to be conformed into the image of Christ bearable.

Since refreshing is likened to rain, I determined to understand the characteristics and benefits of rain. Interestingly, in reading general materials, these are some of the conclusions drawn about rain's value:

- The lightning in rain clouds charges the soil with large amounts of nitrogen when it strikes.

- Rain may provide as much as 40 pounds of sulfur per acre per year.

- Rain contains carbonic acid, which forms carbon dioxide in the soil.

- Dust is another beneficiary of rain. It contains minerals, organic matter, and beneficial organisms (bacteria) important to healthy soil. Dust is considered one of the most significant factors in restoring vital minerals to exhausted soil. It is also a source of yeast and other spores essential to decomposition that rots dead vegetation and turns it into fertile humus.

Without necessarily having an advanced degree in meteorology, it's simple to understand the value of rainfall. It adds nutritional and restorative value to the soil. Even a trifle like dust has restorative powers lodged in its fine, dry particles. If we first understand the natural, then we may more readily comprehend the spiritual application. Rain, in the natural, is refreshing and extremely important for the earth to be fruitful and productive. In the spiritual, refreshing brings nourishment and refreshment to the spirit and soul of man. God stamps His approbation upon His people when the heavens rain refreshing.

> *I will make a covenant of peace with them, and cause wild beasts to cease from the land; and they will dwell safely in the wilderness and sleep in the woods. I will make them and the places all around My hill a blessing; and I will cause showers to come down in their season; there shall be showers of blessing* (Ezekiel 34:25-26).

> *You visit the earth and water it, you greatly enrich it; the river of God is full of water; you provide their grain, for so you have prepared it. You water its ridges abundantly, You settle its furrows; You make it soft with showers, You bless its growth* (Psalm 65:9-10).

A JUST BALANCE

God loves a just balance (see Lev. 19:35-36; Prov. 11:1). Just as rain in the natural brings balance to the earth, the ethos of refreshing is the philosophy of how God balances the weight of His glory on the earth utilizing refreshing. Weather systems act and react to bring balance and equilibrium to the whole earth. So does refreshing. It rains on all the earth! God's glory is for all the earth! I define *glory* as "the weightiness of His thoughts and activities expressed in all the earth." No one nation has a complete market on all God is doing in the earth; therefore, no one nation experiences all of God's glory. Too much weight in one place will produce an imbalance and will tilt the scales toward ungodly human attitudes in those receiving the imbalance. Because of man's overt tendencies to destruction—himself, his neighborhood, his nation—God is constantly balancing everything. The nature, then, of refreshing is that it does not remain in the same region forever, for that would negate the truth of balance. If it rains in the same place in the natural all the time, the rivers probably would flood, the soil would become waterlogged, thus negating the blessings the rains were intended to produce.

For instance, during the 1980s and 90s, revival was very prevalent in Toronto, Canada; Pensacola, Florida; England; Africa; Argentina; China; Australia; and many Arabic-speaking nations. God moved in all these places at once to keep a just balance. He was straddled between the East and West, the Northern and Southern Hemispheres. The wave of refreshing eventually ebbed, the glory lifted, and the showers rescinded. It was now time to properly process what the Lord had been doing.

The Coming of the Lord as Rain

One of the most misunderstood subjects in the Bible is the coming of the Lord. Because of its many peculiarities, this subject may become a tinderbox instantly. God's children are either authorities on the subject or don't have a clue. We haven't finished school yet, and haven't processed all the subject matter. Many people are visual learners; therefore, God couldn't have chosen a more definitive metaphor to explain the coming of the Lord than rain. It doesn't rain once or twice—it rains many times. The Lord has never locked Himself into just a first and second coming; He comes many times with great diversity. Rain doesn't come with the same amount of force or intensity every time. Rain is refreshing. This is called the moderate level of refreshing. At this level refreshing is scalable, regulated, predictable, and consistent. The apostle Peter said, "God will send Jesus Christ!" You can't receive the presence of God in any greater consistency or intensity than the person of Jesus Christ. Jesus is the same yesterday, today, and forever. Behold! He comes in clouds—the clouds bearing rain!

God has operated in the cloud from the Flood of Noah and the rainbow in Genesis to the One who sits upon the clouds in the Revelation (see Gen. 9:13; Rev. 14:14-16). The primary nature of the cloud is to empty itself once full (see Eccles. 11:3). When God becomes full of the passionate pleas of desperate intercessors and prayer warriors—purpose-driven people, He empties Himself in drenching refreshing. The Book of Job declares a cloud is built in proportion to the amount of vapor it receives (see Job 36:26-28). Asking, or fervent prayer, becomes the precipitous energy for the development of lightning-filled clouds of refreshing. This is just another metaphor to describe men and women of God in the present economy of the Kingdom. The Bible calls people "clouds"!

God promised to come as the former rain and the latter rain to a people who returned to Him (see Hos. 6:3; Ps. 72:6; James 5:7; Joel 2:23). Prayer is one method of returning to the Lord. Pentecostal people spoke often of this promise because it was consistent with the operation of God in Pentecost. From its Hebrew definition, the early rain is a teacher of righteousness, or teaching as a flow of waters. If a person has strayed, and he or she returns to the Lord broken, the teacher of righteousness restores that person to right standing with God. That person is reminded that all New Covenant righteousness is centered in the person of Jesus Christ. Rarely will that person struggle with the righteous demands of faith from henceforth. Grace sustains them rather than the performance of the law.

Latter rains are *gathering rains*. It's the teachings that announce God's determination to gather His body into one body—a teaching that eradicates division. The prophet Joel said, *"And He will cause the rain to come down for you—the former rain, and the latter rain in the first month"* (Joel 2:23). "Month" is italicized in the New King James Version, indicating an addition by the translators for readability. "First" implies the beginning or headship principle. God is giving a first-fruits people a two-in-one experience to maximize their ability to harvest quickly. The result is a refreshed land and a people restored to their place of special significance. Since Israel and the Church are parallel stories, what applies to them in the Old Covenant applies to us in the New Covenant.

> *Let us know, let us pursue the knowledge of the Lord, His going forth is established as the morning; He will come to us like the rain, like the latter and former rain to the earth* (Hosea 6:3).

> *He shall come down like rain upon the grass before mowing, like showers that water the earth* (Psalm 72:6).

> *Therefore be patient, brethren, until the coming of the Lord. See how the farmer waits for the precious fruit of the earth, waiting patiently for it until it receives the early and latter rain* (James 5:7).

The Lord is coming as a double portion of rain! What a comforting thought! This doesn't sound like any of the modern catastrophic images painted by carnal interpretations of the Scriptures. A logical thought may be: *But too much rain may become a destructive flood!* We have a promise from God that He'll never destroy the earth by a flood again—that's history. (See Genesis 8:20-21.) Obedient believers may find great security in this promise. Insecure and rebellious believers alike may be greatly agitated by it. The coming of the Lord is not an automatic fire escape from troubles. It is the coming of the Lord, not the disappearing of the saints. Somehow, we have supplemented the beauty of the Lord's coming with the Church's disappearance from planet Earth. If that happened, there would be no biblical overcomers. The Lord has great patience, receiving only a ripe, overcoming product. Until there is a unified body that processes the former and latter rain together, the Lord will wait patiently (see James 5:7).

The land of Israel, like all farming regions, was unproductive without rain. It was not some lush, tropical rain forest with an abundant water supply. Water and wells were most precious, often the reason for great contention between herdsmen. In order for the Old Covenant people to reap their harvests (grain, new wine, and oil), they unquestionably needed rain. Note that this is a threefold harvest, with the grain harvests first and the fruit harvests last. The first rains prepared the soil for sowing, whereas the final rains prepared the maturing crops for harvest. Both the former and latter rains (a double portion) were essential to bring forth the full results in God's heart. Rains were the outward indication of God's favor and willingness to secure the land from recession. Lack of rain left them at the mercy of drought, scorching winds, and essentially no crops.

The prophet Zechariah speaks of the need to discern the timing of God during the rainy seasons. If there is no rain, then mankind has the responsibility to ask for it. When there is no refreshing or reformation, the Church has the responsibility to ask as well. Although God knows what we need before we ask, it pleases Him for His children to express their trust in this manner.

Ask the Lord for rain in the time of the latter rain. The Lord will make flashing clouds; He will give them showers of rain, grass in the field for everyone (Zechariah 10:1).

Our heavenly Father relishes the idea of His children asking. It becomes a prerequisite to precipitation and the development of clouds as bearers of precipitation. Zechariah spoke of "flashing clouds" or clouds of lightning. They are clouds with illumination. This speaks to the true nature of the vessel that brings the refreshing nature of God. Because of the intensity of their own spirits and a willingness to stand repeatedly in God's presence, men and women metaphorically leave that encounter flashing like lightning—beaming with wisdom, knowledge, and understanding. Moses was a powerful example of this point. There was a glow about him as he came down the mountain from absorbing the presence of the Lord. The people of God are greatly benefited because such vessels bring much refreshing.

Refreshing in the spirit of man results from man standing under the artesian waterspout of an uninhibited release from the throne of grace. Its objective is fruitfulness in the recipient—not chills, thrills, goose bumps, jerks, laughing, running, falling, or being slain in the Spirit. Many interesting and bizarre manifestations have always found expression in people intoxicated by the Holy Spirit. However, this is not the primary purpose of refreshing. Refreshing is a face-to-face encounter with Almighty God while intoxication may be the result of that. Intoxication means losing control of one's faculties. Good Southern slang says, "You're smashed on the Holy Ghost!" It prevents flesh and carnality from dominating a person's life for a short span of time and gives the Holy Spirit total control.

The primary reason for various manifestations, when they're present, is to persuade men concerning the authenticity of divine intervention into the moment of time. Most people are not accustomed to yielding to the Holy Spirit's presence because of traditional teachings that assign various manifestations of the Spirit to a previous age. By doing so, we short-change ourselves of some very precious experiences with the Holy Spirit. In fact, this is such a carnal age of Christianity many that Christians have no history of knowing how to respond, or if they should respond. They become like the proverbial neatly wound hose once the water faucet is turned on full blast. The hose moves uncontrollably in various directions. It's a very unpredictable situation. Time and experience will often change this in the lives of people. Yielding to the Holy Spirit produces a *flow* rather than *forced* actions.

Later on, as we mature in our experience with God, some manifestations will happen with less frequency, or maybe even abate. God focuses His attention on developing our characters, and not, necessarily, stirring up our curiosities. If manifestations happen, well and fine; however, refreshing can't be measured by their presence or absence. Also, dogmatic and doctrinally laced discussions about the scriptural legitimacy of unusual manifestations are fruitless. Nature teaches us that rain triggers not only positive vegetation, but also weeds, briars, thorns, and thistles, etc. Everything germinates! Rain compels the earth to express uninhibitedly what is already there. We must accept that godly and godless things will happen in the midst of refreshings. The following scriptures extol the significance of rain and its refreshing reality.

> *For as the rain comes down, and the snow from heaven, and do not return there, but water the earth, and make it bring forth and bud, that it may give seed to the sower and bread to the eater* (Isaiah 55:10).

> *Sing to the Lord with thanksgiving; sing praises on the harp to our God, who covers the heavens with clouds, who prepares rain for the earth, who makes grass to grow on the mountains* (Psalm 147:7-8).

> *Who in bygone generations allowed all nations to walk in their own ways. Nevertheless He did not leave Himself without witness, in that He did good, gave us rain from heaven and fruitful seasons, filling our hearts with food and gladness* (Acts 14:16-17).

> *The Lord will open to you His good treasure, the heavens, to give rain to your land in its season, and to bless all the work of your*

hand. You shall lend to many nations, but you shall not borrow
(Deuteronomy 28:12).

*If you walk in My statutes and keep My commandments, and per-
form them, then I will give you rain in its season, the land shall
yield its produce, and the trees of the field shall yield their fruit*
(Leviticus 26:3-4).

Refreshing, as the coming of the Lord, yields manifold blessings. It also has within its fabric the power to release wealth. History records that each time God visited His people with refreshing
it resulted in a profusion of spiritual and economic abundance. God
doesn't just open the windows of Heaven; He opens the Heavens.
He doesn't just pour out stuff; He pours each of us into a greater
reality of Himself. The greatest view when the Heavens are opened
is the *presence* of the Lord, not the *presents* of the Lord. When He is
present, there are many blessings. The Lord's presence is consummate wealth (see Genesis 15:1)—for there is no abundance more
outstanding than He.

In both texts (Leviticus 26:3-4 and Deuteronomy 28:12), Moses
attests to God's plan of financial enhancement for a covenantal people. Economic empowerment is a necessary force to operate in the
Kingdom of God. A servant of God may have great wisdom, but if he
has no financial power, very few people will listen to him. Certainly,
this is not the covetous spirit of *wanting more, having more, and getting
more.* Isaiah spoke specifically of the wealth of the nations coming to
the children of God—coming from afar (see Isa. 60:5). However, these
verses speak of abundance from the expenditure of labor. Does this
sound like a free meal to you? I can hear apostle Turnell Nelson
preaching in Freeport, Bahamas, "God has placed you on this green
Earth to work, not to rest!" Refreshing is like the final approval of the
Master signifying His pleasure in our work ethic. Rains precipitate
productivity, and no rain means nonproductivity. The same is true of
spiritual refreshing. God's concentrated, manifest presence is approval
of our repentance, and no refreshing indicates His intentional absence.

The only reason we ever experience what appears to be an absen-
tee God is disobedience. It is said that absence causes the heart to

grow fonder—or more tender. In these circumstances, it's not God's heart that needs tenderizing—it's man's. We are tenderized to be lavished with His grace. Father God has voiced His intentions to dwell in our midst, both Israel and the Church (see Exod. 25:8; John 14:23). Why, then, would He be absent? The Scripture speaks with clarity on this matter.

> *"I also withheld rain from you, when there were still three months to the harvest. I made it rain on one city, I withheld rain from another city. One part was rained upon, and where it did not rain the part withered. So two or three cities wandered to another city to drink water, but they were not satisfied; yet you have **not** returned to Me," says the Lord* (Amos 4:7-8, emphasis added).

> *Therefore the showers have been withheld, and there has been no latter rain. You have had a harlot's forehead; you refuse to be ashamed. Will you not from this time cry to Me, "My Father, You are the guide of my youth?"* (Jeremiah 3:3-4).

Between the Feasts of Pentecost and Tabernacles, there were four months—with Pentecost being in the third month and Tabernacles in the seventh. Amos states that the interim was a time of no rain—no refreshing. Those cities (churches) receiving rain had met the mandate of repentance (returning to the Lord) and conversion. Others stiffened in rebellion and were subjected to wandering and searching for rain.

This reminds me so much of most North American revivals. Rather than people building God a suitable dwelling place, they traverse land and sea seeking out those places where others have paid the price for His presence. A believer can never be satisfied siphoning the labors of others and wandering from revival to revival. That's not God's divine order, period! We each have the capacity to maintain a personal relationship with Jesus, thus securing His continual presence. We also have Heaven's permission to build our own altars and fill our own bellies with living waters. Therein lies the principle of refreshing and revival.

When men are sensitive to divine order, and why God has introduced seasonal changes into Kingdom dynamics, seasons of dearth will facilitate brokenness and repentance. Repentance marches us squarely into the arena of a new encounter with the grace of God. Previous wet seasons allowed the rain (refreshing) to become life within the earth (each believer).

Palestine has six months of dryness, from May to October, in which very little rain falls. The whole land becomes dry, parched, and brown. Similarly, my home, Southwest Florida, has both a dry and a wet season. Because it is semi-arid, the winter months and the early spring constitute the dry season; and the summer and the early fall, the wet season. Our environment instructs us to be wise and cautious during the rainy season because drought is coming. Believers must allow these natural signposts to teach us. Just as the earth drinks in the rain, believers must imbibe the spirit of refreshing when it's present. And when we do, together the saints become a watered garden.

> *For the earth which drinks in the rain that often comes upon it, and bears herbs useful for those by whom it is cultivated, receives blessing from God* (Hebrews 6:7).

As the divine clock ticks toward the spiritual fulfillment of the Feast of Tabernacles, out of necessity, a stern warning has been issued in the Book of Zechariah. It says, *"All nations must worship the Lord in the Feast of Tabernacles!"* (see Zech. 14:16) "All" means any place you go on this earth. God's purpose behind this exhortation is to prevent man from incorrectly discerning His seasons, patty-caking in religion, and therefore missing the refreshing that comes from the Lord. Believers are refreshed in the new birth, and receive many more refreshings between the banks of conversion and destiny's fulfillment. The prerogative of Jesus Christ's lordship gives Him the sovereign right of releasing refreshing when He chooses.

The Feast of Tabernacles speaks of Christ, the Head and Body, in His fullness. At that point in time, all of the in-part revelations of Him have completely served their purpose. The greatest refreshing of all requires the Church to embrace that dimension in God that doesn't need to be refreshed at all. When someone lives in the state of fullness, that person is never empty or in need. Christ, in the Feast of Tabernacles, will both qualify and quantify us to experience this measure of life. The only criterion necessary is accepting the gift of grace. Grace has led us thus far, and grace will lead us on!

> *And it shall come to pass that everyone who is left of all the nations which came against Jerusalem shall go up from year to year to worship the King, the Lord of hosts, and to keep the Feast of Tabernacles. And it shall be that whichever of the families of the earth do not come up to Jerusalem to worship the King, the Lord of hosts, on them there will be no rain. If the family of Egypt will not come up and enter in, they shall have no rain; they shall receive the plague with which the Lord strikes the nations who do not come up to keep the Feast of Tabernacles"* (Zechariah 14:16-18).

At this point, your head may be attempting to interpret the seismographic readings of an unusual theological earthquake. Purportedly, this Scripture applies to the Millennium Era according to conventional fundamental theology. Since we have entered the beginnings of the seventh millennium from Adam, and the third from Jesus Christ, we may need to rethink some of our ideas. Spinning out of the epicenter of God and the new creation is a ring of fellowship for the 21st-century believer. The river flowing out of the throne of God is bombarding us with tidal waves and not leaving many of our ideologies and canned theologies intact.

Traditions obliterating the commandments of God don't die easily! As long as peddlers of traditions wear the religious garments in the spirit of denominationalism, and sell the company merchandise, there will be much prophetic warfare to shake the earth free of tradition's trappings. (This by no means implies that everyone in a denomination is religious or seeks to minimize the commandments of God.) We, the Church, have come to the hour of the Feast of Tabernacles. Some brethren choose to call this the postmodern Church era, and some call it the Third Day from Jesus Christ. Regardless to what we call it, may we repent of our biblical illusions and submit to the Holy Spirit as He places us into a self-effacing position. Father God is revealing many important truths to His searching sons. He winked at us in our ignorance, but now commands each of us to repent in a day of enlightenment. Remember, the apostle Peter said, *"Repent and therefore be converted."*

REPENTANCE AND REFRESHING

Refreshing is the direct object of the action involved in conversion. Conversion is the means by which God safely conducts the believer from a state of bondage to freedom, from death to life. It is inclusive of the new birth experience, but not exclusive of the process required to change into another state or purpose, thus living with a heavenly orientation. While preaching, the apostle Peter assures us that true refreshing does not precede repentance. Any believer desiring a personal season of refreshing had best prepare to repent of the things that aided in their deterioration. The Bible says, *"To be carnally minded is death"* (Rom. 8:6)! I see a divine imperative in Peter's preaching: *"Repent and be converted!"* This constitutes marching down humility's pathway before rising in spirited celebration to joy unspeakable.

Multitudes of sincere believers throughout the world are praying for revival or refreshing. Because of a misunderstanding of the true nature of refreshing, the word "refreshing" has fallen into great misuse in modern Christianity. Among some groups, it is gauged by the bevy of unusual spiritual manifestations. Oftentimes, it seems the stranger the manifestation the more glorious the revival. God is to be praised for the numerous times He has moved by His Spirit thus far. However, the refreshing believers so desperately long for—the one they're passionately praying about—will be nothing short of a global outpouring of the Holy Spirit resulting in global harvest. It will consist of the fullness of God in Christ for the fullness of times.

God intends for His glory to exceed every level of glory experienced in the Church in previous revivals. There is one reason, and only one for this: *immeasurable grace!* To all who are pessimistic about the Church's future relevance, this is God's highly acclaimed intention. The greatest chapter of Church history is yet to be recorded because the generation created to experience it has just arrived. Heaven's obscurity kept the 20th-century Church from tainting what God has in His heart. Researchers, such as George Barna, have the data to prove our elaborate prayers couldn't force the hand of God to do what our hearts couldn't sustain. Rising out of the midst of human chaos, when it seems there is nothing to rejoice about, will be a celebrated latter house greater than that of the former house.

The Bible is very deliberate in declaring *times* (plural, not singular) *of refreshing*. There are many times because, historically, the Church completes a cycle of religious death about every 30 years or so. It is obvious that God loves His Church so much that He has prepared seasons, opportunities, or set times for refreshing. If one would care to casually investigate Church history, it would be quite apparent that pockets of revival have been on the earth relentlessly. God continues to release the knowledge of the riches of Christ's accomplishments, subsequently breaking the stronghold of Adam's defeat and flooding a people with unquenchable light. As His illumination pervades each heart, revival breaks out.

Refreshing, one of the children of revival, is the word *anapsuxis*, which means "cooling off, drying out, refreshing, alleviation, relief, or rest."[3] This suggests a recovery of breath—hence, revival. The basic sense of the word is "to refresh with breath" or "to dry out." In medicine, it is treating a wound with fresh air to get a greater volume of oxygen to the wound. Of course, the healing process will be much quicker as more oxygen gets to the wound. Recovery from depleting circumstances is suggested in the Old Testament. Inherent in the sabbatical rest was recovery and refreshing. It is like the Energizer bunny in the commercials to promote the Energizer batteries! We keep ticking as we submit to God's order of entering biblical rest.

Six days you shall do your work, and on the seventh day you shall **rest,** *that your ox and your donkey may* **rest,** *and the son of your female servant and the stranger may be refreshed* (Exodus 23:12).

When there has been a strategically planned expenditure of productive effort, rest is the means by which the heavenly Father renders refreshing and guarantees continued productivity. I love William G. Blaikie's summary of the necessity of the Sabbath: "The Sabbath is God's special present to the working man, and one of its chief objects is to prolong his life, and preserve efficient his working tone. The savings bank of human existence is the weekly Sabbath."[4]

While attempting to accomplish their visions, some ministers labor to the point of burnout. Without hesitation, they'll tell you, "This is the only way to get something done!" In the process, they spiritually wear thin. The Father allows this meltdown because it is one of only a few ways to stop ministers, forcing them to rest and rethink working for Jesus. God never intended ministers to wear so many hats and work themselves down to the raw bone. In other words, there can be no valid refreshing without entering the Lord's rest. Jesus Christ is the Lord's rest in the New Covenant. To continue to expend energy without proper re-creation of used resources is fatal. God has predetermined that man rendezvous with rest in order to renew his strength. Although this may sound legalistic to some, in our present physical state, human beings require one day of seven to regenerate emotionally, physically, and spiritually. I implore you to receive enough grace to unplug for one day!

Major scientific studies have been completed, proving that many people violate this principle; therefore, many are completely broken down in the aforementioned areas. Man is simply too busy to rest—too involved to deactivate himself. Bodily functions strain under such an ominous load; mental genius and creativity stifles. Rest must become a priority to keep the body clicking on all cylinders. God's will is that we disengage the mind and body, and allow the Holy Spirit to replenish our spirit man, thus preparing us for greater accomplishments than ever before.

Six days of man's own activities have exhausted him. Using his invaluable creativity, he has developed every form of philosophy, denomination, device, and division possible. According to Moses, man has "labor and sorrow," and not "labor and joy," or "labor and rest."

Some must enter the Lord's rest after six days (six millennia). Great refreshing lies ahead for the Church in that place. Christ is God's rest—and we have been privileged to enter into Him through His bleeding side. There is a state called revival for those who are tired and worn, beat-up and ready to give up, disgusted and dejected in Him. No matter what the status, God will rain forth refreshing in the appearing of Christ.

SAMSON AND DAVID

The heavenly Father had to oft refresh the nation of Israel in the days when judges ruled. The period of the judges can be characterized as consummate selfishness: *"Everyone did what was right in his own eyes"* (Judg. 21:25). Self-centeredness was their undoing. God raised up the judges as heroes to untie the yokes of their enemies and to restore them to pure worship. At times, the judges' exploits would consume their energies and bring them near exhaustion. A prime example of this is Samson.

> *Then he* [Samson] *became very thirsty; so he cried out to the Lord and said, "You have given this great deliverance by the hand of Your servant; and now shall I die of thirst and fall into the hand of the uncircumcised?" So God split the hollow place that is in Lehi, and water came out, and he drank; and his spirit returned, and he revived. Therefore he called its name En Hakkore, which is in Lehi to this day* (Judges 15:18-19, emphasis added).

Samson, who would be a modern cartoon superhero today, had given himself relentlessly to defeat the enemy. Though he had many personal flaws, he was God's man! Warfare depleted him. He compares well to the so-called superstar men and women of God today, who have demanding schedules, with illusions of invincibility. Constant demands left him without strength, making it impractical to accept one more physical challenge. The last thing he desired was to fall into the hands of the enemy who sought every possible opportunity to destroy him. Sheer exhaustion drove Samson to God. He cried out to God in the midst of his hollow place.

Hollow means, "having a cavity, hole, without substance, worth, character, or lacking in validity and truth."[5] The point is simple: One is desperately empty and needs God to bring refreshing! The ideology behind "a hollow" is recognized lack. God will always meet us at the point of our desperation. Thirsty and hungry people are filled and refilled in the Kingdom economy. He is ready to reload us with Heaven's forces. Samson gave a remarkable testimony in naming the place, *En Hakkore,* which means "fountain of one calling."[6] Springs of refreshing pour out of Christ into every person who thirsts and hungers for Him. The Church, within the last decade of the 20th century, has begun to hunger again. God is answering with times of refreshing.

Another illustration of this principle is David, the anointed king and sweet psalmist of Israel. He desperately needed refreshing during one of the most tumultuous periods of his administration. Probably guilt-riddled from previous mistakes, he needed divine intervention and mercy rather than justice.

> *And as David and his men went along the road, Shimei went along the hillside opposite him and cursed as he went, threw stones at him and kicked up dust. Now the king and all the people who were with him became weary; so they **refreshed** themselves there* (2 Samuel 16:13-14, emphasis added).

Absalom's treason and rebellion manifested with one of David's most trusted advisors, Ahithophel, who also joined the conspiracy. Two privileged men with such awesome Kingdom potential allowed the toxic thoughts of bitterness and resentment to rob them. Men succumb to these beasts many, many times. Together, Absalom and Ahithophel committed the most ignoble deed—treachery. With the constant communion Absalom had with the people, it is no doubt he was more than aware of Ahithophel's simmering anger toward David. There is a saying, "Birds of a feather flock together!" Wise Ahithophel, who had given over to folly, was angry because David disgraced his granddaughter, Bathsheba, and murdered her husband, Uriah.

David was a heartbroken father and reeling emotionally. He must have wondered, *Where did I go wrong?* Rather than choosing to protect his legal right to be king, he abdicated the throne, placing his future squarely into the more than capable hands of the King of kings. David was keenly aware that God gave him the throne and certainly had the right to take it back. When we drop our pride, and sacrifice to God what He gave us, we actually open the door to experience, something exponentially greater. Each time I listen to the voice of the Lord and release an aspect of ministry back to Him, He brings increase. What started, at first, as a loss quickly became a gain.

One of the first prophetic models of this was when Abraham willingly surrendered Isaac. He received him back, in a figurative sense, as raised from the dead, or in a higher state. True refreshing brings us to a higher state. We are refreshed, indicating at one time that we were stale. People and circumstances may trouble us, overwhelm us, or become very wearisome to us. God has a solution! He ordains times when we must pause, put the engine of life in park, let go of the throttle of activities, and allow the Holy Spirit to breathe fresh life into our weary souls. Fresh perspective is regained, and God has the opportunity to complete what He's doing without us attitudinally aborting the process. Emotionally, we may get strained; nevertheless, God gives new vitality as Heaven's therapy.

On another occasion, David sent this particular song (Psalm 39) to Jeduthun, the chief musician. He showed the importance of the lyrics by giving this song to the chief musician, and not just any musician. The Lord Jesus Christ is the Chief Musician in the New Testament. David was in a season of chastening and sought wisdom and forgiveness. This verse captures the height of his musings.

> *"Give me a break, cut me some slack before it's too late and I'm out of here"* (Psalm 39:13 The Message).

> *Remove Your gaze from me, that I may regain strength, before I go away and am no more* (Psalm 39:13).

This Scripture reminds me of the times when my mother's firm hand of discipline ministered so effectively to each of her seven children. In all fairness, she would give us warnings several times before acting. At other times, Mom would give us that gaze. It had such a paralyzing effect on our misbehavior. Imagine fire coming from unhappy eyes piercing through every devious deed you've committed. We knew exactly what the next action would be if we continued in our disobedience. When David asked the Lord to remove His gaze, I can sympathize with what he must have been feeling. That gaze is a powerful deterrent to poor behavior. In addition, when you're on the receiving end of it, it doesn't seem very beneficial at the time.

How many times have you been earnestly broken enough to ask God to give you a break? Refreshing is God responding to our emptiness and ineffectiveness. Man, without God, is nothing but empty, ineffective vapor in his best state. The Church, without refreshing, is a reproach before her foolish, gainsaying adversaries. A powerful Church, such as the Acts model, silences critics. When the Church realizes her position has been compromised, and her function neutralized, there is one thing left to do: *CRY OUT TO GOD!* It is impossible to fulfill the spiritual mandate of *being Church*, not *doing church*, without refreshing. Nowhere in the Bible have we ever been commanded to *"do church."* In fact, once one has been involved in the system of church activities long enough, one may safely do church from a state of rote without ever yielding to the Holy Spirit. Rote leads to routine. Repetitions routinize the things of God, making them common and lacking in awesomeness. When we lose our sense of awe for God, we definitely need a deep, penetrating work of the Holy Spirit.

The psalmist said, *"Hear my prayer, O Lord, and give ear to my cry; do not be silent at my tears; for I am a stranger with You, a sojourner, as all my fathers were"* (Ps. 39:12). He acknowledged his own distant, estrangement from God, when actually he should have been near. These feelings are the stepchildren of a sin-consciousness more so than they are reality. Our Father is approachable; He doesn't skip out on us, and He doesn't disregard our passionate pleas. Sometimes we think His silence is rebuke, when in fact, it is the method by which God extracts repentance from us more deeply. His merciful response happens to be a renewed revelation of His magnificent grace and love. Once that happens, we are immediately refreshed—a refreshing that brings us back to normal sonship, which is supernatural living. Refreshing causes our weary souls to be flooded with relentless grace, sparking a brand-new day in our lives.

ENDNOTES

1. Webster's II New College Dictionary, Riverside University dictionary (New York: Houghton Mifflin Company, 1995), 1022.

2. James Strong, *"Hebrew and Chaldee Dictionary,"* Strong's Exhaustive Concordance of the Bible (Nashville: Abingdon, 1976), #7241, #7231.

3. James Strong, *"Greek Dictionary,"* Strong's Exhaustive Concordance of the Bible (Nashville: Abingdon, 1976), #403, #404.

4. Virginia Ely, *I Quote* (New York: George W. Stewart Publishers, Inc., 1947), 299.

5. Webster's II, 528.

6. Strong's, #5875.

3

Refreshing "in That Day"

The lofty looks of man shall be humbled, the haughtiness of men shall be bowed down, and the Lord alone shall be exalted in that day. For the day of the Lord of hosts shall come upon everything proud and lofty, upon everything lifted up—and it shall be brought low—upon all the cedars of Lebanon that are high and lifted up, and upon all the oaks of Bashan; upon all the high mountains, and upon all the hills that are lifted up; upon every high tower, and upon every fortified wall; upon all the ships of Tarshish, and upon all the beautiful sloops. The loftiness of man shall be bowed down, and the haughtiness of men shall be brought low; the Lord alone will be exalted in that day, but the idols He shall utterly abolish (Isaiah 2:11-18).

The Day of the Lord is the third level, the most intense, of all biblical dealings. *"In that day"* for the Old Testament prophet is the current day of the Church. It is an axe to rebellion and the joy of conversion at the same time. People return to the Lord rather than creating more humanistic, hedonistic systems. It is God in action when spiritual depravity and ethical turmoil have ravished people and brought them to the lowest common denominator. It's a testimony that the real benefits of the New Covenant haven't fully penetrated society at large. It isn't spiritual patchwork to a leaky modern church wineskin; it's actually a discarding of an obsolete dilapidated system, whether religious or secular. Many would-be prophets suggest it is God grinding His axe of justice with humanity. It isn't! Such a philosophy is tainted and 2000 years removed from the truth. That issue was taken care of at the cross of Jesus Christ. Jesus accepted the full weight of God's judgment for all humans. The Day of the Lord is God clearing the debris, mainly pride, which stands between Him and humanity, bringing men back into a Kingdom focus. The reason it appears to be destruction from the Almighty is that every conceivable resistance or rebellion must be banished from the hearts of men. I see the Day of the Lord as the most marvelous outpouring of grace ever witnessed by human beings.

When divine interruption comes as the Day of the Lord, it begins as darkness first, thick clouds and gloominess, before it becomes morning (new day) (see Joel 2:1-2). This contrast is critical because our exposed darkness will enable us to discover His glorious light. Believers experiencing refreshing within the context of the Day of the Lord have pressed on to know the Lord. They are not standing around the shallow, sandy shores of carnal religion—a religiosity that lacks intimacy with the Almighty. This experience is agony before it's ecstasy; in fact, the soul of the refreshed person has been riveted with almost unbearable pain—usually months, maybe even years—before sensing divine relief.

Thus far (in the previous chapter), refreshing has been presented in the positive light of a gentle or continuous downpour of rain from the clouds of Heaven. For believers who heeded the call to repentance, this is primarily the experience they had. However, to other believers, who imperviously trudge along, God refreshes them with a more severe methodology. He employs the Day of the Lord and its entire constituency. The Old Testament prophets often spoke of the Day of the Lord and likened it to a catastrophic hurricane (see Ps. 29; Isa. 2:12-18; Joel 3:14-16; Amos 5:18-20; Zeph. 1:14-18). Hurricanes are tropical cyclones with swirling winds of great strength. When a particular day is ascribed as your day, it is reasonable to believe one may do as they wish with their day. God has determined to fulfill all of His heart in His day. In reverse order, the Day of the Lord is the LORD'S DAY!

The apostle John gives a moving statement of his experience on the Lord's Day. He says, *"I was in the Spirit on the Lord's Day, and I heard behind me a loud voice, as of a trumpet"* (Rev. 1:10). Please note the Lord's Day is not a day of the week as though it can be measured by time. The Lord's Day, the seventh day, is an eternal day; it is timeless. John was transported by the Spirit, not the flesh, into that timeless dimension in which God totally expresses Himself without the constraints of time elements. He heard and saw all the corrections Father God was making in the Church. He equally saw the judgments on the carnal systems of rebellious men.

The Bible marvelously interprets itself. The aforementioned verse (Revelation 1:10) compares trumpets to voices. Since the Revelation is signified, trumpets have nothing to do with brass or silver instruments; that's carnal thinking. Trumpets are clear messages! They are voices articulating the Holy Spirit's heart in the midst of the Church. Numbers chapter 10 gives a powerful progression of the message of trumpets:

- Trumpets were used to gather God's people—leaders and laity (Great gathering).

- Trumpets were used to encourage the journeying of the people (Great advancement).

- Trumpets were used to sound an alarm for warfare (Great struggle).

- Trumpets were blown for appointed feasts, celebrations, and sacrifices (Great celebration).

I have drawn a very practical principle from these combined thoughts. God will gather us to advance us. *If we advance, expect conflict with previous paradigms. As we endure conflict with the right attitude, we will ultimately come to a time of celebration.*

At this point, I would invite you to apply the principle of the Tabernacle of Moses, and its orchestrated furnishings, to understand where John was standing during his encounter. Between visions, John heard the Lord identify Himself as the *"Alpha and the Omega,"* also *"the First and the Last!"* The Lord's operations move concurrently with whatever name He reveals about Himself. By telling John He's *the Alpha and the Omega,* and confirming it with *the First and Last,* the Lord was establishing the fullest extent of all He chooses to be to mankind as He unfolds and finishes His purposes. If the Lord is the beginning and ending of all Christian experience, then He is also everything in between. Christian experience begins with His amazing grace and ends with His astounding grace.

John heard the voice of the Lord in the midst of the golden candlesticks—one of seven dimensions of spirit in the Tabernacle. He turned, or reversed his position to see this fantastic vision. The arrangement of the Tabernacle reveals he was facing the Table of Showbread in the beginning of the vision. (To turn from the Table on the north side of the Tabernacle of Moses is to turn toward the Golden Candlestick on the south side.) The Table is the revelation of the finished work of Christ at Mount Calvary. Anytime we look to Mount Calvary, we will behold the Christ, who is the fullness of the Godhead bodily. The Lord's Day is a revelation of Christ as Lord, and no one else. The Lord is the sum total of everything about His day. Every view and revelation we've had of Him thus far pales in comparison to what is seen within the parameters of the Lord's Day.

The psalmist, in Psalm 148:8, pens a powerful verse that encapsulates the activities of the Day of the Lord.

Fire, and hail; snow, and vapour; stormy wind fulfilling His word (KJV).

Probably the most striking portion of this verse is collected in the idea *"stormy wind fulfilling His word!"* Having lived in eastern North Carolina for many years, and now, Southwest Florida, I can attest to the power of hurricanes with utmost certainty. These awesome storms, mounting up in the Atlantic, Indian, and Pacific Oceans, are rated according to intensity and wind speed, from minimal to catastrophic. Any storm declared catastrophic is loaded with much impending disaster for all in its path. Yet, somehow, I have watched God build an asylum for His people in the midst of them.

I saw this firsthand in Southwest Florida after Hurricane Charley, August 2004. Many church buildings were left standing in the midst of horrific destruction. Even my residence had very minimal damage after dangerous winds toppled huge oak trees. Other places of business were completely blown to pieces. It proved to me that a merciful God spares and delivers the uncompromisingly righteous in such times.

Until our perspectives are adjusted, no one expects refreshing to begin as destruction to secular and religious agendas. Most of the time, we expect the Lord to pour fresh waters on what we are already doing rather than to adjust us. What things have you personally lost in order to find the Lord? We have cut our teeth on a theology that portrays God as a *glorified Santa Claus*; when in fact, He is a Father who delights in blessing and chastening His children. This is another way of looking at the balance of glory.

In the natural, tropical storms are necessary to bring balance to the tropical and subtropical regions. However, many people are affected by such storms (for God rains on the just and the unjust). Our consequences are different based upon our relationship with the Lord. In fact, it is an issue of perception. What appears to be total ruin to the wicked is nothing more than a glorious opportunity for the righteous to observe God's Word fulfilled. The Father turns our pain into gain; we are more appreciative of the crown after the cross.

One of the more comprehensive views of the wicked and the righteous simultaneously in the Day of the Lord is Isaiah chapters 24–26. While admitting these chapters have future implications, there are current applications for each of them now. With each new, radical judgment upon the carnal handiworks of humans, we perceive the present relationship of God's Day. The wicked are judged and overthrown from their iniquity; the righteous are judged and elevated to greater Kingdom responsibility. Wicked men are exposed and turned upside down; the righteous are consecrated and hidden in Christ (see Col. 3:3), enabling them to stand upright. Just as faithful Noah was instructed and protected in the ark during the great watery judgments of his dispensation (see Gen. 7–8), the righteous are preserved in Christ in this present dispensation of the fullness of times (see Eph. 1:10).

The Day of the Lord releases the Lord as the divine confronter and comforter. In the words of the Song of Songs, He's both the north wind and the south (see Song 4:16) Without hesitation, He confronts everything (good and evil); and God comforts those that mourn in Zion. Paul said, *"Each one's work will become clear; for the Day will declare it, because it will be revealed by fire; and the fire will test each one's work, of what sort it is"* (1 Cor. 3:13). The Lord confronts every loathsome, idolatrous practice to utterly banish them from the face of the earth. He equally confronts good things— things requiring dismissal because their purpose concludes. He exalts Himself alone in His great and dreadful day. The storm violently overthrows man-made apparatuses that have circumvented divine purpose and intentions.

The Day of the Lord may also be likened to a *divine roadblock*. God barricades us by saying, "You will proceed no further fulfilling your will masking it behind My Word and self-centered prayers in Jesus' name!" The Day of the Lord is not a flashing, yellow caution light that says, "Proceed at your own risk!" No, it's a red light. Actually, an anointed, sustained red light saying, "Thus far and no more!" Man comes to the end of his doings. This is not just a spot check of God ignoring delinquent behavior; it is a divine commitment to destroy the enemies of divine purposes and reform His people.

Godly prophets and people have already confronted many of God's children many times in each century; but very few prophets have been taken seriously enough for the Church to reverse her carnal ways. (Modern prophets must remember we are turning a great ship and not a canoe!) The Lord God sent many warnings to the children of Israel because He had compassion on them and His Temple. They mocked the messengers, despised God's words, and scoffed at His prophets until there was no remedy. The Spirit of the Lord during the preciousness of worship has dealt with us, and we have never blinked an eye to acknowledge it was He. God has used many methods to talk with us—most to no avail until something disparaging happens. Because refreshing with reformation is imminent, the Day of the Lord is the tool of correction. It is no longer a futuristic promise; it is upon us—like it or not!

In our key text (Psalm 148:8), two contrasts are employed, accompanied by a third manifestation to depict the Day of the Lord: (1) fire and hail, (2) snow and vapors, and (3) a stormy wind. These forces cooperate in assisting the Lord to make known His magnificent power. God is magnified as the Almighty, whether in the progeny of the cold (snow and hail) or posterity of the heat (fire and vapors). Rising and continually falling, congealing and condensing, each of these agencies wreaks havoc on the folly of man's doings. Hurricane winds blast with incalculable intensity and fury, though under divine auspices, to promulgate God's designs and to nullify man's. After such horrific shakings, who can but acknowledge that God alone is great, and greatly to be praised? God's shakings are purposed to immerse the creation with a new appreciation of His power.

As we briefly examine these agencies, we will notice a beautiful plan from God, terminating all flesh and releasing refreshing. The New Covenant reveals that God's corrective measures are redemptive. For every knee must bow and every tongue must confess that Jesus Christ is Lord to the glory of God (see Phil. 2:10-11).

THE DAY OF THE LORD AS FIRE

The Scriptures have an abundance to say about fire. Beginning with the Garden of Eden and its flaming sword to the eschatological furnace of the Revelation of Jesus Christ, man has been subjugated to the blessing and terror of fire. Since my purpose is to implicate fire with refreshing, most of my thoughts will center there.

Hebrews 12:29 says, *"For our God is a consuming fire"*! This verse was quoted from Deuteronomy 4:24. Consuming fire is the passion of God totally engaged and active, revealing unstoppable determination. Passion can be defined as "a powerful emotion or appetite, as love, joy, hatred, anger, or greed."[1] God loves man with a fiery, consuming passion. The Day of the Lord finds God zealously pursuing and confronting mankind in all his ways. If man does not humbly return to God, He becomes the adversary to man's deliberate resistance.

There are four very basic reasons for God's passionate outcry in the Day of the Lord:

- God does nothing apart from passion. The foundation of passion is divine essence: It is what God is (see Exod. 20:5; 34:14; Deut. 5:9; 6:15; Josh. 24:19).

- God has a passion for establishing His sovereign, righteous government in the earth (see Is. 9:7).

- God's passion is always His fiery jealousy; it is never out-of-control extremism, which usually leads to terrorism (see 2 Sam. 21:1-2; Phil. 3:6; Acts 5:17; 13:45; 17:5; Gal. 5:20).

- God has such a passion for His House (the Church), nothing will hinder Him from establishing her as a House of Prayer.

When Jesus arose, filled with righteous indignation, He displayed a zealous attitude, a consuming fire for God's house (see John 2:13-17 KJV). Jesus quoted the first half of Psalm 69:9 in His fervent explosion: *"For the zeal of Thine house hath eaten Me up"!* (KJV) This was radical opposition to a cleverly devised system that was animated and maintained by conniving hearts of pernicious priests protecting their religious heritage. It was a ravenous system—extremely gluttonous for gain. Closing its eyes to the merchandising of God's people, men were never empowered into their purpose: a House of Prayer. Jesus took offense at this. He became especially combustible at this nightmarish practice and confronted it. Jesus became the present reality of the confrontational Day of the Lord.

Jesus Christ emitted a consuming fire in Him for Israel, the Old Covenant house of the Lord (see Ruth 4:11). That fire blazed as the *zeal of God* according to divine understanding. His passion prompted her deliverance from idolatry, which is self-centered service. We must understand that idolatry is presenting God with anything other than

His image. The modern church has excelled in this! Idolatry is a smoke screen that clouds the enormous opportunity to seek the Lord with all our hearts. The Day of the Lord forces us to shake off all the corruption of our idolatry: We lose the stench of our human idols as we behold the beauty of His divinity. We, then, become a people pure in heart who see the Lord. What an advantage! We put to death anything God isn't the author of in our lives. Our heavenly Father conscientiously intends to destroy everything He never told us to do!

As with our Lord Jesus, so it is with the apostolic and prophetic ministries in this modern refreshing and reformation. The apostle Paul maintains that the apostolic ministry has a *holy passion* in watching over the Church, the New Covenant House of God (see 2 Cor. 11:2; 1 Tim. 3:15). Their motivation, since Jesus established plurality in these ministries, is to present the Church as a chaste virgin to Christ. The ministry must model Christ's simplicity in order to accomplish this feat successfully. Overall, the Church is to walk in union with the Lord, joined to Him as bone of His bone, and flesh of His flesh.

As I travel in America and other nations, my heart burns for Christ's Church. I long to see the purity that flows out of grace's muscle rather than the brawn of some legalistic authoritarianism. People are passionate about different things in the world today, but not necessarily the Church. Perhaps that has some merit in the scheme of human activities. However, in the scheme of the divine, my passion keeps me on my knees for the Church. I can't imagine what life on this earth would be like without relationships with God's children living within the context of community. Many brethren have been afflicted and withdrawn from any associations with the local church. Not me! I enjoy being joined— for better or for worse. I'm joined closer to some men than to others by virtue of time, purpose, and years together. What we have built in concert is too precious to throw away. Jesus said our unity would speak much to the truth that the Father really did send Him.

HAIL AND SNOW IN THE DAY OF THE LORD

The Day of the Lord is equally snow and hail. Whether precipitating in winter's economy, or the thunderous cracklings of rain, both weather systems accomplish a sure purpose in nature's cyclic pattern. Each tiny, individualized snowflake and every marbled hailstone, small and great, descend with planned precision from the yielding hands of the Divine Weather-maker. As each flake or hailstone gathers together to form a community of expression, they suddenly become a force to be reckoned with. The suddenness of a hailstorm or the long awaited forecasted snowstorm speaks profoundly. It's the prolonged deployment of the Voice of the Lord ambushing man's structures. The unexpected hailstones fall like heavenly torpedoes; like a merciful messenger each snowflake zeroes in on the target of human mishmash.

Ezekiel saw a time of great hailstones and a stormy wind demolishing a wall built and daubed with intemperate mortar (see Ezek. 13:10-14). Briefly, this wall was built with something never exposed to the fire of God. It is a replacement, a substitution, for the real deal. Prime examples are denominational sectarianism, professional priestcraft, most end-time teachings on eschatology and clericalism. I am convinced these ideas erupted out of the belly of the beastly system called Babylon that has unveiled itself in many different shades of color throughout the history of mankind. They have no scriptural foundations. The antichrist spirit has cleverly made these ideas staples of belief in most church systems, distorting true Kingdom purposes.

The definition of this wall may also range from mere building projects to mental infrastructures resisting the mind of Christ. They all stand as titanic forces coated with steel, daring anything to oppose them other than the Day of the Lord. The Day of the Lord becomes a bashing, blasting tempestuous storm. If we don't discern God's grace in the matter, it will seem like we're *sinners in the hands of an angry God*. In addition, unbelievably, God has no reason to be angry in this manner. When human systems have veered from God's purposes, He stirs things up through apostolic warfare to get humans back on track. Apostolic warfare and words become the earthly agencies employed by Heaven to do eternity's bidding. Since waters are compared to words, when they come from high altitudes, they form hailstones. Prophetic words from the Heavens become great hailstones on man's constructions. God's projected hailstones are great against this wall, as if a great pearl.

Although beautiful in the end, pearls have uncongenial beginnings. Pearls begin as irritants in the shells of certain mollusks, finishing as smooth, lustrous gems. The Day of the Lord is both irritating and excoriating to man's flesh (see Rev. 16:21). It is an overwhelming storm whose purpose is to destroy man's wall (will) and discover his foundations. The idea involves denuding the foundation, bringing everything to the bottom for inspection. Following the Father's spiritual appraisal, He raises up a glorious, incorruptible expression daubed with truth. It is raised in divine order and beauty with nothing added by human inventiveness.

Arriving upon the shattered premises of the Earth during the Day of the Lord is a virtuous woman (the overcoming Church) not afraid of hail and snow (see Prov. 31:21). In fact, she welcomes them! She realizes God's cold, chilly judgments are His means of purification. It reminds me of the severely cold weather in places like Alaska which prevent the germination and growth of certain bacteria that thrive in the Southern states. Our temperatures in the South remain much too moderate in the winter to kill them. The psalmist said that through this storm called the Day of the Lord, which is an invasion of change, God's Word is fulfilled.

VAPORS AND A STORMY WIND

Job reveals that rain falls proportionately to the vapor received in the heavens (see Job 36:26-28). The Day of the Lord is like an onrushing, windy rainstorm, unleashing great fury upon the vices of the wicked (see Prov 10:25). Righteous men are always established and their integrity manifested during such an hour of trial. It is actually the prayers and the praise of the righteous ascending before the throne of God that forms the clouds of the stormy wind. The Lord's breath becomes the steering currents once the winds begin to blow. Since the Charismatic Renewal, God inhaled all the true incense (see Ps. 141:2; Rev. 5:8) of the saints. Our prayers and praise ascend like vapors because of God's holy fire upon us. Now, God is exhaling with the blast of His nostrils. The practical outworking of this is called the Day of the Lord.

Most of God's children had no earthly idea that He would inhale for at least three decades before He began exhaling with intensity. Certainly, there have been short breaths of refreshings and judgments in these years, but nothing comparable to the imminent Day of the Lord. The clouds are formed; they are distilling waters, massing storm surges very unpredictable. Natural prophetic indicators are floods, droughts, volcanoes, violent hurricanes, and El Niño weather patterns all within a short span of each other. Earthquakes and many other natural disasters arrive daily. There is no escape. Every hidden thing is revealed in the Day of the Lord. Even preachers riding the fence of refusal to publicly commit to the truth must arise from politically correct maneuvering in the Day of the Lord. The question before every child of God: "Where do you personally stand in this Day of the Lord?"

A north wind is blowing upon the Church, God's garden (see Song of Solomon 4:16). In this context, only the blowing wind can release the fruit that is sealed in his garden. God is also anointing the Church with glory, breaking the grip of religious familiarity and unproductivity, releasing a **presence of God** revival. The sign of gold dust in various camp meetings is indicative of the presence of God's glory. I assure you it is not the hoofs of horses kicking up the streets of gold preparing for the Battle of Armageddon. There is a different kind of battle going on here! We must fight, without relenting, to finish the work Jesus has assigned to us. The stormy wind is the Father's swift messenger (see Ps. 147:15). A storm surge is washing ashore, purposed to thoroughly wash away all the filth from the sons of the Kingdom. North winds are ferociously driving away every diseased idea in our carnality, calling us to a Kingdom mentality unprecedented.

As in Acts 27, the storm destroyed the ship, but not the people. The storm represented the brute, bestial systems and operations of men. Amazingly, the storm that destroyed the ship also brought forth Paul, the apostolic son of God, into a position of prominence in the

Kingdom. The darkest hour for the worldly is the brightest hour for the sons of the Kingdom. Every possible effort was made to save the ship without success. It parallels many of the conservative efforts to salvage the dying church system out of the hands of purported liberalism today. Settle it! The ship (the current wineskin of the church) is destined for the rocks, being propelled by a stormy wind with a wave (see Acts 27:14). Besieged systems of mankind are impregnated with holy intentions—a date with Christ, the true Rock of Ages. Current leaders will be saved and changed out of this encounter, thus creating a new culture of leadership.

This storm has brought the Church populace to a crossroad. What stands in the middle of the road is the cross. Not His—ours! On one side is tribulation, and on the other is the glory of God. Within the terrain of tribulation are inner, blasphemous desires, suggesting some other alternative to the cross (see 2 Tim. 3:1-7). In addition, you have men reeling back and forth, staggering like drunken men, and coming to their wit's end (see Ps. 107:27). Grief-stricken, the Church has begun to cry unto the Lord in her distress. This prepares her to come to the other side. Joyfully, the Lord has been seeking this response from the Church. Psalm 107:29 (KJV) says, *"He maketh the storm a calm, so that the waves thereof are still."* The stormy wind has produced divine fulfillment.

What appears to be the demise of mankind is the purposeful opportunity of the Holy Spirit. The man of sin (see 2 Thess. 2:3-8) is brought to extinction and spent by the brightness of the Day of the Lord. The beachhead is identified; the battle is won! The 20th century closed a cosmos that will no longer stand on the props of corruption expressed as religion, economics, military might, and political expediency. A tidal wave has been unleashed from the Heavens resulting in a dynamic, spiritual downpour. In all of this, what do you see? Do you see the Lord at work, or are you focused on the global disasters? I see the emergence of a new species of mankind coming forth, not as a relic of the old order, but a man full of divine splendor and relevance for the new day.

What will the Day of the Lord mean to you as a child of God? Will it be night or day? One of the most outstanding truths of the Bible is that God will establish His Kingdom in troublous times. What appears to be the midnight of humanity actually becomes God's love without measure, His grace with no limit. His wisdom in Christ is infinite, and the riches of His power have neither boundary nor horizon in the Day of the Lord. There is a constraining dynamic in God's love: He must accomplish everything He has purposed as an expression of sovereignty. God hears no sweeter music than the chimes of His own ideas fulfilled. Because of the law of love, which is greater than every other law, God has decided man must live at the highest level possible. Our heavenly Father has no regrets about the process it has taken to get man thus far. The Day of the Lord is a tool, an incredible instrument, to get man to that final destination.

The end of the Book of Job gives us some excellent instructions about what our conduct should be in the Day of the Lord. Job grappled with unprecedented dealings from the hand of God and couldn't shake them. His friends did not rightly discern God's dealings or His intentions, and chose to vilify Job. If there were such a thing as libel in those days, Job could have quickly replaced his lost wealth with enormous riches. Instead, much of the Book of Job was spent in diagnosis, debate, and rebuttal. Neither Job nor his friends knew what God had determined to accomplish in the secret places of His own will. God skillfully ascertained His purposes without destroying or marginalizing Job. In the end, He commanded Job to pray for his friends.

One cannot entertain revenge and flow in a spirit of intercession at the same time. Pray for those God has used to help you face things you ordinarily wouldn't even consider. The Book of Proverbs provides much wisdom to a son of God. It counsels us to *"Commit your works to the Lord, and your thoughts will be established. The Lord has made all for Himself, yes, even the wicked for the day of doom"* (Prov. 16:3-4). Everything, positive and negative, has a place in the greater scheme of things in the economy of God. God restored Job; Job prayed for his friends; and the latter end of Job was blessed more than his beginning. The sanctified purpose of all refreshings, whether they are showers, rains, or storms, is to bring each child of God to the same end Job experienced—an end that reveals God's wisdom, His mercy, and His boundless love.

> *In that day the Branch of the Lord shall be beautiful and glorious; and the fruit of the earth shall be excellent and appealing for those of Israel who have escaped. And it shall come to pass that he who is left in Zion and remains in Jerusalem will be called holy—everyone who is recorded among the living in Jerusalem. When the Lord has washed away the filth of the daughters of Zion, and purged the blood of Jerusalem from her midst, by the spirit of judgment and by the spirit of burning, then the Lord will create above every dwelling place of Mount Zion, and above her assemblies, a cloud and smoke by day and the shining of a flaming fire by night. For over all the glory there will be a covering. And there will be a tabernacle for shade in the daytime from the heat, for a place of refuge, and for a shelter from storm and rain* (Isaiah 4:2-6).

ENDNOTE

1. Webster's II New College Dictionary, Riverside University dictionary (New York: Houghton Mifflin Company, 1995), 803.

4

The School of Sovereign Subjects

Education is the knowledge of how to use the whole of one's self. Many men use but one or two faculties out of the score with which they are endowed. A man is educated who knows how to make a tool of every faculty—how to open it, how to keep it sharp, and how to apply it to all practical purposes.

- Henry Ward Beecher[1]

Never regard study as a duty, but as the enviable opportunity to learn to know the liberating influence of beauty in the realm of the spirit for your own personal joy and to the profit of the community to which your later work belongs.

- Albert Einstein[2]

Truth incarnate is the only spiritual truth that makes an effective appeal. Hence every teacher must feel, "My most effective lesson is myself."

- A. H. McKinney[3]

The greatest thing the disciples got from the teaching of Jesus was not a doctrine but an influence. To the last hour of their lives the big thing was that they had been with him.

- John Marquis[4]

The Day of the Lord brought great carnage to Egypt and great reprieve to the children of Israel. Contrary to all the slaughter in Egypt, God was preparing to fulfill a four-century promise. How do you spell *relief* for the Old Testament corporate son? It's spelled with the Day of the Lord's righteous recompense as He made dross of Pharaoh's host! Our heavenly Father preserved His children during the hour of trial; He didn't have to remove them. Gone are the days of the powerful Egyptian empire, both economically and militarily. Pharaoh and his bully pulpit don't exist anymore. Left in the dust are their gods, their troops, their crops, their firstborn children, and their dignity. The only difference between Egypt and Israel was an old man, his stick, and a crystal-clear word from God. God didn't allow Israel to relocate until they had seen His mighty deeds, and His holy arm made bare. The psalmist speaks eloquently to the moment: *"When the wicked are cut off, you shall see it. I have seen the wicked in great power, and spreading himself like a native green tree. Yet he passed away, and behold, he was no more; indeed I sought him, but he could not be found"* (Ps. 37:34c-36). After crossing the Red Sea and entering the lonely desert, the future looked promising and bleak respectively. It looked promising as to the termination of slavery, but bleak as to where this would lead. Israel had no idea they were headed to school, and the heralded wilderness would serve as their formidable classroom.

Metaphorically, the Day of the Lord is like a cyclone used to instruct us concerning God's purposes. Nothing is more indicative of change than a major cyclone sweeping through a region with cataclysmic fury. We gather much information about storms through televised weather reports. These reports didn't exist 30 years ago at the level of sophistication we see them today. Television allows us to witness all the wreckage from one of these storms steamrolling a community. I can only imagine how dreadful one of these storms must have been to people in the early 20th century who had no forewarning. The Day of the Lord compares to one of these events. It brings release for God's children. It's a high-powered storm of righteous judgment purging iniquity. God does forewarn us through His prophets so that it does not become an ill omen to all of us.

Remember, on the positive side, rain recharges the earth with essential minerals for healthy soil. The same rain with the right velocity in its winds can pack a devastating punch to level buildings and disrupt infrastructures. It signals an immediate, significant change. People in the direct vicinity of the storm, are left to grapple with every conspicuous alteration and inconspicuous modification. This is where the principles of transition become vital. Change is evident, and transition induces us to embrace with dignity what can't be undone. Change in this instance is physical, whereas transition is shifting mentally and attitudinally to adjust to the unavoidable.

The Day of the Lord reminds us that Sovereignty's hand has invaded our prized, highly convenient space. Reconstruction and reeducation to comply with the new conditions are paramount. We are forced, not by personal choice necessarily, but by the circumstances to enroll in the school of new beginnings. The old buildings and the old jobs don't exist anymore; they're blown away! There's no assurance the corporation will rebuild and restore the state of security everyone once felt. Maybe the company was entertaining a sweeter deal from some other locality and wanted to bail out anyway. The devastated conditions from the storm served as the catalyst to make the change.

Church folks, because they have been going to church rather than experiencing the transforming power of the Kingdom, also feel lost. What will we do? I believe the answer is obvious! Flow with the change and be renewed through each incremental step of transition. We must enter the school for sovereign subjects. This school will comprise of long-term and short-term stints; it will be exhilarating and excruciating; and it will cultivate and crucify your mind without apology.

MY DREAM AND SOVEREIGNTY'S HAND

One of the great highlights of my early adult life was the opportunity to fulfill a childhood dream by completing a university degree.

After enrolling, what I didn't know was Sovereignty's hand would delay my plans somewhat. The substances of my dreams were nourished while watching our little black-and-white television in the 1960s. I still remember watching all those brainy students from Ivy League universities win the College Bowl—a program in which various colleges would match wits. When you are a child, you have childlike faith and believe all things are possible. I would fantasize about becoming a hero in the College Bowl tournament. Children are able to daydream, walk on clouds, and project themselves onto the highest summits unless someone suggests otherwise. By the time I became college eligible, the College Bowl was no longer on television. Nevertheless, my dream of attending college had not died.

My parents, siblings, teachers, and extended family members had nurtured this wonderful vision in me. It was easy for them to do so because of my academic record. They each, in their own unique way, supported me and persuaded me to believe this goal was, not only possible, but also achievable. At the time, I did not know by experience futures are created by dreams. Most people who support your dreams usually don't caution you about bumps or potholes along the way either. In fact, you're never told until later that there's a cost to marrying your dream.

I entered Coastal Carolina Community College after graduating from high school. Our home was 20 miles from the campus, and I had to hitchhike to class the first two months. That was pretty draining, and I thought about quitting many days, especially when I would see ominous rain clouds gathering in a distance. My mother encouraged me to keep going; she believed the Lord would provide "daily bread" for me each day. Mom had more faith than I did in those days; all I could see was the circumstances. Hardships taught her to trust the Lord. My heavenly Father came through, allowing me to more perfectly appreciate the reality of His name, Jehovah-Jireh, which means, "The Lord will see to it (the provision)."[5]

Two years later, I had an Associate of Arts degree in general education with no money to go further. My father became ill the same year of my graduation, placing a temporary chink in my dream. I had to momentarily cancel my pursuits, get a job, and help my mother provide for the younger children. While reeling from recent events and watching my dream halt in midstream, close relatives kept it from becoming wish-craft! This particular time in my life would become a school of unsolicited beginnings. My heavenly Father would teach me about self-sacrifice, covenantal love, leadership responsibility, God's delays, conflict, and rest. After a short delay, I applied and reentered the university to complete my final two years of a teacher education program. Little did I know what awaited me. Everything God taught me in the interim phase between community college and four-year university was needful for this next step. All things really do work together for good in a son of God's life.

I talked with several incoming students during student orientation who were also pursuing a career in education. They were equally excited about our future and anticipated the day of our graduation. We registered for our classes for the spring semester and were on our way. Veterans in the education program had warned us about an infamous entry-level geography course taught by only one professor, Dr. Duncan P. Randall. I figured it was probably best to take this course at the beginning and get it over with; so, it was among my initial course load. Man! Was I in for a surprise!

Though I had decent study skills, I wasn't prepared to study a simple geography course with the level of intensity this one demanded. Not even the demands of community college prepared me for this. I realized I was in a crucible and my heavenly Father had set me up. Because this course was taught like an upper level climatology course, most education majors were ecstatic just to receive a passing grade in the course. Not me! My dream was at stake. I was convinced with proper attitude, prioritizing, and excellent study habits things would be different for me...and they were!

Geography helped me to understand that university life was very demanding; it's no place for loafers and could become a dream exploder. Reading requirements, comprehension levels, and testing had amplified a thousand times more. High school and community college were history—almost child's play. I was as much enrolled into the school of sovereign subjects as I was in secular schooling. Since all things work together for good, my Father was using this environment to further acquaint me with sovereign subjection. This would give me an opportunity to learn about the abundance of Father God's resources. I was about to be rapt with wonder and in awe concerning the mysterious ways of God. His ways are mysterious until He acquaints us with them.

HELP! I'M IN KINGDOM SCHOOL

Earlier, I stated that Israel and the Church are parallel stories. Our heavenly Father designed a school (more like a crash course in the minds of spiritual delinquents) to prepare His people to become a pattern society reflecting the Kingdom of God in the earth. Before He could introduce the blueprint of the constitution for a *special society*, certain crises were initiated to expose the weaknesses and superficiality of adolescent faith. Walk with Moses and Jesus in the early stages of their ministries. It becomes quite apparent why their followers needed intense instruction. Beneath the hardness of stony hearts is a sculpture of Christlikeness that must be chiseled out. An astute teacher never focuses on the crassness of the stone, just the image within the stone. Do an honest appraisal of the Church today and one must conclude the same. School was in! They were in a *prophetic crucible*—a furnace to change short-lived enthusiasm into deeply rooted assurance. Several quotes will substantiate that great thinkers historically understood the necessity of the school of sovereign subjects. Listen to their words:

> All education should be directed toward the development of character. Sound character cannot be achieved if spiritual development is neglected. I do not like to think of turning out physical and mental giants who are spiritual pygmies.
>
> - Dr. Walter C. Coffey[6]

All education that is not God and Christ centered is the wrong kind of education. Education without the recognition of God makes men fools, and the more of such education they get, the greater fools they become.

- W. S. Hottel[7]

God isn't in the business of producing spiritual pygmies, dwarfs, or fools. Bilious and bloated, fools say *"NO"* to God. The great end of Kingdom education is to make disciples rather than window-dressing man's mind with an accumulation of illustrious thoughts. In order to make a disciple, the Father judiciously exposes us to a variety of learning environments—some thrilling and some rather humdrum. Each will intentionally teach us something about our God, whose ways are past finding out. We must walk through God's character builders with temperance and self-control, also with diligence and strength. Actually, school develops this kind of nature in us.

Spiritual pygmies will accept the path of least resistance, and cannot lead a generation into the 21st century. Many may possess marvelous gifts but are short on character. Rather than becoming fascinated with our budding future as Kingdom subjects, pygmies create a leadership vacuum. The only way to clear this matter up is to reeducate believers and become better qualified to minister in the 21st-century world—which is a world of *change, change,* and *more change*. The world has changed, and the Church is stuck in the throes of little or no change, a mind-set reminiscent of a frozen Ice Age. There are at least three universal classrooms believers must joyfully attend without murmuring. Sovereign subjects are qualified in the crucible of affliction and soothed by the tonic of grace in each school. Cries ricochet from the hearth of refining fires that say, "Help! I'm in school again!"

THE CLASSROOM OF DISAPPOINTMENT

The classroom of disappointment is one of the most powerful tools our heavenly Father uses to either expose the shallowness or to reveal the depth of our faith in Him. It takes us beyond the shallow waters of mental ascent as God plunges deeply into the murky seas of an evil heart of unbelief. The first generation of Israelites who were delivered out of Egypt were frustrated by this classroom. In fact, they immediately faced this classroom three short days after being delivered out of Pharaoh's hand (see Exod. 15:22-26). They aligned with misinformation and plodded in the wilderness for 40 years when the journey to freedom should have taken them 39 years, 350 days less. Why turn a two-week trip into a 40-year journey?

God presents a syllabus to the prospective students covering three major areas: His delays, His methods, and His claims. Lesson plans are filled with repetition. Repeatedly God teaches us many things, line upon line, and precept upon precept. Each student must show a mastery of the subject matter or continue to recycle the same field of study. In addition, Christians would be wise to forget about alternative learning situations when the Lord has chosen to become the headmaster. There are no promotions because of good behavior or length of time in class. Certain cues will reflect in the character of the students indicating the lesson was caught.

The patriarch Abraham renders our first study in the school of disappointment. He was the opening line in the faith saga—a narrative the heavenly Father chose to introduce the legal, messianic lineage. As we are introduced to the call of Abraham, God promises a *seedless* man many descendants. Every other promise and blessing would pale in comparison to this one. Perhaps filled with joyful anticipation over this proclamation, Abraham was ready to journey into the unknown and become the *father of all faithful* children of God. From the human viewpoint, there's a glitch in this story. What God didn't tell him was as important as what He told him. Abraham had no way of knowing God would delay the fulfillment of that wonderful promise for 25 years. Human logic says it's idiotic to wait that long; and one would have a better prognosis with more self-initiative. Besides, doesn't the Bible say, "God helps those who help themselves"? I have searched many years for this phantom verse, and haven't found it yet! Many Christians believe this saying really is in the Bible, when in fact, it is not.

Space, time, fears, apparent failures, and successes are sandwiched between the promise and the fulfillment. This means Abraham wasn't ready to handle responsibly the gift of God without turning it into an anomaly. He would separate from many things during those years and become acquainted with the *"zero factor."* The zero factor means *there's nothing measurable or otherwise determinable we can do to speed up God's planned purposes.* God's movements coincide with His own pre-determined purposes. When they happen, it will be His grace, and His grace alone.

One of the great stories in the New Testament concerning *God's delays* is the resurrection of Lazarus (see John 11:6-32). Jesus, being sensitive to the Father's voice, delayed going to Bethany to minister to Lazarus while he was sick, and yet, physically alive. The Father planned a greater accomplishment in delay while revealing a greater glory of His Son simultaneously. If Jesus had listened to the voice of personal egoism, political correctness, sentiment, or human ambition, He would have hindered a prophetic statement the Father was making about His total victory over death. Jesus delayed two days before going to wake Lazarus up. It was the *kairos* time to establish that the resurrection is a *person* and not just a *day*. The distressed mourners had faith for another day or season, but none for the present. *Faith* and the *glory of God* kissed one another and took center stage that day.

When I was 17 years old, God spoke to me about going to the nations of the earth to declare the gospel of the Kingdom of God. Believe me, I had no actual appreciation of what that meant. Excited, yes! With comprehension, no! After reading about how the Master prepared disciples in three and one-half years for the same mission, I figured diligence and persistence would prepare me in the same length of time. What I didn't consider was: These men were with Jesus every day! Let's just conservatively estimate:

- Hebrew year = 360 days x 3 years and 3 months = 1170 days

- 1170 days x 24 hours per day = 28,080 hours

- Spending an average of two hours a day in our busy world would require 14,040 days to attain 28,080 hours with the Lord.

- Using the Hebrew calendar that would require 39 years.

Most Christians desire to do what the apostles did without this amount of time. I had faith for three and one-half years, which meant my faith was very weak and superficial. Man, was I shocked into reality! I dashed headlong into the brick wall of God's delays. Frustrated because the Father had bunged me in my tracks, I tried other methods to release myself from the divine lasso that had encompassed my neck and restrained my will. I'll never forget the exhortations of William Ambrose, a friend and early mentor. He would often say, "Steve, you cannot outrun your makings!" This homespun wisdom probably saved me unnecessary heartache and steps.

This unmovable lasso remained fixed for 12 years. After school one day, my ever-working mind conceived an idea that amounted to nonsense. Possibly this would be a good day to speak with the U.S. Army recruiter about military service. My logical reasoning, which I thought was rational, said: "Surely God wouldn't mind if I began a military career!" The benefits seemed more appealing than the dreadful classroom.

Once again I had to face the music and quit trying to manipulate my future and current circumstances with good ideas. God's method was to use a heathen to speak forth His purposes to a hardheaded son who had refused to listen to His still, small voice. It happened in my case! The recruiter humiliated me and I left realizing my Father was behind this whole thing. Walking out of that building bewildered, I threw my hands up and yelled, "You win, God!" God's delays had accomplished His prudent purposes. He won convincingly, and my bumbling flesh lost profoundly! Shortly after this acknowledgment, God released me, with the blessing of my pastor and other covenant brothers, into the ministry of Christ. My first trip to the nations happened that same year.

God's delays will bring one into the synchronized classroom with God's methods. His methods are "the means or manner of procedure, especially a systematic and regular way of accomplishing a given task."[8] There is a simple rule to remember here: God's ways are not our ways, and His thoughts are not our thoughts (see Isaiah 55:8-9).

It's possible to mistakenly think He will work in a certain way that is inconsistent with His will. Sometimes we craft these thoughts in our own minds only to be disappointed.

For example, Jesus could have easily shown up two days earlier without suffering the scorn of religious spirits to raise dead Lazarus. However, God's methods, in this incident, didn't mitigate such a safe cushion. Jesus had stopped funeral processions and called a little girl back to life, but never anything like this. A young man, a female, and now a mature man were all raised from the dead. This represented the spirit, soul, and body being raised from the dead. Lazarus symbolized the body encased in sin and death and held entombed by the stone of the Law. All the bandages wrapped around him were the trappings of a legalistic system that ensconced bondage. God's methods were to free him and His delays made it gloriously possible.

The final element in the classroom of disappointment is God's claims. God's claims force each of us to deal with what I earlier called the *zero factors*. We are reduced from our mountainous egos, our improper motivations, and our allurements to success in a zero atmosphere. True Kingdom ministry isn't about these things anyway. Modern America has glamorized ministry through Christian media and falsified its purposes, creating a culture of prima donnas. Many Christians have made the accumulation of things the true measure of God's endorsement. The Scriptures suggest ideas exactly opposite to this. When Jesus was placing His claims on a man, He said, *"Go your way, sell whatever you have and give to the poor, and you will have treasure in heaven; and come, take up the cross, and follow Me"* (see Matt. 19:21). It doesn't matter what our pedigree may be; only Christ and the revelation of Him crucified matters.

Unless one is passionately in love with Jesus, the *zero factor* may eclipse man's consciousness and darken his countenance. His behavior may cause others to doubt the veracity of his faith. Things may have a powerful grip on people's lives and often become meaningless idols. God's claims prevent anything from standing between

Him and us. If we are holding on too snugly to our stuff, make no mistake about it: God pursues us through the medium of the cross to let go. At this point, there is no way to caress our disappointment, or camouflage our anger. As we repent of these human, almost diabolical attitudes, the spirit of revelation, burning with eternal flames, brings adjustment to our minds. God's claims have for a foundation His unadulterated, unfeigned love. It was the height and depth, the width and breadth of His love that He was trying to convey all the time. God's delays, His methods, and His claims are all love issues.

There comes a time in the economy of God when the heavenly Father will say, *"That there should be delay no longer"* (Rev. 10:6c). Delay no longer the ultimate purpose of God as revealed in the finished mystery. Until now, that mystery has been *Christ in you* the glorious hope. The finishing of that mystery is *"Christ upon you,"* manifesting the fullness of all that He is, transforming all of creation. In the days of the sounding of the seventh angel (see Rev. 10:7), which is the voice of the seventh trumpet, our God wraps up His purposeful labors. Psalm 29:9 reveals a clue to what happens when the seventh voice sounds: *"The voice of the Lord makes the deer give birth, and strips the forests bare; and in His temple everyone says, 'Glory!' "*

God births a son (see Rev. 12), and this becomes the hallmark event in the crowning touches of the mystery. The cry of all in His temple is not for more faith or anointing; the cry is consistent with the season of God. It's a cry of *glory!* It is also a world of transparency, for the forest speaks of the collective expression of all of mankind in all his varieties. Mankind fully submitted to Christ has many benefits. For one, we discover a true self-expression centered in the core of Christ. *"It's in Christ that we find out who we are and what we are living for. Long before we first heard of Christ and got our hopes up, He had His eye on us, had designs on us for glorious living, part of the overall purpose He is working out in everything and everyone"* (Eph. 1:11-12 The Message). Perhaps the meaning of the word bare, (to strip off a covering so as to bare what is covered) [9], indicates total transparency in Christ.

THE CLASSROOM OF CONFLICT

Blessed be God, my mountain, who trains me to fight fair and well (Psalm 144:1 The Message).

The classroom of conflict is about moving away from the agony of soulish duality into the stable place of oneness with the Father. It is realizing completeness is in no other source than God's amazing grace. Kingdom advancement comes through the dynamic of conflict (see 2 Sam. 3:1). It is the crossroads between the old and the new; the place in which we think what is considered unthinkable; speak the unspoken; do what has never been done before; or we travel the beaten path of the usual, the ordinary, the safe path of mediocrity. During conflict, the new order will swell stronger and the old order will wax weaker.

In practical terms, that means there are many things in our past that blessed our lives but will not bless us now because their season is completed. They have become a *spiritual* and *natural oxbow*. Webster defines oxbow as "a U-shaped bend in a river."[10] Sometimes the forces of nature will cause the river to move in another direction, leaving the oxbow as an indication the river once flowed there. Allow me to paint a picture of this in both the natural and the spiritual. Let's draw upon the preponderance of evidence from the Industrial Revolution and the early days of the Protestant Reformation.

As important as the Industrial Revolution of the 18th century was, it's a bygone idea, an extinct modern dinosaur. During this period, extensive mechanization of production systems resulted in a shift from home-based manufacturing to large-scale factory production. The grand accomplishment of this era was radical modernization, social and economic changes. Factory worker was a most desired occupation at the time for common men seeking to improve themselves. Millions of citizens flocked to major cities to improve their economic status. Serving God wasn't, necessarily, in the picture. The initial phase of the Industrial Revolution is no more because the factories have locked their gates and moved into developing nations at cheaper prices. In the United States, the Industrial Revolution has been succeeded by the information age and the technology revolution, and now, the informational/digital age respectively. What was once a flooding job market has now become an ebb tide of joblessness.

Nothing creates mental, emotional, and moral *conflict* quicker than the suddenness of unemployment brought on by a changing world. It's overwhelming to wake up one day and realize you may be unemployed. Lost jobs destabilize the economy and every other aspect of society. Every industry and service-oriented business depends upon a strong economy. Even nonprofit organizations and charitable donations are equally dependent upon a strong economy and people's liberality. When there's no money, there are no gifts. The problem may be eliminated, but not without great cost. United States citizens must adapt and reeducate themselves if they are to connect with a global society with its many opportunities. Most baby boomers, like me, must make some serious adjustments! Our brains must cast off the rust of inactivity and get out of the gear of mosey. It's a technological world requiring greater math skills and in-depth critical thinking. People who have strong computer skill are some of the most attractive draws for employers. Let the manual typewriter die gracefully, and get in step with the times. I am moved with compassion repeatedly as I hear about the pain of Americans because of joblessness. Permit me to ask you: How are you preparing yourself for the 21st century? Are you willing to change? Are you willing to think global?

In the realm of spiritual exactness, the *showers* of the Lutheran Reformation created great conflict in the 16th century and are history. These showers subsided, being replaced by the *fiery rains* of Pentecostal fervor in the 20th century. Pentecostal people created great conflict, curiosity, and chaos. They're also responsible for great spiritual advancements in the Kingdom of God. The renowned physicist Albert Einstein thought humans should never lose holy curiosity. Speaking in tongues became a modern stone of stumbling to many people. Shall we dare say that the Pentecostal Movement, not the experience, is history? Now, the creation is being inundated with the *storms* of the Day of the Lord flowing out of the Feast of Tabernacles. Christianity's challenge is to receive the influx of overcoming grace by cooperating with God in the employment of His limitless resources of grace. God will teach our hands to fight and our fingers to make war! There's one interesting dilemma, though, in this: *THE WAR TO RESTORE MANKIND'S RIGHTFUL CREATED STATUS IS OVER!* Jesus Christ restored man's dominion in the earth. In the real battle, King Jesus has won with a convincing victory, flattening serpentine subtleness, death, hell, and the grave along the way. Jesus triumphantly placed His feet upon all of the above mentioned. What, then, is the remaining war?

The modern conflict for the children of God consists primarily of the struggle for our whole man (spirit, soul, and body) to come home to Father God, after being absent for so long. The mixture of *legalism* and *irresponsible grace* for the last two thousand years has misrepresented the integrity of Father God's intentions toward all mankind. I see this so clearly in the episode of the two prodigals in Luke 15:11-32. There were two sons bespeaking two different orders. The older son, representing the previous move of God, was proud, religious, reticent, and compliant; *he was very insecure.* The younger son, symbolizing the new wave of God, was immature, therefore arrogant, rebellious, and full of revelry; *he was overconfident.* The father divided the *inheritance* with *both sons* because he loved both equally. Neither the older son nor the younger son had a revelation of grace because both were *wasters.* The profound truth of grace will not allow us to misconstrue the generous gifts of God. The old order did *nothing,* whereas the new order strayed and played. Let's open the classroom of conflict by telling the story of the younger son.

The younger son became deceived, left his father, and *journeyed into a far country.* The first man, representing all men, gave up his citizenship in the Heavens, trading it for carnality and naturalness. He traded the immediacy of God's immanence for distance. Man's sense realm governed his desires and appetites. He no longer had the opportunity to develop intuitively and just enjoy the spontaneity of fellowship with the heavenly Father. Man, now, had to depend upon the ability to gain carnal education based solely upon external stimuli. As communion with the Father ceased, communion with the physical increased, becoming perverted. His conscience was stained with the consciousness of sin and no longer knew the holiness of God. It was corrupted with a diluted perception of good and evil, which is duality. (We will discuss duality in detail in a later chapter.)

In this unconscionable state, man became an extravagant waster. Once the portals of the Heavens closed, and man arose in carnality, he began to dissipate spiritually. Man became fragmented, detached, and incomplete. By feeding on the presence of the Father during sweet fellowship, man would have remained an integration, which means "to make into a whole by bringing all parts [spirit, soul, and body] together."[11] After disobeying, man was shipwrecked and dead in his spirit man (no communion with Father God). The process of dissipation continued in the first man until his spirit finally separated from his body in physical death. He was alive in his soul, yet perverted in knowledge based upon the sense realm, thus demonstrating total disintegration.

Mired in the slippery soil of carnality, a quagmire of humanism, man discovered that sin, *mistaken identity*, is costly. This was no misdemeanor; in fact, it was a felony temporarily costing everything. When a man feeds from the carnal process rather than the Spirit of God, he becomes a casualty in the making. This rickety process is burdensome, exhausting, and will drain all the life from a man. God wanted man to understand the value of what they had together; so, He permitted him to sink deeply. Instead of spending all in a godly sense to gain progressive, spiritual understanding, man lost all because of improper fellowship with the wrong sources.

When that happened, destitution, scarcity, and famine became man's portion. One cannot continue the corrupted pathway of sin without experiencing the dead-end city called famine. Inevitably, there was no spiritual food in this city; there were just enough crumbs to sustain life for 70 or 80 years. The cry of everyone present was for rations. Eating the emptiness of vanity was the daily portion of every citizen of the city of famine. There was a great need for deliverance and freedom in this realm. All but forgotten was the loving, lasting, and satisfying meal at the Father's banquet table in which He's both the Host and the main course.

Man was in a horrendous, ghastly state. After becoming enslaved by the habits developed because of the presence of death, he became an alien in his own mind to the heavenly Father. He became *political* (not in a Kingdom sense), bouncing between anarchy and tyranny. Weaknesses in character became the catalyst for bias based on illusions and immorality as a natural disposition. Man was now operating as a citizen of the same country with the serpent, the beast nature, the false prophet, death, and hell. This pseudo-fivefold expression was a constant companion with him, influencing every vital decision. Man plunged into the darkness of night, the blight of his soul. The veil of fleshly imaginations blinded his mind from its enormous possibilities. Repentance alone would turn him from the blot caused by dimness of perception, and allow the glorious light of Christ to shine into the confusing maze of his mind.

The trap for the final plunge into selfhood was positioned, ready to spring with unmerciful results. The highest expression of anything is to become the thing. When we choose to chart our own course, we already have a predetermined ship ride into the lowest hell. The prodigal fed swine and ate swine's food. This was total assimilation, which means "to absorb and incorporate into the body; to make part of one's own thinking."[12] Literally, becoming a pig was the result of living in such a malapropos environment. Man wasn't just associated with uncleanness; he had become consummate uncleanness. Herein completed the matured manifestation of what it means to become antichrist. From this depressed condition, there remained no place to go but upward. Repentance was the next step. Before we access Father God's solution, let's look at the older son.

The older son was a workaholic, constantly trying to merit the love of the father. Like most compliant personalities, he tried to be inoffensive, tractable, fruitful, and useful. Buried beneath this acceptable façade were mountains of seething, volcanic anger. While others were loafing, this son spent his time in the field *"working for"* instead of *"working with"* the father. He was doing the work of the ministry by gathering crops. Although this was an excellent work, the father's heart primarily was for him to prioritize his relationship with him. I have found this to be the general rule of Kingdom operation: Out of relationship comes ministry. The sentiment of the father's heart is relationship first, then production later.

The deadness of the older son's efforts (produced by a horrific, religious attitude) caused alarm in him. When the younger son, the new order, was restored, something new and fresh happened. The older son was bewildered by the celebration, the exuberance of joy. Joy was contrary to the somberness and grief that had been the daily portion of the older son's rote activities. In fact, if this was a worship service, this effervescing presence was quite contrary to traditional ways of expression. The older son was so entangled in the rote and formalism of each day's endeavors that the spontaneity of joy and the newness of life could not be properly appreciated. There was an inability to celebrate the father's mercy. He concluded this new wave of exuberance definitely was not from God; no, it was just not authentic. Religious spirits most often take this posture. This new move of God must be smothered at once by anger and consternation. If it's not suffocated, it will expose my religious spirit.

Of course, the younger son needed some adjustments in his character. While the father was heartbroken about his dastardly deeds, hellish experiences became a ways-and-means committee to develop lasting character in the son. The younger son's demanding spirit, which was openly expressed, was broken by adversity. Contrary winds produced a fulfillment of the word called "discipline." Deeds of sin could not destroy his remembrance of his father. Indelibly, a blueprint of the father was burnt within his memory. The love of the father, not the law of the father, drew him back home. Grace washed his weary soul with a regularity that axed all the pathological deeds of the past.

Although a worker, the older son had character flaws also. Perhaps he harbored resentment and bitterness toward his younger brother.

In fact, he hated his own compliant nature. Speaking of jealousy! It really is as cruel as the grave. The older son needed the father to adjust him likewise. When the father came out to him, he was seeking to bring him home although he was already in the house. Apparently, he was insecure in his relationship with his father. He supposed love was based upon *doing*, rather than *being*. The father entreated the older son to become one with what he was doing. This truly illustrates the impartiality of the father's love. Moreover, the father was equally concerned about both sons.

The voice of resentment (*Why did I have to do this?* or *Why me, Lord?*) is a law-keeper, control freak, and a manipulator supreme. Our heavenly Father will walk us through whatever is necessary to train us in the graces of true sonship. If the older son had known that it was all based upon grace, he probably would have entered blatant lawlessness just as the younger son. His *fear*, rather than his *love*, caged and controlled him.

The voice of accusation cannot forgive or forget the past, thus manifesting the lower, carnal nature of man. Satan, the adversary, is an accuser of the brethren (see Rev. 12:10). Walking in condemnation is no different from walking in lawlessness. Although they are polar opposites, one religious, and the other unrestrained, neither reveals a heart of love and obedience. A son must learn the balance of walking in love and agreement with whatever the father is doing, even if it is adverse to his doctrinal persuasions.

Interestingly, the father addressed the elder son as *teknon* (see Luke 15:31). This word implies relationship, but lacks the wholeness of mature relationship. The son had chronological age, but he lacked spiritual age. He was an heir to all the father had (see Gal. 4:1); however, he would be no different from a slave until he matured. All his labors amounted to no more than slavery, saturated with gripes and complaints. Though he was "lord of all," he would be under tutors and governors until the time appointed of the father. He never realized that he was the hindrance to his own growth and happiness. Selfishness had crippled him. He needed an adjustment from his own egoism, an opportunity to master his own emotions.

111

The father, both caring and compassionate, ministered to each son. The classroom of conflict was to bring each son to the place of rest. The younger prodigal came to a place of resolve, a place of immense determination. His return to the father, and subsequent restoration, is a marvelous picture of the Dispensation of Grace. The father fell on his neck (will) and kissed every bit of condemnation out of him. Although this son wasted some things, it did not bankrupt the father's desire to give him the best inheritance he had. It solidifies the truth that severed fellowship does not denote severed relationship.

Despite their destitute conditions, their spiritual insolvency, the father loved both of them unconditionally. If there's such a thing as eternal security, this is it! Definitely, it was time for the older son to understand his father in this manner. The fatted calf represents the immense quantity of God's grace ready to be lavished upon His creation. A person rapidly progresses toward maturity when one becomes other people-centered. Other than stinking selfishness, why is it so harrowing to see others are blessed as much as we are? The innate tendency of the carnal man is to be self-absorbed and self-centered. Love of self must know it was crucified with Christ in order for our relationship with the Father to perpetually develop.

THE CLASSROOM OF REST

And so this is still a live promise. It wasn't canceled at the time of Joshua; otherwise, God wouldn't keep renewing the appointment for "today." The promise of "arrival" and "rest" is still there for God's people. God Himself is at rest. And at the end of the journey we'll surely rest with God. So let's keep at it and eventually arrive at the place of rest, not drop out through some sort of disobedience. God means what He says. What He says goes. His powerful Word is sharp as a surgeon's scalpel, cutting through everything, whether doubt or defense, laying us open to listen and obey. Nothing and no one is impervious to God's Word. We can't get away from it—no matter what (Hebrews 4:8-13 The Message).

In the Old Testament, Joshua was given the task of leading God's people into the Promised Land, into the rest promised them by the heavenly Father. As with most Old Testament experiences, this was something temporary at best. The Book of Joshua describes for us the certainty of Joshua's fulfilled task. However, the fuller meaning of rest does not lie in some external, natural experience. God's true rest is a *powerful person*, and His name is Jesus. Jesus is the everlasting rest that the Sabbath Day, the Sabbath Year, and the Promised Land prefigured. He is the greater Joshua who invites His brethren to release their weatherworn conditions of unfulfilled works. By the time He came, He knew the creation was wounded, weather-beaten, and weary. Despite every imaginable combination of human effort, we have had surprisingly very few true experiences of rest. There is a freeing word in His mouth for us: *COME UNTO ME!*

The word that flows out of God's rest is sharper than any two-edged sword. In this season, for all practical purposes, the word flowing from any other realm is dull to the degree it has failed to remain current with God's times. It has been dulled by noxious mixture and a denial of spiritual realities, and at times, by a callous heart that is indifferent to God's love for His entire creation. Believers will not find the fullness of God's rest by simply keeping the Feasts of Passover and Pentecost. Both feasts are powerful, but will only get us a fraction of the way there. Being born again and filled with the Holy Spirit must give way to a greater reality. The place of God's rest is beyond the veil—the Most Holy Place, the Feast of Tabernacles. One of the most promising aspects of journeying through the wilderness is the fact that the journeys will conclude, and we'll enter the Lord's rest. The Lord's rest is not a place of inactivity—just check the many things Jesus did on the Sabbath. Conversely, it is a place of immense Kingdom activity. We must labor to enter that rest—the labor of love, and not the sweat of humanistic strength browbeating us into a frenzy of labors the Master never commanded us to do.

Since every New Covenant principle and reality find fulfillment in Jesus Christ, He respectively is God's rest. Jesus was a servant of consecrated activity, but also one who never moved from self-efforts. He also had times of active contemplation and quiet worship. Leaving the wilderness, where there's the conflict of soul and spirit, with little time for meditation, brings us to Christ. Like Martha in Luke 10:40, many of God's children are distracted with much serving, worried with and troubled about many things. They've yet to understand that there's a true labor to enter into the Lord's rest. Mary, Martha's sister, had chosen the better part by sitting at the Lord's feet. Sitting is the posture of rest—resting from everything.

I have seen and met many Marthas during the course of more than 30 years walking with God. Most of them are driven with a real sense of duty. Martha must come to understand that acceptance, security, and significance have very little to do with the quantity or quality of work she does. They only produce self-satisfaction, which is a false sense of security. A question Martha must answer is *"Do I want chores or Christ?"* Christ has given us an unimpeachable position in Him. Christians must be rooted and grounded in His boundless love—His extravagant grace. Attempting to find fulfillment through any other method is futile and wasted.

The word that flows out of rest emphasizes the finished work of Jesus Christ. This is the only word that is accurate or consistent with the current seasons of God. The Father purchased us and brought us to another mountain—Mt. Zion. *"For out of Zion shall go forth the law, and the word of the Lord from Jerusalem. He shall judge between the nations, and rebuke many people; they shall beat their swords into plowshares, and their spears into pruning hooks; nation shall not lift up sword against nation, neither shall they learn war anymore"* (Isa. 2:3b-4). The word of rest is the word declaring the end of our carnal warfare, and the amassing of weapons, usually indiscriminate words, of mass destruction. This word changes the hearts of men; it's not the stockpiling of information for the sake of having more fun facts. The rogue nations with lawless hearts will be rebuked by the word that flows out of rest. Out of Zion, the perfection of beauty, God shines forth.

We can ill afford to refuse the voice speaking from Mt. Zion. It is the voice of the Son of Righteousness who has healing in His rays rather than venom in His verbal communication. It is the voice of love, compassion, mercy, blessing, and forgiveness. There was a multitude of prophetic voices speaking in parts from the mountain of the Old Covenant. Every transgression and disobedience received a just reward under that order of things (see Heb. 2:2). The New Covenant rocks the religious populace by holding no grudges and forgiving everyone! It is a compelling message that conquers infantile, juvenile, and adult pathologies.

The Old Covenant voice mainly shook the earth—earthly affairs, kingdoms, and systems of men. In the New Covenant, the voice of the Lord will shake the Heavens and the earth. Principalities and powers are shaken in the Heavens, and principles and powerbrokers are shaken on earth. This indicates the removal of temporal things for the establishment of that which is permanent. The 21st-century Church must receive a kingdom that cannot be shaken. All man-made structures, no matter the amount of creativity and innovation used to produce them, are temporary at best. Only the things of the Spirit are permanent. God's grace teaches us to differentiate between the lasting and the fleeting. All provisional things are just to meet a short-term need. Once that need is met, the Father discards that order of things so that it doesn't become an ordeal. He nudges His children on to the next incremental step in the process of pragmatically leading them back into Himself.

I am amazed at the inept theologies, the interpretations of the last few hundred years, that say, "One day we will come to the city of God in a faraway heaven someplace in outer space!" Please understand I believe in Heaven as the place of God's abode. Nevertheless, the earth is already in outer space. The Book of Hebrews speaks so plainly to this concept, and it's impossible to miss the message. As noble and honest as modern teachers of the Word may be, many teachings do not square with the Scriptures when it comes to our future.

But you have come to Mount Zion and to the city of the living God, the heavenly Jerusalem, to an innumerable company of angels, to the general assembly and church of the firstborn who are registered in heaven, to God the Judge of all, to the spirits of just men made perfect, to Jesus the Mediator of the new covenant, and to the blood of sprinkling that speaks better things than that of Abel (Hebrews 12:22-24).

We have come, and others will continue to come. This would be the proper interpretation for every now generation. This verb is written in the perfect tense representing an action completed in the past but also having continuing results. The city of the living God is not real estate; it's a multidiversified people. There are landmarks in every city that distinguish that city; however, a city is known primarily by the culture and social station of the people in that city. When names like New York City, Los Angeles, Chicago, Miami, Houston, Hong Kong, Seoul, Cape Town, London, Paris, and Sao Paulo are mentioned, what do you immediately think of? Location? Buildings and architecture? Climate? Maybe. In most instances, it is the people and culture of that particular city. The city of God has a command structure, a citizenry, and a culture. Every time someone is born again another citizen is added to the city of God under the command and headship of King Jesus. That's why John, in the Revelation, saw the city of God coming down to earth, not going up (see Rev. 21:2-3).

Security and rest come from the assurance of who we are in Christ and the *finished work* of what we already have as an inheritance in Christ. There is a sevenfold inheritance listed in Hebrews 12:22-24. We have come to:

- Mount Zion, the city of the living God, the heavenly Jerusalem.

- An innumerable company of angels.

- The general assembly and Church of the firstborn who are registered in Heaven.

- God the Judge of all.

- The spirits of just men made perfect.

- Jesus the Mediator of the New Covenant.

- The blood of sprinkling that speaks better things than that of Abel.

If the Church would take the time to carefully examine all that we have come to, we would not be so starry-eyed, looking longingly to the Heavens for something else to come. The reappearing of Jesus Christ in the flesh is not the issue here; there's something more pressing. Our hands must be filled with assimilating everything we already have. The heavenly Father expressed Himself explicitly in Jesus—for Jesus declared the Father. *Declared* means "to exegete or rehearse out loud."[13] Jesus was the Father's full exegesis. This was not some critical interpretation of what it means to be God or Christian; it was a message of unmatched, unquestionable love.

Robert Southey said: "Love is indestructible; its holy flame forever burneth; from heaven it came, to heaven returneth."[14] Love has a name—Jesus! When the apostle Paul expounded the characteristics of love, he was defining a person. He clearly understood that without love a man is bankrupt. Most of the religious leaders in Jesus' day had many advantages, but they lacked the most important one—unconditional love for the poor souls restricted by their authoritarian practices. His ability to love the unlovable infuriated them and exposed their glaring lack of compassion. The holy flame of His love caused people to encounter a God they didn't know existed—a God more inclined to mercy than aspirations to punish what is often valued as the wicked.

> *Love never gives up. Love cares more for others than for self. Love doesn't want what it doesn't have. Love doesn't strut, doesn't have a swelled head, doesn't force itself on others, isn't always "me first," doesn't fly off the handle, doesn't keep score of the sins of others, doesn't revel when others grovel, takes pleasure in the flowering of truth, puts up with anything, trusts God always, always looks for the best, never looks back, but keeps going to the end* (1 Corinthians 13:4-8a The Message).

Of all the things we have come to, nothing is as important as coming to Jesus. There is a real man behind all the principles that are taught about Him. He walked in the higher dimensions of energy and life all the time; He was deathless until He chose to lay down His life to satisfy all the requirements of a kinsman-redeemer.

Jesus Christ is the divine outline; He was coded with the original information of life and godliness. Jesus was truly a renaissance man of peace and reconciliation. While His coming was long after the establishment of the Greek empire and culture, His *renaissance* had nothing to do with the reestablishment of the Greek classics. There is a resurgence, a revitalization in God's concept for mankind in the appearance of Jesus Christ. He's the first man since the deterioration of Adam to never keep score of someone's wrongs, or a log about other men's transgressions. The truth of reconciliation is to not only cancel the consequences of the offense; but also, one must totally erase the fact of the offense.

The purpose of the classroom of rest is to bring us to Him. Jesus unabashedly loves mankind. He plowed through a long litany of hostility to free us. He said, *"Are you tired? Worn out? Burned out on religion? Come to Me. Get away with Me and you'll recover your life. I'll show you how to take a real rest. Walk with Me and work with Me—watch how I do it. Learn the unforced rhythms of grace. I won't lay anything heavy or ill-fitting on you. Keep company with Me and you'll learn to live freely and lightly"* (Matthew 11:28-30 The Message). The Father shakes the Heavens and the earth to bring His children to His uniquely-begotten Son, who demonstrates the unforced rhythms of grace. There is a pace, a tempo, a cadence to grace. Aligning with that tempo is like adapting to the perfect environment of God. The impositions of legalistic tyranny, as it has been passed down by religious men, bring misalignment. All the heavy, ill-fitting garments of the law and legalistic systems have coiled and squeezed us into a system that immobilizes. Rest is the freedom to keep company, to live freely and lightly with Jesus as the center of our lives.

We all must come to the place where Jesus, and His abiding presence, is enough. Jesus is the *desire of all the nations* of the earth. With Jesus and the Church manifesting God's order, a unified desire of the nations is systematically revealed. Many of them don't realize that fact yet; however, they will. He is the key to understanding the culture of the Kingdom of God. God is educating us; that's why we must come to Jesus without vacillation. He's the only one who has fully completed the course of sovereign subjects. Jesus began and finished the race we are in with a rare kind of focus. By coming to Him, we may study His life to understand how He did it. Jesus was able to endure many things in the process of finishing: the cross, the shame, the indifference, the slander, the slurs, the disrespect, and the attempted defamation of character and volumes of vilification. Nevertheless, He stayed focused all the way to the exhilarating finish. When any of us are ready to drop out of class, or maybe flag in our commitments, there is something we may do before that drastic step is taken: Come to Jesus one more time. Jesus will guide us through all our disappointments, conflicts, and turmoil.

ENDNOTES

1. Virginia Ely, *I Quote* (New York: George W. Stewart Publishers, Inc., 1947), 119.

2. Ibid., 120.

3. Ibid., 121.

4. Ibid., 121.

5. James Strong, *"Hebrew and Chaldee Dictionary,"* Strong's Exhaustive Concordance of the Bible (Nashville: Abingdon, 1976), #3070.

6. Ely, 121.

7. Ibid.

8. Webster's II New College Dictionary, Riverside University dictionary (New York: Houghton Mifflin Company, 1995), 689.

9. Strong's, #2834.

10. Webster's II, 785.

11. Ibid., 576.

12. Ibid., 68.

13. Strong's, *"Greek Dictionary,"* Strong's Exhaustive Concordance of the Bible (Nashville: Abingdon, 1976), #1834.

14. Ely, 209.

5

A Noble and Timeless Vision

"Now therefore, if you will indeed obey My voice and keep My covenant, then you shall be a special treasure to Me above all people; for all the earth is Mine. And you shall be to Me a kingdom of priests and a holy nation." These are the words which you shall speak to the children of Israel (Exodus 19:5-6).

The Book of Genesis opens with God introducing the Kingdom of God as He creates the universe. God established the Kingdom on the earth and presented the first Kingdom with man. Adam is called the son of God (see Luke 3:38); therefore, he is under the authority of his Father and God. Shortly thereafter, a malfunction came into the brightness of God and Adam's relationship. Man had fallen from the magnificence of what he had with God because of disobedience, and was banished from the ideal environment essential to his growth. This is a working example of a child in a perfect environment, with perfect fathering, and still becoming dysfunctional. Something had to be done in order to bring about reconciliation and restoration. God, the Father, already had a working eternal plan that would be fully implemented in Christ.

God made it clear after the fall of Adam that He had purposed to raise up an alternative in this world. It was called the seed of the woman. This seed would become a high society—a spiritual, social, and political populace that would manifest the culture of the Kingdom of God in power until it became the norm in the earth. The method of achieving this in the New Covenant was by sending special men and women into all the earth as witnesses of this reality (see Matt. 28:18-20).

The New Covenant calls this an administration, a dispensation, stewardship, a political citizenship, or an economy (see Eph. 1:10; 2:19; 3:9). Please don't bristle about the word *political* and allow it to overthrow or subvert your faith. Political in the natural speaks to a network of interlocking relationships that mutually benefit all participants, chiefly appealing to a carnal agenda in humans. That's worldly, fleshly politics. In the Kingdom of God, the word *political* pertains to *Kingdom citizenship* (see Eph. 2:19). To become a different society is about the high order of Kingdom citizenship enacted in the earth. Every idea God has commences in seed form. In the New Covenant, Jesus Christ and the first-century Church are the first ones to experience restored Kingdom citizenship.

Understanding citizenship isn't necessarily a high priority on most believers' lists. In fact, some of our current theology doesn't make the grade; it doesn't even come close to meeting God's standards. A weakened culture of modern Christianity has evolved rather than powerful Kingdom citizens experiencing the total freedoms of the *finished work of Calvary*. I encourage each believer to despair not! God is raising a priestly generation, possessing the authority of the Kingdom: a culture that refuses mediocrity, having the capacity to accomplish the impossible and fulfilling the great commission. A message beats in the breasts of that priesthood that says, *"Thy kingdom come, thy will be done in earth as it is in heaven."* Only Kingdom citizens understanding their dominion assignments will accomplish this noble cause.

In the Book of Genesis, God selected individuals and families; however, in regards to the exodus from Egypt and onward, God selected a nation, with the ultimate intention of including all nations in the Messiah (see Rev. 11:15). Abraham, Isaac, Jacob, and Joseph are wonderful models of individuals, and yet, corporate family purpose.

They are like four rivers flowing out of the Eden of God's heart. The last quadrant of Genesis deals with their development as Kingdom subjects. God's methods were to develop them by faith.

> *By faith Abraham obeyed when he was called to go out to the place which he would receive as an inheritance. And he went out, not knowing where he was going* (Hebrews 11:8).

> *By faith Abraham, when he was tested, offered up Isaac, and he who had received the promises offered up his only begotten son, of whom it was said, "In Isaac your seed shall be called," concluding that God was able to raise him up, even from the dead, from which he also received him in a figurative sense* (Hebrews 11:17-19).

> *By faith Jacob, when he was dying, blessed each of the sons of Joseph, and worshiped, leaning on the top of his staff* (Hebrews 11:21).

> *By faith Joseph, when he was dying, made mention of the departure of the children of Israel, and gave instructions concerning his bones* (Hebrews 11:22).

It is very interesting that each verse of Scripture in the above listing begins, *"By faith."* That's why the faith-worthies of Hebrews 11 form a faith hall of fame. These are not, necessarily, independent relationships as though everything ended when the individual died. Their purpose was always corporate and their destiny generational. Each process and outworking networked back into the life of the previous vessel of God, and into the succeeding vessel. Primarily, we're raised in a culture of individualism and sometimes do not see the big picture. Participating in God's Kingdom involves faith for the unknown, faith for supernatural miracles, faith for blessing another generation with a sense of familial destiny, and faith for the transgenerational fortune of your descendants. These four principles produce a family legacy, which is always greater than one's destiny. For instance, I may personally reach my destiny, and yet, pass nothing on to the next generation. If so, I will have no legacy. Our Father desires that we combine destiny and legacy together. Faith and vision are keys. It takes both to reach a destiny, and both to touch another generation in your lineage. God gives us powerful lessons in faith toward

Him in each of these Kingdom subjects (Abraham, Isaac, Jacob, and Joseph). The noble purpose of faith is to focus us *toward God* (who is the object of our vision), and not, necessarily, the procuring of things or gifts from God.

God's premise for sovereign selection was: *All the earth is Mine!* Our heavenly Father moves because He desires to reveal His glory in the earth. First, God deputized Israel from a focused corporate level, and then the Church, to become the vessels bearing His glory. Of course, this became a multitudinous undertaking. Because an infinite God cannot be contained or explained completely from a finite perspective, He always provides many creative ways to express Himself beyond our previous experiences or expressions. Sovereign selection consists of "those subjects over which God's Sovereignty extends as He guides and influences their thinking, speaking, attitudes, motives, and conduct; thus creating a new person" (author's definition). This indicates the rites of passage into Kingdom citizenship. When you are sovereign, you don't have to manipulate; rather, you influence subjects and allow them to participate in your reality. Subjects share your wealth, which creates a commonwealth.

When a sovereign has this kind of attitude, he isn't intimidated to share his realities or his space with others. This leads to the experience of glory. The reason this leads to glory is the magnified influence of God's presence. We are more apt to experience the tangibility of God's presence the heavier His presence becomes. God's glory is the weightiness and volume of divine nature or its perceptible manifestation, tangible to the senses, as God moves from the invisible to the visible, from the abstract to the concrete; thus saturating the realm, the people, and the arena He enters. God's glory is *Jesus Christ!* When He enters a place, He fills it with Himself. He's the only man who perfectly fits this definition.

Kingdom dispensing begins with vision, and that vision must be a view of the eternal vision of how God sees us in Christ. *"If people can't see what God is doing, they stumble all over themselves; but when they attend to what He reveals, they are most blessed"* (Prov. 29:18 The Message). The vision is *the Kingdom—a kingdom whose citizens are priests, and have become a divine embassy in the earth for Heaven's interests!* The people of the Kingdom are an orderly, structured society with labor that flows out of rest, and proper interpersonal relationships. The first official statement Jesus made after entering public ministry was concerning the Kingdom. He clearly understood the Father's priority and official concerns for His earthly subjects.

> *Now when Jesus heard that John had been put in prison, He departed to Galilee....From that time Jesus began to preach and to say, "Repent, for the kingdom of heaven is at hand"* (Matthew 4:12,17).

> *Now after John was put in prison, Jesus came to Galilee, preaching the gospel of the kingdom of God, and saying, "The time is fulfilled, and the Kingdom of God is at hand, Repent, and believe in the gospel"* (Mark 1:14-15).

God, in Christ, was commanding humans to change their minds and receive a renewed vision through the gospel of the Kingdom. The word *gospel* means *"good news."* Men have preached the good news of salvation, healing, prosperity, deliverance, etc. throughout the earth. However, they, basically, have not fully preached the gospel of the Kingdom of God. The Kingdom requires each one of us to become a subject of King Jesus without personal rights. Without a doubt, that kind of demand bothers a Western, independent mind-set. Therefore, some modern teachers have judged the Kingdom message, in its present context, as an erroneous message. It is my humble opinion that men usually reject messages based upon presentation rather than the substance of the message itself. However, like it or not, the Kingdom of God is the umbrella message to each of these good news strands preached as the gospel. If we preach the Kingdom, it must include healing, prosperity, salvation, and deliverance. However, there's no such thing as a healing ministry apart from the Kingdom message.

This message is a reality always within your grasp—it's at hand also with future implications. Religious men play games with the minds of the simple and the unlearned. They present ideas such as "kingdom now" or "kingdom later" just to preserve a false system that has no biblical base. In this category would be much end-time teaching that probably had a historical fulfillment in the destruction of Jerusalem in A.D. 70. Since God is a *now God*, the Kingdom is always at hand. We must embrace the King and His dominion *now* if we expect to have a future with Him. God is simply commanding us to repent and believe. It's about *faith*, not mental and theological gymnastics. God is not asking us to navigate some theological maze, or intensively study Hebrew and Greek languages, to enter the Kingdom. Just believe it's available now! The first-century believers were mainly unschooled people, and they entered and lived Kingdom realities. By faith, we may also!

If we cannot see what we are *unto* the Lord, it will be impossible to function as we should *among* each other, and *among* the nations. God's vision gives us a sense of identity, which establishes our self-worth, security, and significance. All true vision starts with the understanding that God needs a form truly reflective and representative of Himself in the earth. Mankind is here, on this earth, for the increase of God. God cannot be created or destroyed—He can only be increased as we take our place in the divine plan. Franklin Field says, "Poor eyes limit your sight; poor vision limits your deeds."[1] The deed God is expecting is not a new act of sacrifice that contributes to our redemption, but a participation that reveals the manifestation of His person and fatherhood.

This present generation must take some different steps. The previous one advanced the Kingdom of God as far as they could. For one, we must connect with the truth of biblical sonship, which means, *God is not afraid to share His reality or divinity* (see 2 Pet. 1:3-4) What must we do to bring a greater increase of the presence of God in our day? We must arm ourselves with the same vision Jesus had. That vision is auspicious; it shares the certain reality that a son is *equal to his father* (see John 5:18; 10:30,33). Please, don't tune out at this moment—this isn't spiritual quackery. The sham would be if we don't embrace this as truth, allowing the practicality of it to evade us. Although it isn't something to carnally grasp, it's still the truth (see Phil. 2:5-8). Such a magnificent principle functions best under the guardianship of humility. Vision is the reason men try new things and seek other paths. Our vision must be the Kingdom of God as revealed in Christ Jesus functional in our lives—for He gives us energy, vitality, and life.

Just as He chose us in Him before the foundation of the world, that we should be holy and without blame before Him in love (Ephesians 1:4).

And not holding fast to the Head [Christ], from whom all the body, nourished and knit together by joints and ligaments, grows with the increase that is from God (Colossians 2:19).

The revelation of true sonship is to know we are chosen for greatness in Christ. Do you see this? This vision is also a Kingdom whose citizens are priests, and has become a divine embassy in the earth. An embassy is the position, function, or assignment of an ambassador: the function of a messenger. The key word in this definition is *ambassador*. The Hebrew definition for *ambassador* is "a hinge (as pressed in turning); also a throe (as a physical or mental pressure); also a herald or errand-doer: pain, pang, sorrow, hinge, messenger, ambassador."[2] The New Testament Greek (G#4243) defines *ambassador* as "to be a senior, act as a representative."[3] Webster defines *ambassador* as "a diplomatic official of the highest rank appointed and accredited as representative in residence by one government to another."[4] Based upon these definitions, only mature Christians qualify for this position. Ambassadors are chief influencers; and chief influencers should bear the marks of time and spiritual experience. We are God's messengers and senior representatives.

Most nations send ambassadors to represent their interests or goals. They are always citizens of the representative nation. To keep things in proper perspective, ambassadors are in constant communication with headquarters. Rarely are they young, inexperienced people. Usually, they are mature people with many years of public service. They understand the protocol of governmental operations and policy procedures. The ambassador never reflects his or her own personal views. Their statements will always reveal the will of the homeland administration.

Ambassadors have very little to be concerned about as far as personal needs. The sending government will provide all things necessary for them, their families, and their staffs. A military presence is garrisoned about the embassy for security purposes. They don't worry about shelter, food, clothing, transportation, hospitalization, insurance, retirement plans, etc. These benefits go along with the job. Their financial status and living quarters never reflect the nation they have been sent to; it will always reflect the sender. As I have traveled into other nations, it is comforting to see the American embassy truly representative of America's economic strength and ideals. Even if the indigenous people are extremely poor near the embassy, it doesn't affect our ambassador, his family, or his staff.

Are you getting the picture? All churches, and more specifically apostolic ministry teams, are to be Kingdom ambassadors sent from the governmental headquarters of Heaven. As we seek the Kingdom, we are to be anxious for nothing in our current assignments. Our heavenly Father knows what we need, and has already made Himself our full provision in Christ. We are safeguarded by His ever-abiding presence, which no enemy can penetrate or destroy. The benefits are wonderful, at least most of them: houses, lands, relationships, persecutions, and in the age to come, eternal life (see Mark. 10:29-31). Our sole purpose is to represent the interest of King Jesus and His Kingdom. Serving our own interests at His expense will not work. In the natural order of things, if ambassadors do that, they will be recalled and replaced without an opportunity to rectify their deeds. This is not necessarily so in the Kingdom of God. The Father provides corrections filled with grace, and He allows His subjects who yield to continue.

Our priestly function is to represent King Jesus as ambassadors. We must properly represent His vision for creation. He has committed to us a *message* and a *ministry* of reconciliation. A message requires insight, whereas ministry requires involvement. God has reconciled humanity and the creation back to Himself through Jesus Christ, the Arbitrator. We now have reconciliation through arbitration. Arbitration occurs when there is no mutual ground of agreement for different parties to stand firmly on together. A gap is created and a bridge builder with a stake in both sides must arbitrate the situation. Jesus was such a man, for He is very God and very man. "For there is one God and one Mediator between God and men, the Man Christ Jesus, who gave Himself a ransom for all, to be testified in due time" (1 Tim. 2:5-6). Apart from Jesus Christ, there could be no mediation or arbitration. As the apostle Paul said, *"For if, when we were enemies, we were reconciled to God by the death of His Son, much more, being reconciled, we shall be saved by His life"* (Rom. 5:10 KJV).

This is why Kingdom ambassadors must be mature; and they must understand the mercy-gifts of God in this operation. Otherwise, they could misrepresent the integrity of God's heart and preach doctrines contradictory to the seasons of God. Coming out of Romanism and performance-based religion, men didn't always understand the full mercy of God. We have entered the season of the Holy of holies administration. It has a mercy seat as one of its most appreciative expressions. All judgments and truths must flow from the mercy seat. Ambassadors link with the mercy seat and plead with the creation on behalf of Christ to be reconciled to God. I love the way The Message describes this whole operation:

The old life is gone; a new life burgeons! Look at it! All this comes from the God who settled the relationship between us and Him, and then called us to settle our relationships with each other. God put the world square with Himself through the Messiah, giving the world a fresh start by offering forgiveness of sins. God has given us the task of telling everyone what He is doing. We're Christ's representatives. God uses us to persuade men and women to drop their differences and enter into God's work of making things right between them. We're speaking for Christ Himself now: Become friends with God; He's already a friend with you. How? you say. In Christ. God put on Him the wrong who never did anything wrong, so we could be put right with God (2 Corinthians 5:17-21 The Message).

These verses reveal God's intent to establish His creation with right standing or right positioning with His divine government. To be righteous carries this connotation. Kingdom ambassadors bear this message in their hearts and mouths. Can you imagine how much peace this message will bring to the hearts of all who still believe God has some vendetta with mankind? Will you believe God has no further issues, and that all accounts are settled? Jesus Christ was the complete payment. The slate now reads: *Paid in full!* God has no log of our trespasses, so forget the idea that there is some angel recording all your misdeeds. Retaining inventories serve as the cesspit for bitterness and revenge. Our Father is neither bitter nor vengeful—He is just! The Church is the righteousness of God in Christ, and besides, God took His full vengeance out on Christ.

I foresee an army of Kingdom ambassadors, moving like soldiers, who do not break rank. They are speaking a message of reconciliation without the threat of the consequences of sin being greater than the mandate of grace. The Message says, *"When it's sin verses grace, grace wins hands down"* (Rom. 5:20). The negative will not be the emphasis of the declaration; instead, it will be the positive message of peace that Jesus Christ has procured and released through His personal sacrifice. This is a message of properly receiving from God what He has accomplished through His Son without the mixture of religion. No doubt, the outcome in the hearts of people will be very different. Rather than responding out of fear, people could receive the love of God freely.

The 21st-century Church must be just as faithful to the message and ministry of reconciliation as she was to the other messages preached in other centuries. I have found that truth usually comes in layers: Father God will place emphasis on one thing and then another. Sixteenth-century reformers reclaimed true Bible regeneration; Pentecostal reformers majored in renewal and restoration; and now we must unearth the truths of true biblical reconciliation. Where there are wars and rumors of war, it will take peace and peacemakers to change things. The writer of the Proverbs says, *"Like the cold of snow in time of harvest is a faithful messenger to those who send him, for he refreshes the soul of his masters"* (Prov. 25:13). Remember, the validity to any message is not so much how men accept or abuse a message. Credibility comes from God the Giver!

First, we must refresh the Lord with that in which He gives us to minister. God's righteous requirement is that we be faithful to Him! All true ministries are to minister unto the Lord and allow others to listen. In doing so, our motives don't become messy, and our actions performance-oriented.

Paul stated that he was an ambassador in chains (see Eph. 6:20). He was acknowledging the fact that he was a prisoner of the Lord. He had gone from being of note among the apostles to a jailbird preacher (see Eph. 6:20 The Message; 2 Cor. 11:5) It did not matter what Rome or Jerusalem were doing to him; he realized his incarceration was ordered by the court of justice in Heaven. If we each will remember that our steps are ordered by our heavenly Father, we too will admonish fellow-believers to pray for us rather than complain about our circumstances. Kingdom ambassadors release personal rights with the acceptance of their positions. Our most effective labor as an ambassador may be in chains. That's something to pause and consider carefully.

Kingdom vision surpasses normal, modern church vision. The Kingdom touches every facet of society. It supplies practical instructions for secular government, the arts, education, and the business world—essentially, the marketplace. If Kingdom citizens are faithful, they will refresh our Master with their obedience to participate in these broad areas. God needs a body of citizens, a diplomatic core, truly representative of Himself in the earth. Ambassadors are here on earth for the specific purpose of being the Lord's heavenly outpost. Through our faithfulness, we see the *increase of Christ in the earth*. There is a maxim in the New Covenant: God cannot be created or destroyed—He can only be increased! The apostle Paul stated, *"Now, therefore, you are no longer strangers and foreigners, but fellow citizens with the saints and members of the household of God"* (Eph. 2:19). As fellow citizens and members of God's household, we give definition to the increase of Christ. Every time someone awakens to their legal rights of Kingdom citizenship, Christ increases. Our adversary trembles in fear when someone under the spirit of revelation declares Kingdom citizenship. On another occasion, Paul said: *"For our citizenship is in heaven, from which we also eagerly wait for the Savior, the*

God's Kingdom

Lord Jesus Christ" (Phil. 3:20). These are very comforting words. One of the highest recognitions anyone can have is citizenship. Even in the old Roman Empire, citizenship was something treasured very much in a conquering, imperialistic society (see Acts 22:22-29). A person would be less apt to receive abusive treatment once their Roman citizenship was known.

When Ann and I travel abroad, we carry our passports that indicate we are citizens of the United States of America. The Secretary of State has asked other nations to recognize this legal document and afford us all the privileges that they would grant citizens of the United States of America. Next to the personal identification page of the passport is this special message:

The Secretary of State of the United States of America hereby requests all whom it may concern to permit the citizen/national of the United States named herein to pass without delay or hindrance and in case of need to give all lawful aid and protection.

If trouble should break out, we immediately may have refuge at the American embassy until we can be transported out of that country. Our citizenship is our legal protection. Another important factor to understand in all this is that our passports are not necessarily our private property. Passports belong to the United States government. They may be revoked when necessary. This is also a protective measure for both the government and its citizens.

Jesus Christ purchased us, and we are not our own. Our passport, as we travel in these temporary bodies here on earth, is the Bible. The Bible is God's legal document. It speaks to our citizenship and does not personally belong to any of us. It is the Word of God. God compels principalities and powers to honor our citizenship. Just as the heavenly Father protected Jesus in the midst of trouble, He will also protect us. This assurance we have from the Word of God. Note the examples in the life of Jesus, and the prayer He prayed for us.

So all those in the synagogue, when they heard these things, were filled with wrath, and rose up and thrust Him out of the city; and they led Him to the brow of the hill on which their city was built, that they might throw Him down over the cliff. Then passing through the midst of them, He went His way (Luke 4:28-30).

Jesus said to them, "Most assuredly, I say to you, before Abraham was, I AM." Then they took up stones to throw at Him; but Jesus hid Himself and went out of the temple, going through the midst of them, and so passed by (John 8:58-59).

Therefore they sought again to seize Him, but He escaped out of their hand (John 10:39).

I do not pray that You should take them out of the world, but that You should keep them from the evil one (John 17:15).

Jesus Christ walked as a true Kingdom ambassador while here on earth. His adversaries could not touch Him until His assignment was completed, which was to accomplish a state of reconciliation and redemption (see John 7:30,44). Neither can the adversary touch us until our assignments are completed! Our Kingdom citizenship is one of the greatest privileges we have guaranteeing security and personal preservation. Jesus asked the heavenly Father to guard us from the evil one. Nowhere in this verse is it indicative that the Father would have to remove us from this earth in order to protect us from the onslaught of the enemy. This has been one of the greatest deceptions alleged in modern Christianity, and now carried over into the postmodern era. God is more than able to guard and keep us from the intentions and assignments of the evil one. The Church must exercise the highest trust in God when it comes to this. Antichrist spirits and systems shouldn't have us petrified in fear and emaciated with phobias. We are citizens and have a right of existence on this earth, which belongs to the Lord (see Ps. 24:1-2; 1 Cor. 10:26) If anyone must leave, it will be the devil and his cohorts. Their days of being squatters on the earth are near finished. The Father's heart and vision give us the right to minister until all nations are at peace with God through the truth of Bible redemption and reconciliation.

It is important at this point to distinguish between *reconciliation* and *salvation*. Reconciliation is the event, whereas salvation is a process out of the event. Reconciliation occurs as we appropriate the truth of the *finished work*. Salvation requires learning how to apply *Christ's life*. Many strange fires have erupted throughout the history of the Church because of a lack of distinction in these terms. Because both experiences are factual through the blood of Jesus Christ (see Rom. 5:9-10), some brethren treat them as though they are synonymous, when, in fact, they're not.

God reconciled the *whole world* to Himself through Jesus Christ—which is an objective statement. What reasonable person will argue against this truth? This decision was uninfluenced by human emotion, opinion, or surmise—it's a matter of sovereignty and predetermination. God sent His Son in the fullness of times. Reconciliation is an exchanged status—things have turned from a state of fragmentation to harmony. A breathtaking recovery occurred through this gracious act. Forgiveness and blessing were released upon all of mankind as illustrated by the guilty people Jesus pardoned during His earthly ministry (see John 8:10-11). Jesus' obedience was what mattered in this transaction. Just as the first Adam released a condition of sin through his disobedience, Jesus released a condition of reconciliation through His obedience (see Rom. 5:12-21). In both cases, we as individuals had nothing to do with those decisions; one, as a federal head, was deciding for *all*. The Message says,

> *"Here it is in a nutshell: Just as one person did it wrong and got us in all this trouble with sin and death, another Person did it right and got us out of it. But more than just getting us out of trouble, He got us into life! One man said no to God and put many people in the wrong; one Man said yes to God and put many in the right* (Romans 5:19).

May I illustrate reconciliation in this manner: Every month, when personal bank statements come, reconciliation is necessary. This is the simplest illustration I know of engaging in reconciliation. My purpose is not to execute some vendetta against the bank or my checkbook—it's to produce harmony. Its purpose is to begin each month even and in agreement. For instance, if my bank statement says that I have one amount in my account and my checkbook says another, there's a need for reconciliation. God's account had one thing in mind when He sent Christ, and our old Adamic account had something else. God's account was filled with grace, mercy, unity, harmony, peace, and justice. Man's account had wrath, injustice, disunity, disharmony, confusion, sinfulness, and human laws aplenty. Jesus Christ, by being both God and man squared both accounts and harmonized them. He brought God and man back to the same page. His death satisfied the just demands of a righteous God and released the grace essential to reconnect man with God again without a guilty conscience. Christ's act of reconciliation brought us near to God again. Man's account is no longer in arrears.

Salvation, on the other hand, is slightly different. New Testament salvation works because of reconciliation. Once one has been brought near, then, and only then, does the process of experiential salvation begin. The objective of salvation is God's gracious choice to be Savior to us through Jesus Christ our Lord first, and then, conform us into His image. It is through the application of the principles of Christ's life, *putting on the new man* that causes salvation to become effectual. God primarily saves us from the old man, the old system, and ourselves. The difference in these two terminologies unfolds this way: Reconciliation is the gift of an arbiter through grace's arbitration, whereas salvation is the gift of a redeemer through the grace gift of sacrifice, particularly in the realm of having the legal rights of purchase power. A redeemer purchases someone from an unredeemed situation. From all of the stories in the Old Testament, the unredeemed has no power to redeem themselves. Someone must have not only the desire, but also, the legal authority to purchase. For us, that person was Jesus Christ. It is important to know that there's no parallel word for New Testament reconciliation in the Old Testament like there is to salvation. There were kinsmen-redeemers in the Old Testament, but never kinsmen-reconcilers.

There is, however, a practical similarity between reconciliation and salvation: Both have an objective and subjective ramification. Reconciliation and salvation both require participation from their recipients. This is the subjective end of each. With reconciliation, it spins out in these words: *"We implore you on Christ's behalf, be reconciled to God"* (2 Cor. 5:20b) "Be" isn't something you do; it's an acknowledgment of an exchanged state. It's entering into an alliance with the truth. The subjective end of salvation involves a corresponding action in the redeemed—it demands the obedience of faith to Christ's sacrificial, atoning work. We call that receiving Jesus Christ as your personal Lord and Savior, thus coming into agreement with the truth.

Every person and nation that is reconciled is not necessarily saved yet. Salvation is multidimensional, having relevance for the whole person. It is a combination of experiences because of man's tripartite nature. It commences practically with the new birth (spirit); continues with the renewing of the mind (soul); and consummates with the transformation of the body (body). Salvation requires repentance (a change of mind and behavior) and faith. God provides what we cannot in both reconciliation and salvation: His wonderful, matchless ocean of grace! *"For by grace you have been saved through faith, and that not of yourselves; it is the gift of God, not of works, lest anyone should boast"* (Eph. 2:8-9).

Conversely, salvation by works speaks a foreign, unintelligible language to the New Covenant citizen. Works suggest we deserve something. It presupposes the dynamic of performance rather than the reception of a gift resulting in relationship. The apostle Paul, in particular, was speaking of the works of the Law economy. They will never save any of us. Only faith in the efficacious work of Jesus Christ will. The heavenly Father cannot repent and believe for anyone, which commences salvation and deliverance. Jesus Christ redeemed us, reconciled us, and saved us by His life; but amazingly, He will not force our hearts to believe. The work of the Holy Spirit in salvation is to lead us to Christ the Savior, which is an antecedent to the overall salvation process. However, He too will not compel us to believe. The Scripture speaks of individuals losing their souls because of unbelief, but it never speaks of mankind losing the reconciled status gained through Christ.

Consider the difference using an episode from United States history. After the horrific United States Civil War (1861–1865), several amendments were shortly added to the Constitution. One idea behind amending something is to say the current instrument was obsolete as it existed. One of those amendments gave former slaves the status of citizenship. The statement could have read this way: "Now that you are citizens, *be citizens!*" That's reconciliation, or peacemaking. Most ex-slaves and their immediate descendants were uneducated; therefore, they could not appropriate what was rightfully theirs, and many were abused by American apartheid until almost one century later. They were set free by the law, but did not experience freedom until many began to demand their freedom after understanding the inalienable rights of all free people. Because many risked their lives by refusing the new system of institutionalized slavery, freedom came to many. The working out of freedom was like the working out of one's salvation. Nothing, other than another amendment, could change the status of citizenship and freedom. However, as men participated in their freedom, they really became free. That's the truth of salvation: You must participate in that which was freely given to you to know the full outcome of your freedom.

Before we conclude this thought, the apostle Paul never commanded us to work out our reconciliation with fear and trembling. Jesus Christ cleared the slate in reconciliation. However, he did say, *"Work out your own salvation with fear and trembling; for it is God who works in you both to will and to do for His good pleasure"* (Phil. 2:12c-13). Each believer has a responsibility to be responsive, reverent, and obedient to our heavenly Father. Prompted by grace, this truth may be illustrated in the daily disciplines we exercise as believers. Be mindful that all that we do is because of the deep energizing work of the Holy Spirit in us—multiple layers of grace.

Our labor is not in vain when the Holy Spirit is prompting our actions. If we are driven by a spirit of pride in our works, they become nothing more than dead works. This is where the philosophy of the church must be careful. We teeter-totter with a message of salvation by works at times. The Scripture is clear about Abraham's faith being perfected by his works (see James 2:21-23). The original context (see Gen. 15:6) shows that it was God working in him and prompting the entire matter that precipitated his obedient response. Therefore, even in our working with God, it really is the grace of God working in us. The best humans we'll ever be is yielded vessels.

A POSTCARD TO PHILEMON

My wife, at times, purchases postcards in various places when we travel. Sometimes it's for collection purposes and at other times, mailing purposes. If we send them out, we usually make some comment about the joy of our travels or how we miss family and friends. The epistle to Philemon is a vastly different kind of spiritual postcard. In comparison to most of the other books of the New Testament, this Epistle is no larger than a postcard. With much diplomacy and gentleness, the apostle Paul asks Philemon to embrace Onesimus, a once useless slave, as Philemon would embrace Paul. Art Linkletter described diplomacy this way: "Diplomacy: The art of jumping into troubled waters without making a splash."[5] This was necessary because Onesimus was a runaway slave when he met Paul. Of course, Paul ministered to Onesimus who became a child of God. This book is a superb visual of the ministry and message of reconciliation. Paul, the icon of the message of grace, was confident that Philemon would respond to his imploration with brotherly love, forgiveness, and respect for their relationship.

The apostle Paul begins by commending Philemon's faith and love toward Jesus and all the saints. The vertical relationship we have with Jesus Christ should be horizontally lived with the saints. That gives veracity to our witness. It was his zesty, life-giving faith that produced great joy and refreshed the saints. *Refreshed* means "to give an intermission from labor." Philemon was the kind of brother who could give you a fresh drink of water in the midst of laborious conditions by his mere presence. Paul's approach was actually a setup. He was appealing to his goodness, not from the basis of law, but love. This is where the spirit of reconciliation enters on a practical level.

Paul, the aged, is now a prisoner of the Lord, and a representative of reconciliation. *Aged* comes from the Greek word *presbutes*, meaning "an elderly man."[6] It is in the same word family as *presbeuo*, which means, "to be an ambassador."[7] Just from looking at the closeness of these words, there is a strong implication that an ambassador must have the knowledge and experience of life in order to be an elder. Very simply, *elder* is an old man in specific contrast to a young man. Because of various reasons, modern congregations have made younger men elders, rather than leading men among the brethren (see Acts 15:22). Obviously, this has produced a strain on congregations and unnecessary hardships. It is inconceivable to think a young man, still rearing a family, can have the experience of an older man who has reared a family. Likewise, younger women should not be expected to have the wisdom of older women. Young men and women lack the wisdom and sturdiness of older men and women because of one simple reason: time!

As in Eastern cultures, the West must rekindle a value for agedness. Older people are certainly beyond the seasons of life younger people must walk through. Acquiring wisdom and prudence along the way, they are more apt to suggest peace between brethren rather than hostilities. Aged people will more readily count the cost of drastic decisions before acting; whereas younger people are more prone to act and then regret some decisions and consequences. Because of the work of reconciliation, it is very important to commit this matter to someone mature. This is why Paul, the aged, appeals for peace rather than a justifiable punishment. As a younger man, Paul had refused to reconcile with Barnabas (see Acts 15:36-39). He learned the Christ-like posture is always to forgive and to release. Jesus said we are to love and to release rather than express hate and retaliation. The ministry of reconciliation gives us the opportunity to do this.

> *You're familiar with the old written law, "Love your friend," and its unwritten companion, "Hate your enemy." I'm challenging that. I'm telling you to love your enemies. Let them bring out the best in you, not the worst. When someone gives you a hard time, respond with the energies of prayer, for then you are working out of your true selves, your God-created selves* (Matthew 5:43-44 The Message).

When we come out of our God-created selves, we will manage the opportunity for reconciliation correctly without the corruption this word has been tainted with in the past. There can be no ulterior motives, self-seeking, political maneuvering, or dishonorable living. We will recognize the value in restoration versus the pathos of broken fellowship. Paul was willing to sacrifice some personal ministry in order that Philemon and Onesimus might be reconciled (see Philem. 13-14) Sometimes we must sacrifice personal comforts, or maybe even a desire to be right in order to be reconciled. It was abnormal for a slave owner to release a slave solely based on love as Paul was suggesting. This was a radical social change in philosophy. This could also have been disturbing to other slave owners, placing pressure on them to treat runaways with dignity rather than with brute force. From a Kingdom basis, he is no longer a slave but a brother. New birth had shifted the structure of their relationship. Now Philemon must have a mental paradigm shift in order to agree with the heavenly shift. This may not have been good for business, but it was good for Kingdom development in the love of God.

The Promise Keepers Movement recognized the need for reconciliation between brothers just as in the message to Philemon. During the decade of the 1990s, Promise Keepers had a noble and gallant vision. That vision can be simplified in these words:

Promise Keepers is a Christ-centered ministry dedicated to uniting men through vital relationships to become godly influences in their world. Throughout the nation, men are making the following commitments to this ministry of reconciliation to God in all areas of their lives.[8]

This Movement was able to amass vast numbers of men in some of the modern sports stadiums in a very short time. Prophetically, this attested to the fact that the heavenly Father had shown many men the need for unity and reconciliation. But once again, the ugly need in man to control things with personal preferences tarnished what could have been a powerful tool of reformation in the Church. Although a para-church ministry, the benefits of this ministry directly benefited local churches everywhere. Men were stepping up to the plate and becoming accountable in the family of God. Many wives were excited about their husbands' newfound commitments to Christ and leadership in the home.

In our local region, as we dug into some of the issues that separated brethren, it became very painful to be totally honest and transparent. Old issues, which blocked reconciliation, ran deep like still waters refusing to be unearthed. What started out with hundreds of men gathering in regional meetings was reduced to just a few men, in comparison, meeting in smaller groups or accountability groups. Although rough and tough externally, men proved to be too fragile for such a rigorous, emotional undertaking. Many academic studies have proven men are afraid of confrontation in this manner and feel violated when it happens. In general, men do not value closeness as women do and are intimidated by it. Promise Keepers was advocating closeness in order for brethren to reconcile. Frankly, we missed a tremendous open door of opportunity one more time. At some point, our timing will totally synchronize with God's desire and timing.

Much of my public ministry has been involved in the ministry of reconciliation. In fact, we have no earthly excuses not to be at peace with one another. It is good and pleasant for brethren to dwell together in unity. My earliest recollections of prophetic words being spoken over me were to this effect. I have come to appreciate the peacemaking ability Christ expresses through me. I am under no illusions; it is truly a gift of grace from God. One brother said, "God has put something in your heart that inoculates young men against hate. As they relate to you, they will come out of you as men of love, understanding, and wisdom." That pretty much sums up the ministry of reconciliation. The greatest delight in life is to identify with the Lord in the ministry and word of reconciliation. As recent circumstances have compelled me to reevaluate most of what I have done in ministry, I am still most pleased to co-operate with the Lord in His peacemaking mission with His creation.

WHAT HAPPENS WHEN VISION
DOESN'T HAPPEN AS EXPECTED

And when John had heard in prison about the works of Christ, he sent two of his disciples and said to Him, "Are You the Coming One, or do we look for another?" (Matthew 11:2-3)

These are the words of John the Baptist, a quintessential prophet, once regarded as the vanguard minister of his day. Now, he has been reduced from this elevated place in the Spirit to Herod's jail cell. John is in prison, and alone. Perhaps discouragement and disillusionment hampered him from remembering what the Holy Spirit had revealed to him several months earlier (see John 1:29-35). His introduction of Jesus, in effect, terminated his ministry. John was like the court hearld. Running in advance of Jesus, he had one responsibility: *announcing the King!* He experienced vision failure and seemed to be doubting the truth of what he first saw. Jesus reassured John by pointing to super-natural evidence as proof of the veracity of his initial vision.

Something most men and women with vision hate to think about is temporary vision failure, or the turbulent waters of unful-filled vision, much less someone else replacing us. Because we live in such a success-driven culture judged by natural standards, we may complicate things by thinking the Kingdom of God functions with the same complicity. It is difficult to trust the validity of a vision until it has been tested. Usually, a vision storm will hit us with a surprise attack and pinpoint accuracy. Our prophetic senses, maybe, did not warn us of impending danger, nor the severity of its landing. On the other hand, we were too stubborn, perhaps too busy, to listen to the still small voice of the Holy Spirit signaling danger. Attitudes between the ministry's inner circle and family are shifting with every gust and gale force wind. How do you deal with this imminent low-pressure system energized by low morale, negative attitudes, and spiritual indifference within the family? Can we prepare to ride out the foul weather and reconstruct the vision? We had to answer these questions unexpectedly.

It was a few years before a team in our local church crafted a vision statement for our ministry. In light of the great command (see John 13:34) and the great commission (see Matt. 28:19-20), we wanted to be accurate and consistent with God's vision and heart for our community and us. After much prayer and collaboration, we compiled this statement:

> Present Truth Ministries is to be a church, a body of believers interwoven by love, faith and hope in Jesus Christ. This church is established into the community to present King Jesus in His completed, triumphant victory. It is dedicated to reaching and touching all aspects of our current population...old and young, families and individuals, all races and economic levels. We are to be a ministry without prejudice; thus presenting the creation with hope; reaching them in faith, and touching them in love.

We felt this statement best represented our contribution in response to God's mandate for the ministry and word of reconciliation. Amazingly, after this statement was presented to the entire body for ratification, things began to happen. We wrote the vision and it tried us! Because there was a wonderful cross section in the developing and planning stages, problems did not mount because of a lack of involvement, or a lack of vision ownership by the church family. Most people now understood we had a tool in our hands that clearly identified our cause. One person alone, namely a pastor, could not fulfill this vision. Others would need to become hands-on, place their hands to the plow, and sacrifice in order for this vision to flourish. As positive as that was, it also had a negative effect. Insidious forces began to work deviously against the unity of the group to disrupt the vision. Culturally motivated issues surfaced on both sides that threw us for a loop. Now, we had to fight tooth and nail just to remain a thriving body of people. A vision tempest was on the horizon.

For two years, I tried to dodge the mounting thunderheads before they became a humungous cluster. My wife, like a modern Deborah, was giving me fair warning about what was going on. Like some men of God, we believe in prophets as long as it isn't our wives, who, by the way, usually love us, anointed or not. It became obvious, after a while, that we were going to suffer the shaking of a storm spawned by personal ambitions, a general lack of integrity, and some mistakes on my part as the primary leader. The coordinates of the storm had lined up and were making a beeline straight toward us, gathering momentum with each passing day. I felt like Job. I wanted to ask God: "I know You are for us, but where are You in this?" Pain, sometimes, has the ability to cloud our discernment. Because of the hurt and regret, our vision became blurred and many questioned its trueness. We wanted to present a victorious Jesus although we were highly defeated for the moment. Humiliated and abased, we received a baptism in weakness. Long-term relationships were tossed around and washed away because of diabolical misinformation. Despite a colossal effort in damage control, we had little control over the circumstances, and we were directly in the center of the tussle of a spiritual conflict. When things finally subsided, we had to reevaluate our position and renovate the vision. Storms never come just to give us practice in replacing blown-away things. They come for one reason: *CHANGE!*

As of today, we are beyond the defensive crosscurrents of self-pity, condemnation, a sense of failure, or retaliation. Our failures are just opportunities for us to begin again more intelligently in the purposes of God. I, personally, refuse to cross-examine the situation any longer. The past cannot be changed or improved. We have seen the good hand of God in it all. Hindsight is always twenty-twenty vision. Some are still trying to heal and clean up. In the aftermath of the storm, most of us are attempting to learn to trust others all over again, and provide them with the wide margins of grace we first gave them. Even trusting God with childlike dependency is an intensified challenge for some. My wife and I are hearing the voice of the Master in all of this and moving on with our lives. Though the lines of communication, at times, hum with the static of our own emotions, we are sure of His unconditional love. God's love has a way of slowly clearing our cloudy vision—and the intent of the original vision is beginning to come back with necessary adjustments. As the apostle Paul so clearly says:

> *We don't yet see things clearly. We're squinting in a fog, peering through a mist. But it won't be long before the weather clears*

and the sun shines bright! We'll see it all then, see it all as clearly as God sees us, knowing Him directly just as He knows us! (1 Corinthians 13:12 The Message)

The one question people asked was: "How do we get back on track with what God assigned us to do?" Said another way: *"Where do we go from here?"*

Identifying the source of the tempest with an attitude of grace was the first thing we needed to do. As with the first man Adam, most storms begin with lust in someone's heart that refuses to yield to the Holy Spirit and His work. The serpentine spirit uses flesh and blood to block, cloud, and distort visions. This is important to note, but may be dangerous because people will think you are judgmental and unforgiving. For a true God-fearing man or woman of God, that's not how you wish to be labeled. However, it will be fatalistic repeatedly, if one doesn't realistically learn to locate and determine breeding grounds for storms. If ministries just pray and forgive without pinpointing the obvious signs of vision storms, you will have the opportunity to chart another one in the future. It's not to say that proper diagnosis will prevent anything from forming in the future. However, we sharpen our discernment and develop our attention for detail through becoming proactive in the reevaluation process. In the natural, only through locating the eye of a storm will we be prepared to take emergency measures and maneuver beyond its cumulative devastation.

Very important operational decisions had to be made. There was a greater requirement to become more transparent, more direct in leadership, and refuse to make any excuses as to why this storm happened. After spending days in prayer and seeking God's face, I emerged from those encounters with one message: *We must forgive everyone for everything!* Rather than concentrating on the rubble, I desperately desired to build the leaders and people we had left. We had more leadership training sessions that dealt with the tactical end of leadership. It was my hope that all of us would be freed from any residual effect of the past vision storm. New focus was employed to get us beyond the hurt and disillusionment. We steadily moved toward a corporate mind-set although we were much smaller than before, and somewhat weather-beaten. I knew if we could redefine, re-chart, reorganize, and re-envision, we could begin to make positive strides again.

Now, if you're thinking I'm naïve, please don't! It would have been asinine to think we could just pick up and go on as if nothing had happened. Where we were and how we got there were no longer questions—we were there! I took the people back to the original vision, before they were totally rapt with confusion. The vision was the thing that excited us; it was what we believed our contribution could be to the Christian community. If we had been oblivious to our strengths and weaknesses, we no longer were. Our vision was what we saw as a vital need in our community. We knew firsthand how segregated Southwest Florida still was, even as the 20th century closed. The need for reconciliation between the races and denominations was critical. Every natural and spiritual signpost pointed to this need. Slowly, we are trying to redeploy our vision. We have come to terms with several vital understandings:

- The Lord must build the house (give the vision) or our labor is in vain.

- After all the planting and watering is completed, God must give the increase.

- The vision must have definable leadership and monetary resources to be achievable.

- We must trust the Lord to refresh His children and reestablish proper morale and momentum.

- The vision must be practical, specific, and finally measurable.

- The leadership and people must have a sense of fulfillment and fruitfulness in redeploying the vision.

By God's grace, we are being faithful to the heavenly vision. Our hearts are open to all who have challenged us with their personal decisions. The focus, without sacrificing the results, of our ministry has changed: *We seek to build big people rather than a big ministry.*

Undoubtedly, Jesus took this approach as He mentored the apostles. God's vision of the Kingdom, coupled with the ministry of reconciliation, is life changing. It is a radical turn to God with everything that it means in everyday life. God's love working in and through us will help the vision to prevail—no matter where we are. This anonymous quote sums up the sentiments of what we believe God would have us to do with His vision: "Love is a fabric that never fades, no matter how often it is washed in the waters of adversity and grief."[9] Love helps us to continue.

> Love is the dove of peace that soars out on the wings of the morning to greater spiritual heights. It is the angel's flight to a higher world of beauty, lifting life from its dust to meet the sunrise of God. It is beauty incarnated, kindness glorified, and goodness sanctified.
>
> Rosalie Mills Appleby[10]

ENDNOTES

1. Virginia Ely, *I Quote* (New York: George W. Stewart Publishers, Inc., 1947), 352.

2. James Strong, *"Hebrew and Chaldee Dictionary,"* Strong's Exhaustive Concordance of the Bible (Nashville: Abingdon, 1976), #6735.

3. Strong's, *"Greek Dictionary,"* #4243.

4. Webster's II New College Dictionary, Riverside University dictionary (New York: Houghton Mifflin Company, 1995), 35.

5. Vern McLellan, *Wise Words and Quotes* (Wheaton, IL: Tyndale House Publishers, Inc., 1998), 259.

6. Strong's, *"Greek Dictionary,"* #4246.

7. Ibid., #4243.

8. Geoff Gorsuch with Dan Schaffer, *Brothers! Calling Men Into Vital Relationships* (Boulder, CO: Promise Keepers, 1993), 2.

9. Vern McLellan, 172.

10. Ely, 213.

6

Signs and Wonders—God's Marketing Agents

God said to Moses, "Get ready. I'm about to come to you in a thick cloud so that the people can listen in and trust you completely when I speak with you" (Exodus 19:9 The Message).

When I first came to Southwest Florida, the gospel of the Kingdom of God, in relationship to the Feast of Tabernacles, was a foreign language to most Christians; and the region was mainly virgin territory in that regards. Without being presumptuous, I am sure you know there were a number of strong Evangelical and Pentecostal churches already functioning. Home groups here and there, along with small, struggling churches were preaching what is commonly called the *Kingdom message*. I understood this to be a message centered in the lordship of Jesus Christ, and manifesting His life in practical terms. Others labeled the message cultic, *wild kingdom,* or the message of Jehovah's Witnesses because of a fundamental lack of biblical understanding. Perhaps the previous messengers had communicated unclearly and left a horrid taste in people's mouths because of immaturity.

What I thought would be a swift work has become an 18-year spiritual quest. Father God knew I had many things to learn to get beyond presumptuousness about certain things. I am learning the importance of the principle of buy-in, after many lamentable leadership struggles, after many shifting winds in congregational commitments, and after many gales of turbulent winds producing change after change. Truthfully, I was very naïve when it came to the technical end of leadership. Desire alone doesn't make one a great leader, no matter how noble your intentions, how spotless your integrity, how righteous your pursuits. Leadership develops through time and effort. Fellow parishioners thought people would run to the truth. Truth alone does not lead people. Without people buying-in, a leader's vision will go no place. More than likely, he or she will become discouraged, disillusioned, and wonder if this is a God situation for them.

In the third month, when the children of Israel had gone out of Egypt, God announced a solid, long-term vision for them. This was a vision of greatness and acceptance. They were about to become a kingdom occupational force—occupying the land once held by the Canaanites. Now, they had to move beyond their circumstantial conflict, evaluate what God was saying to them, and buy into the vision. There was just one problem: Would the children of Israel connect with the man bringing the vision first? People will not buy into a vision until they have bought into the visionary.

Previously, Moses had bought into the God of the vision because of what he had seen. Jonathan Swift has said, "Vision is the art of seeing things invisible."[1] The writer to the Hebrews said Moses had seen Him who was invisible (see Heb. 11:27).

Now Moses was tending the flock of Jethro his father-in-law, the priest of Midian. And he led the flock to the back of the desert, and came to Horeb, the mountain of God. And the Angel of the Lord appeared to him in a flame of fire from the midst of a bush. So he looked, and behold, the bush was burning with fire, but the bush was not consumed. Then Moses said, "I will now turn aside and see this great sight, why the bush does not burn." So when the Lord saw that he turned aside to look, God called to him from the midst of the bush and said, "Moses, Moses!" And he said, "Here I am." Then He

*said, "Do not draw near this place. Take your sandals off your feet,
for the place where you stand is holy ground." Moreover He said, "I
am the God of your father—the God of Abraham, the God of
Isaac, and the God of Jacob." And Moses hid his face, for he was
afraid to look upon God* (Exodus 3:1-6).

God used a *supernatural manifestation* rather than the enticing
words of man's wisdom to cause Moses to receive the new thing He
was doing. We could certainly establish this as the pattern of God
as revealed in other occasions (see Acts 9:3-9; 1 Cor. 2:4-5) This
was not some fancy mental or emotional footwork. Moses would
have been less apt to sacrifice his life for God's cause without some
overwhelming reason. Remember, he had gone far, far away from
what he perceived to be his purpose, and possibly had no ambitions
to reclaim it. Moses' earlier disappointment probably could be
described this way.

He had met hell's fury and human reaction all at once. The
vision, the original star that he was following, led him into rough seas
and uncharted waters. What accumulated momentum he had was
snuffed out with one stroke of impetuosity. His calling, vision, identity, placement, and commitment were about to be overhauled.
Rejection had left him wounded, afraid, and weary. To add insult to
injury, Pharaoh had banished him to the scorpions and beasts of the
desert. Anyway you look at it, the desert is not an atmosphere to
build a man's ego. The depth of what he was feeling was difficult to
describe, hard to verbalize. Although what happened wasn't eternal,
yet he felt the residual effects in his spirit and every sphere of his
existence. It would require a supernatural manifestation to motivate
him to action again.

The Lord used the same principle of the buy-in with the nation of
Israel and Moses. *"And the Lord said to Moses, 'Behold, I come to you in
the thick cloud, that the people may hear when I speak with you, and believe
you forever.' So Moses told the words of the people to the Lord"* (Exod.
19:9). God utilized His own glory and greatness to create a buy-in
between the leader and the people. When there has been little basis for
trust between the people and the leader, something extraordinary

must happen. It was pivotal that they connect, and do it quickly. With the assistance of the Lord's Angel, Moses held the navigational charts to their destination. Then again, Moses had a speech impediment; therefore, he wasn't the eloquent spokesman who would cause people to hang on to every word he spoke. Effective in speaking, yes; powerful and moving, that's debatable. His power of presence came from spending time in the Lord's presence. The Father actually used Moses' weakness to introduce him and the nation to the supernatural. Also, it opened the door for Moses to team with Aaron in ministry. This would help to quell ecclesiastical abuse of power, illegitimate authority, and impure ministry motives.

ONLY THE LORD BE WITH YOU

Just as we heeded Moses in all things, so we will heed you. Only the Lord your God be with you, as He was with Moses" (Josh. 1:17).

Most men and women of God have had well-intentioned people tell them, "I will be with you wherever you go!" Several individuals have spoken that to me. Generally, this has been before any trials or offenses. The moment there seems to be one spiritual misdemeanor by the leader, all the commitments fall between the cracks. If that is not enough, try following an exceptionally gifted vessel of God who has demonstrated great spiritual aptitude. Comparisons linger for many years. The only standard of leadership people have is the one that used to be, but is no more.

It is extremely difficult to follow a man of God who has been a mighty instrument of the Lord. More than likely, people are always comparing the new leader to the previous leader, especially when the former leader excelled in the things of God. Pressure may be a gross injustice to a new leader. It can stunt his or her strengths, produce resentfulness or weariness. It is impossible to flow in your own personal uniqueness when you're being compared to someone else all the time. How do you get beyond that point and go further in the purposes of God?

The Master had a wonderful plan to help Joshua cross this hurdle. Just as Moses and Israel had passed through the Red Sea, now Joshua and Israel must pass through the Jordan River. It was not the most opportune time to cross when God commanded them to arise and cross the Jordan (see Josh. 3:15). Without contradiction it was another one of those divine set-ups—a defining moment. The heavenly Father had already uttered these words to Joshua: *"And the Lord said to Joshua, 'This day I will begin to exalt you in the sight of all Israel, that they may know that, as I was with Moses, so I will be with you"* (Josh. 3:7). Exalt means "to make you great!"[2] Joshua was about to be elevated in the minds of the people from commonness to greatness. The Lord would remove people's natural proclivity to judge harshly a second-generation leader. The onus of leadership would no longer rest on Joshua's neck.

Joshua pointed the children of Israel toward the Ark of the Covenant. Since the Ark pointed to Jesus Christ, he was persuading the people in type to be Christ-centered in their vision. A man or woman experiences greatness in God's Kingdom when they de-emphasize themselves and aim people toward Christ. To point people toward yourself is inviting them to exploit your weaknesses at the opportune moment. Joshua commanded the people to keep their eyes on the priests bearing the Ark.

When the priests bearing the Ark stepped into the Jordan River, the waters stood still and heaped all the way back to a city called Adam. Our heavenly Father was bearing witness of a future date when He would deal with all the issues of life dating back to our progenitor Adam. Twelve memorial stones were taken from the Jordan as a sign to future generations of what the Lord had done. This was prophetic of the resurrection of Jesus Christ and how He would become the firstfruits of all who would arise from the dead. The resurrection bespeaks the supernatural power of God. Joshua's leadership was being affirmed by the supernatural. The legitimacy of all Jesus attested was confirmed when the Father raised Him from the dead also (see Rom. 1:3-4). God was using the supernatural to avow His servants, and He still does. Signs and wonders have a way of arresting people's doubt and releasing them to believe God for the impossible.

COME SEE A MAN!

"Come, see a Man who told me all things that I ever did. Could this be the Christ?" Then they went out of the city and came to Him (John 4:29-30).

And many of the Samaritans of that city believed in Him because of the word of the woman who testified, "He told me all that I ever did." So when the Samaritans had come to Him, they urged Him to stay with them; and He stayed there two days. And many more believed because of His own word. Then they said to the woman, "Now we believe, not because of what you said, for we ourselves have heard Him and we know that this is indeed the Christ, the Savior of the world" (John 4:39-42).

Activities within the Kingdom of God often surprise some of its most loyal, yet uninformed, subjects. The disciples, who were trainees at the time, often misunderstood Jesus' mission. Kingdom work, at times, is unpredictable business, especially since God's ways are not always our ways; and His thoughts are not our thoughts. On His way to Galilee, Jesus made one of those seemingly abrupt stops by going through Samaria. It must have been something to have Jesus drop in on you, especially when you had been viewed as God's stepchildren by the current move-of-God people. Our Lord showed great compassion for the Samaritans through the numerous times He cited them as examples for the Jewish people. For instance, Jesus used a Samaritan to illustrate a true neighbor (see Luke 10:30-37), and the grateful leper to expose the ingratitude of the Jewish nation (see Luke 17:11-19). One of His sharpest rebukes was to James and John for desiring to incinerate a Samaritan parish for inhospitality (see Luke 9:52-56). Jesus wanted them to understand rejection was no reason to destroy people. When you are secure in the heavenly Father's provision, lack of responsiveness from man will not rattle you.

This is such a rich and potent story of a buy-in. It goes something like this. Jesus had come into the city of Samaria near Jacob's well. The Samaritan woman had come out to the ancient well for water while the disciples were gone to purchase food. Jesus asked the woman for a drink, knowing the Jews and Samaritans had no dealings with each other. It is obvious the woman became suspicious of this stranger's motives, but continued the conversation anyway. Possibly, she was hoping for assistance from the strenuous task of carrying water. When Jesus confronted her about a secret He should have known nothing about, she turned at once to religious arguments and theological debates. The fathers had been in a longstanding dispute over what mountain God had sanctified for worship. Jesus affirmed that true worship was in neither place, and God's true sanctuary was the heart of man. The accuracy of His prophetic flow convinced the woman this might be the Messiah. The woman bore witness of Jesus, and He stayed near Samaria for two days. He actually laid the groundwork for the harvest of Samaria that would come several years later.

The one prevailing question we must ask is: "Why did the Samaritans buy into Jesus so quickly when He was with them for only two days?" Was it only His words, or the density of the Man with the words? Or, maybe both? Perhaps they had never met a man who had refused to judge them based upon carnal reputation. We must consider the auspicious powers of spiritual manifestations in the mouth of a genuine prophet who ministers by the power of unfeigned love. Used correctly, with a sense of integrity, *the spirit of knowledge* has the ability to disarm people's defense mechanisms immediately. The words Jesus spoke were the grassroots seeds for what happened as a citywide harvest in Samaria almost a decade later when Philip came there (see Acts 8).

The ministry of Jesus continued through the apostles and the Church once He returned to Heaven. He commanded them to make disciples in Jerusalem, Judea, Samaria, and the utmost parts of the earth. Philip, one of the seven (see Acts 6), was the vessel who labored with the Lord to reap God's harvest in Samaria. The results are startling and worthy of our consideration to observe what happens when a city turns to God. Samaria could serve as a prototype of what God desires to do in our modern, ghetto-filled cities, which appear today as sophisticated jungles.

Acts 7 closes with the death of Stephen, the first known martyr in the Jerusalem Church. When great men pass away, it is like a seed corn for a greater work of the Lord. Men such as Abraham Lincoln and Dr. Martin Luther King, Jr. understood this principle: Their lives would probably serve as the seed for a new beginning. There was great lamentation in the Church, which served as the precious seed for great joy about to be reaped. Saul, the great persecutor to the Church, had already been released by the words of forgiveness uttered from the mouth of a dying Stephen. When he said, *"Lord, do not charge them with this sin,"*[3] these eight words removed judgment off someone who would later become the great defender of the faith.

After the death of Stephen, there was a great scattering of some of the sons of the Kingdom. They became scattered seed for evangelizing the nations. The Church in Jerusalem had been contented to fulfill only one half of their mission thus far. Samaria, which became the third quadrant of their mission, represents all the great outcasts of every generation and society. They were a culture of mix breeds that nobody wanted to associate with. Because of acute disenfranchisement, Samaria became open to many occult practices through the wizardry of Simon. They became a community overpowered by the devil. Philip preached and demonstrated the power of the Kingdom of God, which broke the power of evil in Samaria. The key to Samaria buying into Philip, and the message of the Kingdom, was the God-signs and miracles that were manifested.

> *Then Philip went down to the city of Samaria and preached Christ to them. And the multitudes with one accord heeded the things spoken by Philip, hearing and seeing the miracles which he did. For unclean spirits, crying with a loud voice, came out of many who were possessed; and many who were paralyzed and lame were healed. And there was great joy in that city* (Acts 8:5-8).

The citywide crusade in Samaria was so powerful it broke the chains of darkness and its draining effect upon society. All it took was one man, who had caught the spirit of the apostles, who had caught the spirit of the Master, King Jesus. Philip bought into the apostles, who had bought into Jesus. The proof of this is Philip was able to do the things that the apostles did. They preached the Kingdom of Heaven is at hand by healing the sick, casting out devils, cleansing lepers, and raising the dead. The presence of the Lord broke the city's fascination with a false power. Simon, the sorcerer, represents the control that modern drug cartels have over cities and countries. The word *sorcerer* comes from a Greek word in which we get our word *magic.*[4] In sorcery, the use of drugs, whether simple or potent, was generally accompanied by incantations and appeals to occult powers, with the provision of various charms, amulets, etc. This crusade was so astounding that even Simon believed and submitted to baptism (see Acts 8:13).

Our cities will be restored through the preaching of the gospel of the Kingdom with power. Spots commonly called dens of iniquity can be recovered. Every ministry must share their particular part with Jesus receiving the glory as He delivers the people. In the early days of the New Testament, buy-ins occurred because the gospel was accompanied with signs and wonders following. If we remotely desire our cities to buy into our ministries, we must do more than just talk. Rhetoric alone has always been cheap. The Kingdom is a kingdom of words certified by corresponding actions.

Look—Paul Didn't Swell!

The apostle Paul's experience on the Island of Malta is one of the most interesting stories of a buy-in in the whole of the Book of Acts. It was one of those unexpected additions in a trip. He happened upon this island because of a ship-ride that had gone dreadfully wrong. This story parallels some of those fierce storms fishermen have faced off the coast of North Carolina. My father was a commercial fisherman and shared some of those stories with me. It gave us respect for the powers of the wind and the ocean.

We could almost subtitle Acts 27 as: *Rome Bound—Turbulence Ahead.* Anytime God opens an effectual door for you, there will be tribulations—the greater the door, the greater the tribulations. Paul appealed to Caesar for justice (see Acts 25). He was on his way there. His earthly purpose would conclude in Rome, not in some ferocious northeaster storm. Storms have an uncanny ability to reveal a man's character. They do not hide God or hinder His purposes. Storms are opportunities to serve others and to bear witness of the faithfulness of God.

It is very important to remember a man's purpose is determined by his Creator and Maker, and circumstances will never alter that. It is incorrect to judge one's destiny based upon a specific season in one's life. God stated His purpose for Paul, his anointed one, and the devil stirred up an unholy conspiracy against him to thwart it. Paul bound his destiny to himself through his testimony. Words have a way of establishing things in Heaven and in earth. Bearing witness before three different governmental officials, he confronted three specific spirits:

- Felix was a type of many whose consciences are stirred by truth, but whose hopes are ruined by procrastination (see Acts 24:22-27).

- Fetus was a type of many who characterize full commitment to Jesus Christ as madness. In his testimony, Paul fellowshipped Christ's sufferings (see Acts 26:24).

- King Agrippa was a type of those who attempt to walk the fine line between being politically correct, yet noble to religious heritage (see Acts 26:27-29).

Paul overcame each of them, along with the ship-ride, the storm, and the possibility of a premature death at sea. Overcoming various obstacles is essential to making progress in the Kingdom of God; in fact, our greatest opportunities come with our greatest adversities. He, along with all the others on that ship, came out of those cold, bone-chilling waters of the Adriatic Sea, possibly suffering from hypothermia. Temporarily delayed, he was still on schedule to fulfill his destiny. This is where the story really gets interesting.

They came upon the island called Malta. The inhabitants were called "barbarous," which Webster defines as "primitive in culture and customs: uncivilized."[5] That was not the original meaning. The term *barbarous* was applied to all non-Greek-speaking peoples, who were regarded as foreigners. It was also applied by the Romans to non-Romans. This word carried the nuance of any culture in contrast to whatever was the dominant culture of the times. The men gathered wood and built a fire at once on the island. A venomous viper suddenly came out of the fire and fastened itself to Paul's hand. Paul shook off the beast because there was no dust in his life for the beast to feast on, for dust speaks of carnality and the old nature (see 1 Cor. 15:44-49) The fire is the only thing that will reveal and consume the beast at the same time. God's holy fires will reveal and consume the beast nature in man through the brightness of His appearing.

There must arise a body of people in the earth who are immunized against snakebite. The devil may show up, but he must find nothing in them. Paul didn't swell or puff up when bitten; and he didn't die! Men who have experienced the deathblow of the cross do not swell in pride when the supernatural is manifested. Paul's stock elevated in the heathens' minds when they beheld his status. He was no longer viewed as an escaped robber from the sea who finally received due process. They repented and he became as a god in their eyes. The opportunity for a buy-in was now available.

And it happened that the father of Publius lay sick of a fever and dysentery. Paul went in to him and prayed, and he laid his hands on him and healed him. So when this was done, the rest of those on the island who had diseases also came and were healed. They also honored us in many ways; and when we departed, they provided such things as were necessary (Acts 28:8-10)

It only took three days for the people of Malta to buy into Paul, therefore treating him, his traveling companions, and fellow-shipwrecked travelers with dignity. The island magistrate received them as guests with friendly thoughtfulness. For three months Paul was honored because of the manifestation of the Spirit of God. This is just one more illustration of how the power of the Holy Spirit will open people's hearts to a man or woman of God.

And my speech and my preaching were not with persuasive words of human wisdom, but in demonstration of the Spirit and of power, that your faith should not be in the wisdom of men but in the power of God (1 Corinthians 2:4-5).

Paul displayed the power of the Holy Spirit. The Holy Spirit affected the hearts and lives of his hearers in a manner human strength and wisdom could not. It contrasted the attempted methods of proof by rhetorical arts and philosophical arguments. The Roman world, influenced by Greek sophistry, was filled with rhetoric and homilies. These tedious speeches were very showy, entertaining, and placed emphasis on eloquence. The schools of logic taught students how to speak admirably on any subject at any time. Debate was common, and students had to learn to argue convincingly. Logic appeased the Greeks' thirst for knowledge, and was more theoretical than practical. Paul refused to establish converts into the Kingdom of God on this faulty method. He refused to become a *wordsmith*. Polished grammar may impress your head; however, it will not transform your heart. Men of God are most effective when they point people toward the Spirit of God and trust Him to establish them in the faith. There can be no greater buy-in than this.

Let's extract a very important factor from this story. Paul illustrated how to get over the carnal "I-am-god disease" in man. Certainly, he was not a member of the "me cult," which follows the hubristic lure to deify self without the transforming work of the Holy Spirit. He did not change in character or attitude even though uninformed people thought he was a god. He knew exactly who he was! One of the last tests men of God must overcome on the route to fulfilling their destiny is the "god-treatment" as though they're the Almighty God. Make it clear to people: Without Jesus, a man of God can do nothing! Though we are a part of the full God expression, no individual is the Almighty God. When people seek to make us a god or a king, we must do what Jesus did while here on earth: Refuse them. *"Therefore when Jesus perceived that they were about to come and take Him by force to make Him king, He departed again to the mountain by Himself alone"* (John 6:15 KJV). Know who you are, based upon the internal revelation of Christ. If men enthrone you, they will eventually dethrone you when someone else comes along who satisfies their lust for power in a greater way.

Now, if you have studied Philippians chapter 2, your mind may be spinning about this question: What do believers do with the command of the apostle Paul in verses 5-6? It reads: *"Let this mind be in you which was also in Christ Jesus, who, being in the form of God, did not consider it robbery to be equal with God."* Does this give us the right to deify self, and create more little gods than Greek mythology? Absolutely not! The key to understanding this series of verses is to know that the only way to properly entertain this mind-set, or attitude, is to walk in humility. Jesus did not have a thirst for being equal with God, although He was, while in His earth-suit. The present conditions of this flesh demand that each believer humbles self and walks the life of oneness with the Lord. Any other approach would be fatal. Walking in an arrogant spirit to this command would lead to the same results lucifer experienced (see Isa.14:12-17).

> *Think of yourselves the way Christ Jesus thought of Himself. He had equal status with God but didn't think so much of Himself that He had to cling to the advantages of that status no matter what. Not at all. When the time came, He set aside the privileges of deity and took on the status of a slave, became human! Having become human, he stayed human. It was an incredibly humbling process. He didn't claim special privileges. Instead, He lived a selfless, obedient life and then died a selfless, obedient death—and the worst kind of death at that: a crucifixion* (Philippians 2:5-8 The Message).

CAUTION—FLASHING SIGNAL AHEAD

It is necessary to issue this caution since God employs the supernatural in order for us to understand the power and coming of the Kingdom. Have you noticed how people who often move openly in the supernatural sometimes end with disgraced, shipwrecked lives? This puzzled me as a young minister. After all, none other than Jesus said that signs would follow believers (see Mark 16:17-18) In studying the Scriptures, and questioning the Lord about this bizarre phenomenon, I have come to some solid judgments about the supernatural.

The initial operation in the Holy Spirit was primarily by the handpicked apostles of Jesus Christ. It is an assumption to think signs followed all believers who had never been developed in the character of God. After years of sitting at the feet of the apostles, some trainees finally began to come forth who could do what they did (see Acts 6). According to the storyline, they probably excelled in management as mature businessmen. Their emergence was the result of years of ego dismantling and destruction of human ambition. The primary work of the Kingdom among the churched is fruit development, not miracle-working. If the fruit of the Holy Spirit develops properly in a person's life, there won't be much need for miracles undoing what diseased character has produced. A change in our inner dispositions of heart and lifestyles is sometimes the greatest miracle one can receive.

Phenomena are only necessary in the most urgent cases. If you have no grace to bear persecution, please don't attempt to operate in them. The natural process is usually the most advantageous to a person because of the deep dealings of God that change the heart along with the health. This is more of a spiritual therapeutics, which agrees with one of the very important New Testament words for healing. Therapy requires time and endurance. One look at the nation of Israel proves this thought: The first generation received a miracle every day of their lives in the wilderness and still missed their purpose. They had no sick, no starving, and no social welfare system. God met the necessities of life for them in one of the most hostile environments. Most of Israel rebelled against His commandments anyway!

When ministers present miracles as customary to undisciplined believers, they seem to lose their sense of awe and effectiveness. The green light into the supernatural tends to promote prison cells of self-glory, especially to those who know nothing of the crucified life. God intended for signs and wonders to amaze us and cause us to wonder. They are not Kingdom publicity stunts, or credentials for someone attempting to become a god or approved of other men. We are not called to sideshows or magical displays. This has nothing to do with theatrics and Hollywood showmanship. Often Jesus would do something mind-boggling and say, *"Tell no man"* (see Matt. 9:27-31;

Mark 1:40-45). He realized carnal curiosity was never an ideal atmosphere for people. How many men today do you hear saying, "Tell no man about the miracle wrought in your life"? To the contrary, many men of God are hoping to polish up their résumés with just one authentic miracle.

I'll never forget the day when a certain woman called and asked me to visit with her in the hospital. She had just been diagnosed with aggressive breast cancer. I knew of her values and belief system, and was hesitating about going. My natural mind said, "Don't go," but the voice of the Holy Spirit was saying, "Go!" After fussing with my own rational mind for a while, I finally relented and obeyed the Lord. As I walked into that hospital room, the presence of the Lord met me there. The dear lady shared her story and asked for prayer. I agreed. The Holy Spirit touched her in a powerful way; God received the glory, and my attitude a needed adjustment. She felt the presence of God during prayer, and I felt nothing. I couldn't use that situation to promote myself as a miracle-worker because God moved in spite of my ugly attitude and me. He performed a miracle privately, and there was no glamorizing of the situation. I experienced what it was to enroll into God's silent society that day. Needless to say, I left the room humbled and perplexed.

A very interesting pattern unfolds as you study the Book of Acts concerning signs, wonders, and miracles. Most recorded power manifestations occurred outside the *four walls* of the church's gathering places. Miracles occurred in secular settings rather than sacred environments. After seeing this, I understand now why modern men violently oppose them. We have witnessed the modern media attack miracle-workers with vicious vindictiveness. Joining with spiteful religious spirits, a mockery is made of the power of God. Carnal men have always contested miracles because the hidden force behind carnality contests the power of the Kingdom of God manifested. The adversary doesn't want men to know the authority of the King, and subsequently the believer. Note the pattern:

• The miracle of the lame man (see Acts 3:4-8) — opposition to the miracle (see Acts 4:1-2).

- Miracles from Peter's shadow (see Acts 5:12-16) — opposition (see Acts 5:17-18).

- Stephen's exploits (seeActs 6:8) — opposition (see Acts 6:9-15).

- Saul's miraculous conversion (see Acts 9:19-22) — opposition (Acts 9:23-25).

- The miracle of the crippled man (see Acts 14:8-10) — opposition (see Acts 14:19-20).

- The miracle of the girl's deliverance from the spirit of python (see Acts 16:16-18) — opposition (see Acts 16:22-24).

- The miracle of conversion and opposition in Thessalonica (see Acts 17:1-8).

- Miracles because of handkerchiefs from Paul's body (see Acts 19:11-12,18-20) — opposition (see Acts 19:23-24).

Jesus knew the negative effect that public marketing could have on people. He was well aware of the snare the enemy would set for unscrupulous performers. Things like pecking order (greatest man of God?), defensiveness, covetousness, and greed would be difficult to overcome. I have had to caution certain individuals at various times about this. It forces people to become too dependent upon a *man of God* rather than the *God of the man*. In addition, many times there are no other men or women able to bring balance or correction to the man of God. He often becomes a law unto himself, and an influential voice in areas of Scripture in which he lacks understanding. God's pattern is to team miracle-workers with teachers, who can ground God's people in the Word of God so that diseased thoughts may be unearthed out of the soil of their souls. Because miracles are so impressive, people will often devalue instruction. We must teach people to value every tool God uses.

Sensational things in people's lives will often provoke them to think and speak too approvingly of themselves. They often forget miracles are clearly acts of God—grace fringe benefits, having little to do with whether one deserves one or not. In this sense, divine healing is still quite a mystery. I have seen wicked people get unimaginable miracles, and righteous people die inconceivable deaths needing miracles. We must leave things like that into the hands of our wise and prudent heavenly Father. Father knows best! Jesus, our Elder Brother, showed us how to do it. He did only whatever He saw the Father doing. Subsequently, He was not self-absorbed with a performance mentality or bent on producing original things. Jesus did not give the enemy an opportunity to feast on egoism because of His total self-surrender to the Father. Imitating Him will help each ambassador of the Kingdom to utilize the power of buy-in honorably. May the Lord give us the right vision, and may we utilize the power of buy-in appropriately. We are here on earth to *occupy until Jesus comes*! Let us make His name great and not our own.

ENDNOTES

1. Vern McLellan, *Wise Words and Quotes* (Wheaton, IL: Tyndale House Publishers, Inc., 1998), 279.

2. James Strong, *"Hebrew and Chaldee Dictionary,"* Strong's Exhaustive Concordance of the Bible (Nashville, TN: Abingdon, 1976), #1431.

3. Acts 7:60 - New King James Version (Nashville, TN: Broadman & Holman Publishers, 1996), 965.

4. Strong's, *"Greek Dictionary,"* #3095, #3096.

5. Webster's II New College Dictionary, Riverside University dictionary (New York: Houghton Mifflin Company, 1995), 89.

7

Love: The Firm Foundation of Morality

The only morality that is clear in its course, pure in its precepts, and efficacious in its influence, is the morality of the gospel. All else, at last, is but idolatry - the worship of something of man's own creation, and that, imperfect and feeble like himself, and wholly insufficient to give him support and strength.

- John Sergeant[1]

Morality and ethics! Nothing provokes greater passion or ire, except, maybe, religion, secular politics, and sexuality. In the post-modern world, there's a humungous debate continually existing in the field of morality. When there are so many cultures, with so many dissimilarities, how do we come up with an agreeable moral structure suitable for all cultures—something we could call absolute? Sounds pretty impossible, doesn't it? There are cultures in which to kill the enemy of your cause is an honorable, moral obligation. Others reject any type of killing, including State-supported executions. Some celebrate millions of gods and goddesses, while most Judeo-Christian cultures are monotheistic. Some even permit many wives, if your financial position is strong enough, while others maintain the idea of one wife—period. A question most people may entertain one time or another is: Does it ever become permissible to lie or steal? How about committing murder? If we stacked some of these ideas together, would it be right to lie in order to prevent someone from committing a murder? Does the Lord expect us to approach some of these things hierarchically if it serves the greatest good for human beings? Will any of these issues prevent us from having a proper Kingdom morality and foundation?

THE TEN WORDS OR SAYINGS

God's initial answer in addressing some of these matters, from a documented Kingdom perspective, is what we call the Ten Commandments, which were called the "ten words" in Hebrew. If we were studying ethics, they would fall into the category of *normative ethics*—which provides general rules and principles of conduct. Israel had reduced themselves to performance-based religion rather than relationship-based experiences (see Exod. 19:8). They supplanted *doing* for *grace*.

In reviewing each command, God's character was reaffirmed in each statement. The words the Lawgiver spoke were reflective of His nature; they had very little to do with doctrines, creating proof text, and establishing commentaries for latter generations. There's no way Moses would have ever thought he was fueling future U.S. Supreme Court cases and judicial reviews with what he wrote. Maybe if Christians would focus on the nature of God, they wouldn't concentrate on the prohibitions, or the restrictions, these words seem to present. The Bible says, *"A good man out of the good treasure of his heart brings forth good; and an evil man out of the evil treasure of his heart brings forth evil. For out of the abundance of the heart his mouth speaks"* (Luke 6:45). The Lord was teaching us to use our minds, creative potentials, and gifts of speech correctly. Time and experience have taught me that purposeful words truly represent a purposeful heart. The Lord was giving practical, workable, relational ideals to the developing culture He had just called out of darkness and unto Himself.

Through and through, the Decalogue provides a framework to repeal various forms of idolatry. The heavenly Father was saying, "This is what the face of idolatry resembles, every shade of it!" All honest men will tell you that it is impossible to keep any of the commandments without a change in carnal man's nature. The Bible discloses idolatry as carnal mankind's greatest moral weakness, the root of all historical moral diseases. I simply see it as man's compulsive infatuation and excessive adoration of self without properly giving God His rightful love and adoration. The first letter in the word *idol*—"I"—reveals the center of idolatry. Man tries to be a god unto himself outside of the one sovereign God. This is expressed in all forums of life, particularly using philosophy and the creative arts as two of its greatest scholastic venues. Other avenues are the extremes men will go to in acquiring wealth, stripping other people of economic empowerment, or controlling the lives of others by keeping them at certain economic levels while increasing their own economic strength. Thus, the power and powerful feeling men get motivate them to accrue what can be the greatest idol of all: *money!*

After Adam left the Garden of God, he moved more deeply into selfhood, and idolatry increased. Idolatry has grown with every generation and matured into a concept we call humanism, which refutes the existence of the Eternal God. As an organized system of influence, it began as a cultural and intellectual movement of the Renaissance that emphasized secular concerns because of academics tracing back to previous epochs in Greece and Rome. The morality of humanism is the morality of man, by man, and for man. Since humanists reject the reality of God, there is no God; and there's no ordained moral strategy for man to follow or be concerned with in this philosophy.

The first and last commandments (see Exod. 20:1-17), particularly address idolatry. They show us the perils of distorted images and covetousness. (Covetousness will be treated more fully in another chapter.) Since humanism is the idolatry of self, any godly commandment would be an affront to it. Self is crowned king in humanism and can do no wrong. Could we say self is the taproot of idolatry, then? When man is seen in any image other than the image of God, the foundation is laid for distorted, wrong images. Graven images are the artistic forms of mentalities submerged in wrong imagery, which is idolatry. Within the context of this notion, man releases himself from under the auspices of God and seeks human fulfillment, which is a measured freedom of unstable conditions and consequences. He creates lifeless gods to appease the emptiness, the hollow in his soul, because he has forsaken a living relationship with a living God. The dignity of the individual and the extensive continuum of human rights become the basis of all actions. This fluctuates from situation to situation, thus producing a situational morality. Nothing is absolute; everything is relative to what satisfies a human. When this happens, man has placed another god before God's face; and this is the genesis form of idolatry.

A FIRM MORAL BASE

The heavenly Father began to establish a firm moral base for Israel after He presented His vision of their corporate enormity. (Read Exodus 19–20.) Morality is "the quality of being in accord with standards of good or right conduct."[2] These principles are measurable and grounded in the indescribable character of God, which should become the nature of God's children. They have been around for many centuries. Since God breathed into man the breath of life, man was given the spirit of morality in this gift of conscience. For example, when Cain murdered Abel, he didn't need legislation that said, "Do not commit murder." This principle was clearly rooted in his conscience as supported by his retort to God's question, "Where is Abel your brother?" He intrinsically knew he was his brother's keeper.

The Bible testifies that many of the patriarchs walked morally before there was a written code. When Abraham lied to Abimelech about Sarah, he was rebuked sharply. The finger of God had written upon the tables of men's hearts a code of divine morality. Behavior contrary to His nature was unacceptable. The Scripture says, *"The integrity of the upright will guide them, but the perversity of the unfaithful will destroy them"* (Prov. 11:3). Even heathen leaders lived with a sense of moral integrity (see Gen. 20:1-6) Man was expected to conform to these principles and preserve a morally unbreakable, unbendable foundation for all of mankind. He would be responsible to other men, guaranteeing a society of love, care, and equality. That's the Kingdom of God!

When the Kingdom of God isn't produced, men substitute a variety of moral and ethical theories. One of them is utilitarianism, which is the ethical theory proposed by Jeremy Bentham and John Stuart Mill. It postulates that all moral, social, or political action should be directed toward achieving the greatest good for the greatest number of people.[3] Christians would be totally amazed at how much this philosophy has bled over into our thinking and behavior. Under this philosophy, morality is no longer reckoned by an authenticated divine, absolute code. It is one of the many theories with a variety of choices that sprang up after the Renaissance Period. Great thinkers moved away from divine, Kingdom-oriented law and began to concentrate on natural law and secularism.

I saw one of the most powerful applications of this moral theory in the dramatic series, *Law and Order.* Television is a powerful tool to reflect our present culture. In that particular episode, the parents had two sons, one healthy, and the other with a deadly disease. Apart from special medical intervention, the younger son would soon die. This was where the story line backed utilitarian thinking. The parents allowed a wealthy pedophile to spend time with their healthy son for an astronomical fee. Their rationale was that the healthy son could get over that incident and continue with his life. He was physically and emotionally raped and sacrificed, scarred unmercifully for the good of the whole family. The family moved from a very poor neighborhood, and the younger son received treatment that saved his life. Thus, you have an action that supposedly achieved the greatest good for the greatest number of people.

What do you think God's opinion would be in this? Would He be a silent partner or a solicitous judge? It is highly unthinkable to justify the gruesome deeds of pedophilia just to make a few others jubilant. Somehow this doesn't square with the righteous, character-building intentions of a holy God. Gratifying the majority has never been His aim. Majority rule is of no concern to Him—He's theocratic.

Theocratic is God-ruled, which means "out of God, through God, for God, and unto God" (author's definition).

The Church will shortly face more potent, court-supported forces right out of the cradle of utilitarianism. Our theocratic views and practices will be challenged repeatedly. Because of their economic strength, there's a strong push to make homosexuality as acceptable in postmodern America as heterosexuality. By accepting this practice, won't the financial strength of the homosexual community benefit more people than narrow-minded, financially strapped heterosexuals? It is a fact that homosexuals are becoming one of the most powerful economic forces in the global market. They are steadily gaining ground in all of the strongest economically enriched occupations. The Church needs to take notice of this. The logical conclusion of utilitarianism would say, "Yes! Let them have what they want!" The money will create new jobs, or better jobs, which in turn will benefit society in general. They are very creative people, and we need their creativity to benefit humanity. Whether this behavior is unnatural, sinister, and threatening to family values is another story. When there are no moral absolutes, we appeal to reason to figure things out for us. Moreover, reason may at times deceive us. My appeal goes to a higher court of love and concern for all human beings.

I make my appeal to the timelessness of true biblical morality, which is centered in man's initial oneness with God, and not secularism. It provides each generation with the security that God's moral structure is uncompromisingly safe—safe from all the manipulation current moral trends are postulating. Biblical morality is tamper-proof: We don't have to worry about someone becoming belligerent or intelligent enough to break the spiritual seal and poison God's order. God has always preserved His principles, even in the darkest of times, and passed them on to each succeeding generation. His principles will never be massaged by the perverted impulses of warped human nature to fit some relative, non-absolute standard that changes with every human whim. The postmodern neo-moral engineers will never be able to daunt God's absolute standards, which are absolutely founded on love. The Church's responsibility is to present and model

God's standards without hypocrisy. The true challenge before us is: We must make sure they are His, and not our own creations.

VISION AND MORALITY

Vision without morality becomes a farce. The apostle Peter, in the New Covenant, encouraged moral excellence to be added to faith (see 2 Pet. 1:5) I don't believe this was one of those times, either, when he was dangling between law and grace. Without biblical morality, men will employ whatever means necessary, whether noble or sadistic, to achieve their ends. It is the old cliché that the results justify the means. David A. Noble quoting Lev Kopelev sums up the practical application of this thought concerning communism. He said what was proven an acceptable refrain in communist ideology.

> With the rest of my generation I firmly believed that the ends justified the means. Our great goal was the universal triumph of Communism, and for the sake of that goal everything was permissible—to lie, to steal, to destroy hundreds of thousands and even millions of people, all those who were hindering our work or could hinder it, everyone who stood in the way. And to hesitate or doubt about all this was to give in to "intellectual squeamishness" and "stupid liberalism," the attribute of people who "could not see the forest for the trees."[4]

This philosophy reminds me of a modern attitude that says: "You will either join us, get out of our way, or get run over." It says, "We're coming, whether you think we're nasty, sadistic, psychotic, aggressive, vicious or etc." Of course, Russian communism ran its course after 70 years. Their moral code could be summed up in this anonymous quote: "Morals without religion will wither and die, like seed sown upon stony ground or among thorns."[5]

Theocentric, or God-centered, morality is just the opposite; it is absolute, non-circumstantial, peaceful, and eternal. It isn't polluted with ethical strivings and morally good efforts, attempting to obey the scrupulous commands of God. It eludes all human fussiness and meticulously draws strength from grace. The purpose behind a theocentric morality is righteousness, or right standing that aligns with divine government. Righteousness is always joined to peace (see Rom. 14:17). It presents core values that will underpin a culture wherein its citizenry will properly manage themselves, their desires, and their possessions. It doesn't have an unholy world supremacy notion centered in humanistic values such as communism and other 20th-century aversions. Conversely, it posits a self-effacing one that submits to the lordship of Jesus Christ and the mandates of a holy God and Father, who longs to flood us with grace. This is key because the greatest impasse of freedom is the management of self, which is the basic unit of society. Without a relationship with Jesus Christ, the management of self is all but impossible. We may have a firm conviction, a moral track, and a will of steel; and yet, still miss God's higher order.

When a nucleus of self-managed people, under the authority of the Holy Spirit, unite, they become, literally, the mainstay of that society—something of a community of Kingdom righteousness. They collaborate and present governable principles that benefit everyone. Please keep in mind these must be communities governed by the law of the spirit of life. In the spirit realm, they actually become a covering presence for the community from the strategies of evil. Even derelicts tap into the acceptable mores and live somewhat under this influence. Though homeless and shackled with abject poverty, in their own world, they respect one another's bags, carts, and sleeping spaces. When principles work throughout the fabric of society like that, most purists, leaning from a God consciousness, would call these principles absolutes. *Absolute* means "perfect in nature and quality."[6] Only the Eternal God is absolute and can give something absolute—touching every social stratum of human beings. If it isn't absolute, by nature it becomes humanistic.

Various reforming movements have arisen to counteract the claims of humanism. They have attempted to utilize moral absolutes centered in Christian principles rather than a morality flowing out of a divine nature. Right principles will not work apart from the right nature. One such example is Moral Rearmament, which was an international movement calling for moral and spiritual renewal.[7] Its leaders (Frank Buchman in the 1920s and the Oxford Group) enrolled supporters to practice absolute purity, absolute unselfishness, absolute honesty, and absolute love. This group became a proactive voice of resistance during the Cold War period when its anticommunist demeanor found a receptive mood. With the tremendous amount of social engineering happening today, this group, under new leadership, may rise again, attempting to thwart the postmodern redefinitions of marriage, family, and sexuality.

Although the previously mentioned absolutes would make a fine group of core values in any society, first, they must be birthed in the hearts of people by the Holy Spirit. Honest men try to legalistically impose a system of ideals that can't transform them internally—it only suppresses them externally on a temporary basis. Because we see the need for people to behave wisely doesn't necessarily mean they will. The practice of purity goes beyond the impositions of a legalistic system. The key ingredient to make an absolute workable is an impartation and a revelation of the nature of God, which is love. The Holy Spirit, the means of revelation, imputes agape love, which is unconditional love for God and our fellowman. Pure love alone is the strength of a moral correctness demanded by Moral Rearmament. Highly sensitive political and social issues affecting mankind can only be governed by a flow of life from the throne of God, not rearming morally from a carnal or even Christian agenda. Remember, Christian doesn't necessarily mean Christ-like to people anymore. Many people call themselves Christians and have none of the fruits of biblical Christianity.

THE OVERRIDING REVELATION

The purpose of this chapter is not to discuss each individual commandment per se. That would be unnecessary for this writing, though not pointless. Many excellent works have been written on them already. We must see the overriding theme of the Decalogue as revealed by the spirit of revelation. By doing so, it affords each of us the perfect opportunity to abide in God's love knowledgeably.

In addition, it empowers us to manage ourselves without the necessity of written rules and regulations. We grow relationally to the point we don't need them anymore because our nature is transformed. In God's economy, transformation leads to conformation: We are conformed into the image of Christ! All rules, essentially, are temporary; they are like yokes borne in our immaturity to prevent self-destruction. The Law economy, in its beginning with Moses, and in its ending with Jesus, bears witness to the importance of God's love at work within Kingdom people. With or without rules, love is the best assurance we will respond to the Lord correctly, and work for the common good of all men.

> *Hear, O Israel: The Lord our God, the Lord is one! You shall love the Lord your God with all your heart, with all your soul, and with all your strength. And these words which I command you today shall be in your heart* (Deuteronomy 6:4-6).

> *"Teacher, which is the great commandment in the law?" Jesus said to him, " 'You shall love the Lord your God with all your heart, with all your soul, and with all your mind.' This is the first and great commandment. And the second is like it: 'You shall love your neighbor as yourself.' On these two commandments hang all the Law and the Prophets"* (Matthew 22:36-40).

Moses commanded the fledgling second generation of Israelites to hear the sacred command of God's righteous requirements of heartfelt love. When questioned by the probing inquiry of an analytical lawyer, Jesus quoted from the same thought. He taught that all commandments could be reduced to two. All the Old Testament's commandments are not official obligations or duties for Christians. Inherent within the spirit and sphere of love is the mandate to keep the Lord's words with joy—for God's commandments are not grievous. Although every commandment is just and righteous, human nature uses them to exploit the exceeding sinfulness of the sin nature. Redemption frees us to love God and man freely without the impositions of the legal code. We best conform to God's love by keeping His great commandment of pure, unfeigned love—highlighted by a giving nature (see John 3:16). Conversely, to resist keeping God's commandments is a refusal to love, which is contrary to a Christ-like nature. Today, rites of purification and ceremonialism have absolutely nothing to do with loving God or our neighbor. These things were part of a system that passed away in the finished work of the cross.

> *By this we know that we love the children of God, when we love God and keep His commandments. For this is the love of God, that we keep His commandments. And His commandments are not burdensome* (1 John 5:2-3).

To be without love or core values is to create a culture with anarchic behavior, with the results being uncontrollable human appetites and practices. Many call this *eros*. In an erotic world, self is what matters. It is the seedbed for a theory called solipsism,[8] which says self is the only reality. The Book of Judges closes with a bleak analogy of almost five centuries of Israel's history lived this way: *"In those days there was no king in Israel; everyone did what was right in his own eyes"* (Judg. 21:25). The children of Israel during this volatile period were gods unto themselves or magnified other more appalling, idolatrous practices. When people refuse to share the love that belongs to God with idols or self, they prohibit the development of such a culture of individualists. The fact of society implies that people must work and choose to coexist together on the basis of principles that are higher than individual interests are. This is an impossible task apart from loving others as one would love self. The early Church is a sterling example of a proper Kingdom society and people living out the ideals of vital interest for one another.

> *Now all who believed were together, and had all things in common, and sold their possessions and goods, and divided them among all, as anyone had need* (Acts 2:44-45).

> *Now the multitude of those who believed were of one heart and one soul; neither did anyone say that any of the things he possessed was his own, but they had all things in common* (Acts 4:32).

Because of the baptism of the Holy Spirit, and choosing to cooperate with Him, people were able to live the selfless lifestyle described in the Book of Acts. The Holy Spirit is the agency that pours the love of God into the hearts of people, thus enabling them to live this way. Love was, is, and always will be the motivational force for all genuine

Kingdom activity. Motivation is the inner drive, impulse, and intention that cause a person to do something or act in a certain way. This is why God judges the heart of a matter and not with the recklessness of human judgment. The Scriptures are very clear about making inappropriate judgments about others based upon external actions without knowing their motives. Sometimes motives and actions are difficult to square from the standpoint of carnal observation, leaving us in a position to gingerly scrutinize things, and to tread carefully in our judgments. When motives and actions square perfectly, it is because of the proper appropriation of the love of God. This kind of love is the composition of many quality ingredients and spices of grace blended together. Seasoned with mercy and a dash of compassion, we have a special compound.

- Love is patient. It gives us the ability to wait or endure without complaint; patience is steadiness, endurance, or perseverance in the performance of a task.

  But let patience have its perfect work, that you may be perfect and complete, lacking nothing (James 1:4).

- Love is kind. It implies the possession of sympathetic or generous qualities, either habitually or specifically.

  Be kindly affectionate to one another with brotherly love, in honor giving preference to one another (Romans 12:10).

  And be kind to one another, tenderhearted, forgiving one another, even as God in Christ forgave you (Ephesians 4:32).

- Love is generous. Generous is having qualities attributed to people of noble birth; noble-minded; gracious, magnanimous, willingness to give or share and not compete.

  For we dare not class ourselves or compare ourselves with those who commend themselves. But they, measuring themselves by themselves, and comparing themselves among themselves, are not wise (2 Corinthians 10:12).

- Love is humble. Humility is having or showing a consciousness of one's defects or shortcomings; not proud; not self-assertive; modest; unpretentious.

  He has shown you, O man, what is good; and what does the Lord require of you but to do justly, to love mercy, and to walk humbly with your God? (Micah 6:8)

  Likewise you younger people, submit yourselves to your elders. Yes, all of you be submissive to one another, and be clothed with humility, for "God resists the proud, but gives grace to the humble" (1 Peter 5:5).

- Love is courteous. Courtesy is gracious politeness; an act or usage intended to honor or compliment. It is well mannered and considerate toward others.

  Love does no harm to a neighbor; therefore love is the fulfillment of the law (Romans 13:10).

- Love is unselfish. Unselfishness is putting the good of others above one's own interests; concern for the welfare of others.

  Just as I also please all men in all things, not seeking my own profit, but the profit of many, that they may be saved (1 Corinthians 10:33).

  So Abram said to Lot, "Please let there be no strife between you and me, and between my herdsmen and your herdsmen; for we are brethren. Is not the whole land before you? Please separate from me. If you take the left, then I will go to the right; or, if you go to the right, then I will go to the left" (Genesis 13:8-9).

- Love is good-tempered. Good-tempered is having the ability to not easily be angered or annoyed, amiable. It is having a pleasant and friendly disposition, good-natured.

  Therefore, as the elect of God, holy and beloved, put on tender mercies, kindness, humility, meekness, longsuffering; bearing with one another, and forgiving one another, if anyone has a complaint against another; even as Christ forgave you, so you also must do (Colossians 3:12-13).

- Love is righteous. Righteous is acting in a just, upright manner; doing what is right; virtuous. This kind of love hates sin but not the sinner. It is never glad when others go wrong; always gladdened by goodness to others; always slow to expose; always eager to believe the best; always hopeful, always enduring.

But to the Son He says: "Your throne, O God, is forever and ever; a scepter of righteousness is the scepter of Your Kingdom. You have loved righteousness and hated lawlessness; therefore God, Your God, has anointed You with the oil of gladness more than Your companions" (Hebrews 1:8-9).

- Love is sincere. Sincerity is pure and clean without deceit, pretense, or hypocrisy; truthful; straightforward, honest. It is the same in actual character as in outward appearance, genuineness.

And this I pray, that your love may abound still more and more in knowledge and all discernment, that you may approve the things that are excellent, that you may be sincere and without offense till the day of Christ (Philippians 1:9-10).

I speak not by commandment, but I am testing the sincerity of your love by the diligence of others (2 Corinthians 8:8).

THE ONE GREAT COMMAND OF THE NEW COVENANT

Unquestionably, the one great command of the New Covenant is love. Love enables us, with the authority of grace, to pursue God and to respect our fellowman with diligence. While identifying His betrayer, Jesus commanded the apostles to *"love one another"* as He had loved them (John 13:34). It is somewhat interesting that Jesus called this a new commandment in light of all that the heavenly Father had spoken about love in the Old Covenant. Both Deuteronomy 6:5 and Leviticus 19:18 had become a clear injunction for God's people many centuries before Jesus came to earth. In fact, Jesus chose these passages to sum up the mandate of the Law and prophets. How, then, could He say love is a new commandment and be accurate?

The Greek word for *new* is *kainos*. It denotes new, of that which is unaccustomed or unused, not new in time, recent, but new as to form or quality, of different nature from what is contrasted as old.[9] The operative word is *unused*. Jesus was inaugurating a brand-new quality of love in action.

The New Covenant has to be grounded in love, or it has no moral base. Jesus provided the paradigm for this. He didn't function by rules and restrictions—only love that flowed out of a nature not coaxed by human standards or weighed down by ulterior motives. Before giving the apostles the new commandment of love, He girded on the servant's towel and modeled unselfish love and servanthood in a manner unprecedented by a king. His purpose in doing this was to present a pattern of unconditional love that the apostles were unaccustomed to. His love was not only spoken dogma, but also illustrated deeds. The apostles, as part of the embryonic Church's foundation, would love one another on a horizontal plane, thus reflecting their relationship with the Father and the Son on a vertical plane. As they displayed Christ's love, it would truly mimic the pattern of Jesus toward the Father.

The apostle Paul later addressed the Colossian church with these words:

> *So, chosen by God for this new life of love, dress in the wardrobe God picked out for you: compassion, kindness, humility, quiet strength, discipline. Be even-tempered, content with second place, quick to forgive an offense. Forgive as quickly and completely as the Master forgave you. And regardless of what else you put on, wear love. It's your basic, all-purpose garment. Never be without it* (Colossians 3:12-14 The Message).

Love is our all-purpose garment. What a marvelous thought! Love enables us to recognize we don't owe the old life a thing. The old life is like a filthy set of ill-fitting garments ready to be cast into a blazing furnace of grace. Our heavenly Father has customized a new set of clothing for us in the baptism of the Holy Spirit, with a label that says, "Great Grace." What the apostle Paul described was the fruit of the Holy Spirit. The Holy Spirit precipitously pours love into our hearts as we yield to Him. God's love rids us of the old fashions connected with the old man, making them obsolete and superfluous. When we discard the old nature, it isn't difficult to be moral. It's not uncouth, uncivilized, coarse, or ill-mannered. God is love, and so are His children. As we manifest Him, and all of His likenesses, we more perfectly become love personified. And love personified is moral.

There can be no greater morality than the morality birthed out of unconditional love. It is not prejudiced, bigoted, sectarian, fearful, or lacking in equality for all. It has no special interest groups—all men are deemed valuable. All the great moral dilemmas of the present and previous centuries have for their foundation the lack of love overshadowed with the spirit of mammon. Slavery, the great moral divide of the 18th and 19th centuries, was an example of this. Men exploited other men and denied them their basic human rights and dignity. It left certain classes of people looking up at everything from the bottom.

Even the church in general was sadly divided on this issue and didn't cast a clear moral pulse. However, there were certain groups within the church, influenced by the second Great Awakening, which began to publicly oppose slavery. Once institutionalized, slavery became a system of profiteers, profit making, and identity theft through domination and cultural imperialism. The initial precursor to this was the reprehensible heist the serpent pulled in Genesis 3. During slavery, men and women were stolen away from their countries, their cultures, and their identities. In all honesty, we must be aware that tribal leaders were just as guilty in this as slave traders were. Slave owners renamed slaves, whom they considered commodities, therefore making a lugubrious attempt to re-nature them. Slaves were forcibly disconnected from their history and their heritage. Anytime such a system is intact, it will unfortunately create a moral gridlock and conflict in the way God's absolutes are perceived. Such as—is it right to dominate another man without seeing him just as much as the image of God as you are? For example, some men justified their dastardly deeds by believing Black men didn't have souls as other races of men. Therefore, they weren't worthy of basic human civility. Should one disenfranchise a fellow human being just to make a dollar?

The great moral issue of the 20th century was just as divisive and diabolical. Abortion on demand was a gross injustice against the unborn based upon the selfish desires of a few, and a humanistic philosophy that had trapped the world into an anti-God, or antilife juggernaut. The prevailing attitude, justified by a highly aggressive judicial system, saw it as unnecessary to protect unborn children. They were not blobs of tissue—they were children who would have had a unique purpose. Irresponsible people were given the license to commit unjustifiable homicide. I wonder how many apostles, prophets, evangelists, pastors, and teachers were murdered in this monstrous system?

The serpent has insistently sought to destroy the seed of the woman since Father God's pronouncement of judgment upon him in Genesis 3. The abortion industry, which was diabolically instituted to destroy a woman's self-worth, was one more woeful attempt to block the inevitable. Jeremiah the prophet was right when he spoke, saying: *"A voice was heard in Ramah, lamentation, weeping, and great mourning, Rachel weeping for her children, refusing to be comforted, because they are no more"* (Matt. 2:18). Abortion creates a condition where our children are no more. Although every person isn't responsible for endorsing the abortion industry, like the prophet Daniel, we must identify with the pain of humanity (see Dan. 9:3-19) Rather than the Church sitting around lethargic, murmuring, and charmed by the serpent's hiss, we should join mother Rachel in her wail as she experiences this deep wound to her soul.

The great moral issue of the early 21st century will revolve around all the modern technological advances in life sciences, especially in the realm of genetics. What will happen when a known cloned person desires to be saved? Will they have a soul or not? How about the transvestite, or trans-gender person hearing there is love and acceptance in your local church. Will they be welcomed to experience biblical transformation or experience homophobia? Once the scientific gate has opened, it is impossible to undo what is done. We, the Church, must forsake our illusions about future closed gates and not bury our heads in the sand as the proverbial ostrich. When God has allowed something to break through, you cannot un-break it.

Another question overshadowing the previous few is: Will science once again use breakthrough technology to selfishly benefit the rich few, or will this technology benefit all human beings as intended by our Creator? Sincere love for God and for one another is the only guarantee men will respond correctly to these issues. The Church is God's measuring rod, His champion of justice. We must not blunder as in previous generations, or be silent bystanders and fail to get involved in the ethical discussions or classrooms. Our young men and women must be encouraged to get involved in the process; they must have influence in the decision-making headquarters. Like usual, we must not delay either, because procrastination is deadly. And only as we present a united front with God's love as our measuring rod will we get it right.

The Church has one solution: *Jesus Christ, God's love manifested!* We are the current voice that God's Kingdom has been released to humanity. Carnal opinions may be rich with discussions and debates, but the Church has a message rich with love. God's radiating light and overflowing kindness comes through the Church. We are His trumpets of righteousness because of the opulence of His nature within us. We are bearers of a new kind of justice. Because the Father and Son dwell in us by the Holy Spirit, a righteous inner nature has replaced the two tables of stone that the law was written on.

MODERN MORAL ISSUES

If you could make a list of the top ten moral ills of the 20th century, what would your list look like? Without being too presumptuous, perhaps it would look something like this: suicide, homicide, sexual promiscuity (adultery and fornication), pornography, cohabitation, divorce, euthanasia, abortion, homosexuality, and racism. These may not make everyone's top ten; however, their list would be just as viable and disturbing. Once again, conspicuously absent is the one major dilemma that haunted the nation of Israel throughout their Old Covenant history: *idolatry*. Father God was constantly warning them about idolatry. It was the one vice that could cut off the blessing of God upon the nation. Their conduct was very often malfeasant. They were continually creating or adopting idols. By caving in to idolatry, they embellished themselves with many vain imaginations. The imagery of their idolatry depended upon what culture they were cavorting with. I often wonder why we don't see idolatry as the number-one moral failure today.

With over six billion people in the world, and thousands of religions and denominations, moral issues are so numerous they must be grouped. Academia, the church, and society in general are deliberating broad subjects such as personal and family life, education, work, medical choices, community support, and political issues—especially in the context of legal and social regulations, and media challenges connected with the Internet and Global Superhighway. Spinning out of these are such concerns as:

• Reproductive and marital alternatives.

• Private sexual deeds.

• Classroom core curriculum and teacher behavior.

• Racial, gender, and age discrimination in school.

• Admissions and hiring.

• Censorship of free speech, the Internet, and the arts.

• Euthanasia.

• Untested therapies and treatments of new diseases.

• Distribution of wealth and power.

• Civil disobedience and forced military service.

Great defenders of fundamentalism in the Christian faith have valiantly tried to tackle some of these issues with limited success. The defunct Moral Majority (dissolved 1989), a collaboration of inter-esting groups, championed some of them. I admire their courage, although I hesitate to agree with all of their approach. Each of these concerns will require sincere prayer, meditation, searching the Scriptures, and a big heart to love without the spirit of condemna-tion. The greater questions to me are: What standards will be in effect to deal with these complex issues based upon scriptural rele-vancy? Who will set the standards, and what are their motives? If it were just a matter of lusts, impiety, superstition, temper, and appetite, our solutions would be a bit easier to locate biblically. A moral impulse must be established in order to become the definitive props of society in general without repressive regimes and laws. Laws do not change hearts. All the above issues are heart matters just as Jesus taught in the Sermon on the Mount.

However, since society and social orders are more diverse and complex, we all must admit these issues aren't getting any easier with each succeeding generation. The more Bible illiterate postmodern society becomes, the greater our challenge will be. Also, the more peo-ple tap into the destructive end of their creative potential, the more believers must tap into the creative powers of Almighty God to create a counterbalance. Before us is a world that requires thinking outside of our nice tidy, theological boxes; which were mainly hammered out in previous generations without the prophetic edge to see the Church in the 21st century. Many wonderful things were realized in those labors of love; however, we best grab the hammer again and go to work. True Kingdom progression comes with having things old (foundations) and new (future). Martin Luther and John Calvin did-n't deal with the immense technology, its positives and negatives, we deal with today.

DUALITY'S PLACE IN THE MORAL STRUGGLE

There is one important issue that I did not place in either the 20th century list or the one above: *duality*. Duality is the internal barbarism of the soul, which speaks a language and promotes a behavior incoherent and inconsistent with Christ's nature. I propose that duality is the culprit lurking behind every moral dilemma, hoping to go unnoticed. All human problems spring out of duality. This is a lack of oneness with God. When divine morality is added to kingdom development, it tackles the issues submerged in the chaos of duality. For example, we come to grips with the importance of covenant-keeping versus covenant-breaking, giving versus getting, and principled lives versus preference. Grace, as a teacher, will cause each of these ideals to take on new meaning. Only a firm, tested-by-time, moral base, with grace's awning, will give us the solid ground needed to deal with each issue. A moral base is reliable ground for God's children. If reliable ground isn't there, we'll vibrate and sway on faddish non-absolutes; we'll vacillate with reluctance to face the moral earthquakes of our day. Postmodern thinking has created a fault line underneath such time-honored treasures as family, proper sexuality, and the sanctity of life. We can assure ourselves these issues aren't going anyplace until the Kingdom of God becomes the norm in the earth. Every generation has faced duality, knowingly or unknowingly. Our vision for the future must be based in a moral synthesis that will hold us together and produce singleness toward Christ. Studying the first three chapters of Genesis uncovers our heavenly Father's vision for protecting humankind from duality with very little cooperation from Adam and Eve.

If we never move away from duality, morality will be subjective and based upon individual opinion. Whoever has the strongest mind will usually have the strongest opinion and influence. There will be many conflicting moral judgments since strong thinkers rarely see a need to seek God's mind. Given enough time, even the most able thinkers will find some points of disagreement with each other. At this point, people become victims of multiple human reason, which has its foundation in the tree of the knowledge of good and evil. Most carnal people will appeal to logic to help discern which opinion is right for them. Because duality produces no absolutes, moral judgments intending to convince others of a certain point of view must be substantiated by unending persuasiveness to be effective. This keeps human beings on the same slippery slope Adam got all of us on in the beginning. The serpent entangled his reason with his emotions and beguiled him. When these two aren't subject to the guidance of the Holy Spirit, they release unparalleled consequences. Jesus Christ rescued us from this place of sheer pandemonium by living as one with the Father.

YOU BECOME WHAT YOU EAT

Most people have heard this statement, or maybe some form of it: "We become what we eat!" That was certainly true of the first man. Man ate from the *tree of the knowledge of good and evil,* bogging him in duality. This tree was in the midst of the garden. Without a doubt, it was the original source of duality because of the twofold fruit clinging to it. Because duality is the quality of being *twofold,* man is neither completely spiritual nor natural in this state. He's a mixture—and mixture is carnality; and Father God detests mixture (see Rev. 3:15-16). What develops over history as a carnal mind-set is the result of lingering aimlessly in a carnal condition.

Carnality and all its lustful expressions were like crouched lions waiting to pounce upon man once he partook of the tree of restraint. Man now lives in the twilight zone—a zone of neither total light nor total darkness. The apostle Paul said, *"For to be carnally minded is death"*(Rom. 8:6a). Man immediately was the full embodiment of the living-dead. Everything he knew prior to that moment was the singleness of simply walking in the sunshine of a spiritual relationship with Father God. Man's unwise decision circumvented this fellowship and opened something pandemic in his soul.

Duality blocks a proper participation into that which is divine. It literally encases the soul and prevents rays of divine light from entering. It is the most chronic, communicable disease of the soul, transferring hereditarily and environmentally from one generation of mankind to the next. Disregarding color or culture, it attached itself to the seed man and has shown up in everyone. God, through His Word, has given us all things necessary to destroy duality and to reconnect with Himself. I love the way The Message says this:

Everything that goes into a life of pleasing God has been miraculously given to us by getting to know, personally and intimately, the

One who invited us to God. The best invitation we ever received! We were also given absolutely terrific promises to pass on to you—your tickets to participation in the life of God after you turned your back on a world corrupted by lust (2 Peter 1:2-4 The Message).

The serpent proposed that eating from the tree of knowledge would not be deadly to humans. How wrong he was! His smooth-talking, deceptive guile briefly altered a beautiful relationship. God had given the man great latitude and freedom of expression, only one restraint. When Adam accepted the serpent's message, humans fell immediately into death and duality, although the serpent stated differently. Man's soul became *the immoral, seductress woman who flatters with her lips.* Through diminished perception, the soul forsook the companion of her youth, and forgot the covenant of her God. Man suddenly became conscious of good and evil without the benefit of wisdom or of righteous judgment, which comes from experiencing God.

Duality forces man into a condition of unrighteous judgments. Man's spiritual perception becomes dull and dim-witted. He cannot develop intuitively. He becomes locked into ungodly, judgmental practices (judgments considered to be lacking in tolerance, compassion, and objectivity). A tolerant, compassionate, and objective judgment will always have wide margins of grace and deep pockets of mercy, considering as well one's equal potential for human error. Rather than becoming responsible for his own behavior, owning his own decisions, man stepped into the contorted world of accusation and blasphemy. It has been human nature to censure, criticize, and condemn others ever since. Nothing seems to be inviolable or sacrosanct. Man has fallen from his lofty status of sonship. He was left fearful, terrified, and plummeting in duality.

THE DUALITY OF PHILOSOPHY

Duality branches into three basic tracks. It has a philosophy, a theology, and a religion. These concepts are not essentially stackable; however, they do build upon one another, producing a system of thought. Everything begins with a thought. Thoughts become tactile, growing through meditation, intellectual investigation, practical application, and evaluation. They eventually create a philosophy. Philosophy grows into a theology, which is a formalized body of opinions concerning God and man's relationship to God. Theology is the dough of religion, which is a unified system of expression pursued with fervor or conscientious devotion. Let's first explore duality in philosophy.

Duality in philosophy states that the world is ultimately composed of two basic entities—mind and matter. One is visible and the other invisible. To live in these realms is to live imperceptive of the reality or involvement of the Spirit of God in the affairs of mankind. The Bible clearly states God assigned men their predetermined times and boundaries in order to discover Him (see Acts 17:26-28). Stemming from the fact that natural eyes cannot see spirit, most people are landlocked to their five biological senses. They are out of touch with the vast world of spirit—the animating force in all living beings. In the words of the wise sage, life is lived under the sun. What about all there is to know above the sun? Can you imagine being limited to a world of mind and matter without spiritual significance? Such a world sharply compares to the world of the Sadducees in the New Testament (see Acts 23:8).

The material creation is composed of matter perceived by one or more senses in the realm of space. Paul stated that it is an object lesson to teach us the invisible attributes of God's eternal power and Godhead (see Rom. 1:20). Mind is the human consciousness that is manifested in thought, memory, perception, feeling, will, or imagination. In human terms, it is the playground of pop psychology when it actually should be in union life with man's spirit and God's Spirit. God intended a harmonious marriage of spirit and soul and the Fall produced a divorce. The cross removed the curse of divorce and renewed the opportunity of spirit and soul matrimony.

In the earlier listing of things in the mind/matter duality, do you see something conspicuously absent in this listing? I do! It is all the things that people may learn by being connected with the Spirit of God without navigating the labyrinth of carnality. The limited world of mind and matter is another way of describing the restricted world of humanism and all its subsidiaries. It is coifed with the sayings of those who are lovers of words, going back to men such as Socrates, Plato, and Aristotle. The more eloquent one becomes in thought and expression, supposedly the wiser one becomes. Duality in philosophy is nothing more than the wise sayings of humans absent the education the Spirit of God conveys. Eventually, this will produce nothing other than bewilderment and bedlam. Oh, so many words, yet lacking the intrinsic treasure that sound wisdom stores for the upright.

THE DUALITY OF THEOLOGY

The duality in theology deals with one of the greatest charades ever pulled in human history. It is the teaching that there are two mutually *antagonistic* principles in the universe—God and the devil. Webster defines antagonist as "one who opposes and actively competes with another."[10] Mutuality suggests the devil is not a menace, but he and God have a gentleman's agreement to oppose one another. First, what uninformed mind elevated the devil to equal status with Almighty God? Second, what scholar bought this idea? Isn't it common sense to think that any fair competition is engaged in by at least two equals? Even in the Olympics, boxers and wrestlers compete against others in the same weight class, thus preventing an illegal advantage. Father God is sovereign, and therefore, He has no equals or enemies; He has only subjects! Some of them are vessels of honor, and others are vessels of dishonor. Many writers in the Old and New Testaments realized the sovereignty of God and wrote about it:

> *Therefore concerning the eating of things offered to idols, we know that an idol is nothing in the world, and that there is no other God but one. For even if there are so-called gods, whether in heaven or on earth (as there are many gods and many lords), yet for us there is one God, the Father, of whom are all things, and we for Him; and one Lord Jesus Christ, through whom are all things, and through whom we live* (1 Corinthians 8:4-6).

Thus says the Lord, the King of Israel, and his Redeemer, the Lord of hosts: "I am the First and I am the Last; besides Me there is no God" (Isaiah 44:6).

Who has performed and done it, calling the generations from the beginning? "I, the Lord, am the first; and with the last I am He" (Isaiah 41:4).

Bible sovereignty ensconces the idea that there is only one sovereign: *Almighty God! "Hear, O Israel: The Lord our God, the Lord is one!"* (Deut. 6:4) Another way of saying the same thing is: *"The Lord is our God, the Lord alone, i.e., the only one."* The Lord is the only one in His lofty position. He may give commands and require them to be followed without reservation. The devil certainly is not in this position—not in the past, the present, or the future. He is a subject just as man, and must seek permission from Father God before he does anything (see Job 1:6-12). Some believe he is the god of this world, but I choose to differ. The god of this world system is *mammon* (see Matt. 6:24). The devil may be a god of somebody's world, but he's not the god of my world, or any other believer's.

It is high time that believers cast into the abyss these false, carefully crafted, and theologically unsound notions about the devil. He is not equal to God! He cannot walk in and out of our lives as he chooses. From our first glimpse of him and his operations, we see a slithering, insidious accuser of God and man. His greatest tactic is lies and the employment of misinformation. This groveling position doesn't come anywhere near the high and lofty realm of God's existence. In fact, the Scripture seems to suggest that God created a spoiler to destroy (see Isa. 54:16). That would be none other than the devil himself. Jesus said, "He was a murderer and liar from the beginning" (see John 8:44). My pondering mind said: *Beginning of what?* Beginning of beginnings or beginning of his sinister dealings with man?

I know there are and have been great debates over where the devil came from. I choose not to enter that deliberation; I choose rather to acknowledge his defeated existence. Jesus defeated him at Calvary and accepted the keys of death and hell as a sign of ultimate surrender. The Bible says, *"Since the children are made of flesh and blood, it's logical that the Savior took on flesh and blood in order to rescue them by His death. By embracing death, taking it into Himself, He destroyed the devil's hold on death and freed all who cower through life, scared to death of death"* (Hebrews 2:14, The Message). Jesus Christ destroyed the devil! The word for *destroy* is *katargeo*, which means "to reduce to inactivity. Loss of being isn't implied, but loss of well-being."[11] Since Jesus defeated him, the devil isn't well anymore. He is man's sick adversary, and not God's (see 1 Pet. 5:8-9) Therefore, the idea of God and the devil being mutual antagonists is far-fetched and unrealistic.

When I first began to preach this many years ago, I thought Christians would be ecstatic to hear the good news. Surprise! They weren't! Most were so used to magnifying the devil, he had grown from a serpent in Genesis to an almost invincible red dragon in the Revelation. Dust and carnality had fed him considerably (see Isa. 65:25). Satan was that bogus excuse people had always relied upon for failure. Rather than seeing failure as an opportunity to begin again more intelligently, the devil was blamed for almost every problem. Christians must no longer follow mother Eve's example and say, "The devil made me do it!" Hollywood made a movie a few years ago, *Honey—I Shrunk the Kids.* Christians need to adopt this same idea concerning the devil, and say, "Father, we shrunk the devil—we shrunk him by not feeding him!" Rather, we have chosen to magnify Jesus Christ through our words, our works, and our worship. We have chosen to enlarge the Christ and to make this our most important endeavor.

Believers must take complete responsibility for all their behavior if they ever expect to cooperate with God in full freedom and maturity. When we take responsibility for our behavior, we actually give no place or credit to the devil. We rid ourselves from the accursed spirit of duality when we acknowledge God as ordering our steps. The Bible says, *"The steps of a good man are ordered by the Lord, and He delights in his way. Though he fall, he shall not be utterly cast down; for the Lord upholds him with His hand"* (Ps. 37:23-24). I forcefully agree with the apostle Paul, when differentiating what it means to be in Christ. He said: *"Therefore, if anyone is in Christ, he is a new creation; old things have passed away; behold, all things have become new. Now all things are of God, who has reconciled us to Himself through Jesus Christ, and has given us the ministry of reconciliation"* (2 Cor. 5:17-18). If all things are of God within the context of the new creation man, that leaves the devil and his cohorts credit for nothing.

I place my seal of agreement to the words Dr. Karl A. Barden penned so succinctly in *The Enlightened Church* (Destiny Image Publishers, Shippensburg, PA, 1994). He says it marvelously and unmistakably:

> What you believe determines how you live. Revelation or enlightenment of correct Christology and correct satanology releases you into triumphant, radiant Christian living. You truly know your position (in Christ)—and you know your opposition. You quit quavering about the devil and you see him as he truly is, in the totality of his defeat at the cross. That insight explodes within you as confidence.[12]

THE DUALITY IN RELIGION

The most sinister of all dualities is the duality in religion. You see, religion is what's left after men forsake intimacy with the Almighty. A person doesn't have to know God to be religious, or participate in religious systems. Although dualities in philosophy and theology have had some horrible consequences, they pale in comparison to duality in religion. It is the teaching that man has two natures, an old man and a new man, at the same time. He may be controlled by either nature, but not exclusively by one or the other. Nature, in Middle English, meant "the essential properties of a thing."[13] If we are two different men, all at the same time, we have a major problem of immense proportions. There are two major ways this will hinder victorious living in a new civilization. Let's consider their dangers. By knowing the truth, we eliminate their risks.

1. *Duality blocks believers from integrating with their true spiritual genetics and identity.*

Believers must locate themselves in the Word of God and allow that truth to give them full identity, and to connect with their spiritual DNA. Anything else is a lying vanity. Right identity sparks each of us to right behavior. When you know exactly who you are, you don't live in the middle road of duality. The Word helps us to identify our *genesis face*. That face, or source, is revealed in Genesis 1 as the original idea of God's wonderful mind for mankind. This image was lost through human history, circumstances, experiences, and misinformation—through degeneration. Man was delocalized from his native environment, thus declining, as in nature and function, from a former or original state. Regeneration provides each of us the opportunity of rediscovery. In the famous words of the apostle James, we must go back to the mirror and not forget what manner of man we are. Once we see and hear, we must become participants in that word or it is neutralized through forgetfulness.

> *Don't fool yourself into thinking that you are a listener when you are anything but, letting the Word go in one ear and out the other. Act on what you hear! Those who hear and don't act are like those who glance in the mirror, walk away, and two minutes later have no idea who they are, what they look like. But whoever catches a glimpse of the revealed counsel of God—the free life!—even out of the corner of his eye, and sticks with it, is no distracted scatterbrain but a man or woman of action. That person will find delight and affirmation in the action"* (James 1:22-25 The Message).

One way you may know that Christians are living in the bondage of duality in religion is to listen to their conversations about absolute truth. Absolute truth is the Word of God! Often, they may hear something from the Word of God, and yet say, "I know...but...." At this point, the Word bows to their circumstances, at least in their minds. Faith is nonexistent. The catchphrase could read this way: "I think I believe, but help my unbelief." Unbelief has created a void synapse between the Word of God and faith. Many people I have ministered to over the years reside here. God's Word goes into one ear, fails to compute, and out the other. Some of the most difficult cases are those with biological and chemical imbalances. When they are upbeat emotionally, the Word is great; however, when they are depressed, the Word has absolutely no relevance. These people seem to be flighty and disorganized in their thinking and commitment to truth. My friend, it is the result of duality. The Word of God is and remains the means to their deliverance and freedom. Powerful chemicals may alter behavior temporarily; but they won't permanently change the duality.

2. *Duality ties us to the environment of mixture and death—the geography of the old man.*

The second issue deals with how every believer must transposition experientially to cut off all that pertains to the old realm and the old man. To fully understand and appreciate the differences in the new man necessitates an abolished old man merely for comparative purposes. Humankind could not comprehend light apart from darkness, male without female, or peace without turmoil. Adam is dead and Christ is alive! The only reason informed Christians should talk about an old Adam at all is to solidify in their understandings the prestige of freedom in Christ. We communicate to one another the beauty of our victory in Christ through comparison and contrast. Otherwise, there is no reason to mention something that is dead and buried. A person may fail to enjoy or fully understand the place they're in because they're so preoccupied with the place they came from.

Our challenge is to know what happened in the finished work of Jesus Christ. When Jesus Christ finished Adam, he was no more, or simply unplugged. He was fit for one final thing: burial. Like Abraham, we must now get the dead out of our sight (see Gen. 23:3-4). Out of sight constitutes out of mind and out of consciousness. Duality in religion retains Adam, all of his positives and negatives, in our consciousness. Our heavenly Father has a proper burial rite for him— water baptism. Water baptism with the circumcision of the heart was implemented to remove the dead, enacting the full force of New Covenant life. Visualize this with me: When we were lowered into the waters of baptism, we identified with the burial of Jesus; when we came out of those waters by the operation of the Spirit of God, we were raised in resurrection with Him. Resurrection permitted us to enter a new sovereignty under a different sovereign. This experience was not to make us two men simultaneously (the old and new man); but it was to establish the truth of the new man as our only rightful reality, period.

Our old, sin-miserable life was nailed to the cross with Jesus Christ. It met a decisive end, and we are no longer obligated to sin's every beck and hiss. Christians must settle that they were in Christ's death and resurrection. He not only died *for* us—He died *as* us. Now we live as Him. Christ's death was the beckoning of light mankind so voluminously needed. Jesus took the old man down with Him in death, and released us to be restored to the environment of God. We changed our addresses and exchanged natures. If we will remove ourselves from religious theory, songs, and sermons, we'll find the language of the old man is a dead language to us. Our mother language, that pure lip spoken of by the prophets, is from the eternal realms. It's the language of God; and it is what we must learn to speak. Think of it this way: We are dead to sin—the old nature, and alive to God through Jesus Christ our Lord.

Duality in religion has subtly communicated that sin still has a ruling place in our lives and we can't get above it. The focus isn't on the nonexistence of sin, but rather, the ability of sin to reign in human spirits. This philosophy is hoisted like a truthful banner almost every week in some pulpit. An idea like, "The only way to live above sin is to live above a sinner" is trumpeted loud and long. I submit this ideology is flawed and a gross misrepresentation of the truth. To truly be in Christ is to be in a setting above sin. Christ is holy, harmless, undefiled, and separate from sinners. Unless I'm badly mistaken, this list qualifies as above sin, and we are hidden in Him. We must give ourselves around the clock to the new order partnership. The Scriptures often command us to put off the old man and put on the new man. God's thoughts and ways are the only thoughts and ways for us. The old man has no voice in how we live now. The tyranny of the past was swallowed up in the legitimate triumphant victory of Christ. Our greatest challenge is to learn to live freely without organizing any unconventional jobs for the old man.

On the other hand, we may practically choose to build a mental and emotional bridge across the enormous gulf separating the old man and the new man and live in the old realm again. Amazingly, you will find duality there like a hungry young lion ready to pounce upon you. Duality is taken out of gear only in Christ. Choose to accept that truth. Freedom is the spiritual environs of the new man. We all must remember that some of the things that masquerade as freedom obliterate freedom. Once we enter into a confederacy with the old man, we relinquish our rights to any freedom because the old man has never been free. He only knows brutality and rules as a totalitarian taskmaster. In fact, the offering of ourselves to the old regime will be our last free act. Synchronizing with the reality of the New Covenant, we are to never again use freedom as an occasion to the flesh. True Bible freedom demands that we yield to God, and keep on yielding. Duality works when we remain ignorant of the truth. God, through Jesus Christ, has given us a whole life again. As we walk in freedom and resist duality's distortions, we awaken to victory after victory. The voice of God becomes clearer and clearer, and right thinking and living follow suit.

Someone may ask: "What about the apostle Paul's teaching in Romans 7? Doesn't it validate the unconquerable force of duality in human flesh?" I must, at once, say, "No!" Romans 7 explains the purpose of the law as a code to prevent carnal men from guessing and estimating what morality should be. Because it bolted and locked men up, they were constantly producing miscarriages when it came to morality. What was good and sensible produced only rebellion. It's the old idea of *"Thou shall not,"* and the restraint stirs up desire in the restrained, clearly paving a highway for them to be unrestrained. The law, as a succinct, surgical command system, gave clear-cut boundaries. Unfortunately, the boundaries were never regarded as important enough to observe. The power of carnality in human flesh was simply too overwhelming.

Romans 7 also deals with the confusion imposed upon us when we vacillate from the new man to the old man, from law to grace. Maybe we need a modern Elijah to ask us, "How long will you halt between two realities, leaping from the new man to the old man?"

Our heavenly Father never intended us to live in the duality of Romans 7; it is the explanation of our transition from being married to Adam to Christ. Jesus Christ is our new husband. Once Adam died, mankind was no longer bound by the law of that marriage that exacted faithfulness to him. What this amounts to is: We are freed from all ties to that previous covenant. We are now freed from the law and the sin nature. While we were joined to Adam, we were joined to a nature that functioned best in sin. Now that we are joined to Christ, we have merged with a nature that functions best in righteousness.

The practicality of this message is to observe what happens when someone naturally dies. There is no greater transition in this concrete world than physical death. Keeping their pictures and clothing in the closet isn't going to bring them back. Please don't receive this as insensitive or offensive, but it's the truth. They are gone! Constant conversation about them won't resurrect them either. Somewhere closure has to come. In spiritual terms, we must get rid of all the memorabilia of the old man. It's going to be impossible to live with a new husband always talking about the old one, who by the way, is dead. The responsible thing to do is to learn the ways of the new husband, and flow perfectly in that relationship. We must discover his law of life. To say, "My ex-husband used to do it this way," isn't going to cut it! That's called fellowshipping with the dead, or necromancy. Our fellowship must only be with the new man, our new husband: Jesus Christ. Let's forget Adam so that we may effectively get the dead out of our sight.

SINGLE AND SATISFIED

The apostle Paul called the Corinthian church to the place of simplicity, or singleness. What a powerful calling this is! It affords us the privilege of burying the dead. Simplicity is the exact opposite of duality. Only when our perception of reality is beguiled by a serpentine voice are we susceptible to duality. Conversely, when we listen solely to the voice of the Lord, we enter into biblical singleness. It comes from the Greek word, *haplotes*, and means "singleness, sincerity without self-seeking."[14] *Single* evolves out of the word *haplous*, which means "folded together, single, clear, simple with no ulterior motive; it is wholehearted purity with nobility."[15] Singleness is apropos to the king-priest nature within us. Singleness can only be achieved in Christ. He was the first human single toward the heavenly Father. His face was set like flint when it came to a commitment to divine purpose. The prophets of the Old Testament were close but didn't quite achieve the perfection of singleness that Jesus Christ did. From a human standpoint, simplicity was Christ's great strength. This strength lifted Jesus from becoming prey to demoralization; also, it lifts us from a state of demoralization to one of total encouragement. God's sovereign plan was to end duality and restore singleness in the finished work. The death, burial, and resurrection of our Lord provided a merciful release to all of us.

Singleness is pure devotion to Jesus Christ without the interference of other lovers. A person may be pure in their devotion to Christ without necessarily being perfect. Please don't confuse the terminologies. King David was a powerful example of pure, heartfelt devotion toward God. Our heavenly Father never questioned his heart; He simply brought correction and judgment to some of his decisions and deeds. How many people love God so passionately that they want only what pleases Him? In such people, there is no self-seeking in any of their responses to the Lord. They give with liberality and generosity. The first apostles were very much models of this standard.

The Pauline epistles are very clear as they reveal his desperate pursuit of the Lord and sincerity toward God's people. *"For our boasting is this: the testimony of our conscience that we conducted ourselves in the world in simplicity and godly sincerity, not with fleshly wisdom but by the grace of God, and more abundantly toward you"* (2 Cor. 1:12). Considering David and Paul, we find they had what the Song of Solomon calls *"dove's eyes"* (see Song of Sol. 1:15; 4:1). They were not distracted by what they could glance out of their peripheral vision. (In fact, a dove doesn't have very good peripheral vision.) Nothing unimportant or divergent could distract them for very long. When Jesus Christ becomes first in a person's life, he follows Him by this clarity.

It is very important that we, the Church, become single toward Jesus Christ. The old man, the old world, and the old order has left us poverty-stricken and bereft of morality and floundering in carnal, moral theories. Thank God, they no longer exist for a son of God in Christ. Forget all the nostalgia about the law of the old man. We have no legal responsibility to something that is dead. Our relationship to him has terminated. Our full love and affections must be given to the One whom we are given to in marriage to now. That One is Jesus Christ our Lord! We must know Him and explore through the way that we live this inexhaustible message: *"I am my beloved's, and his desire is toward me"* (Song of Sol. 7:10). Christ has wooed us with an inexhaustible love, and we have entered into the joy of intimacy and union with Him. He certainly isn't a pompous polygamist, for He has dove's eyes toward His Church. In the New Testament, it says, *"But he who is joined to the Lord is one spirit with Him"* (1 Cor. 6:17). We have no obligation to any other covenantal relationship outside of Christ. As we are joined to Him, we are single and satisfied. Christ is the only One who can fulfill a person's highest desires, greatest dreams, and most noble expectations. In a lifetime, most people try many other lovers and expend great efforts in various affairs only to come up empty and shortchanged. Nevertheless, if you don't know it already, Jesus Christ is more than enough to satisfy your every need.

Pride makes a god of self, covetous makes a god of money,

Sensuality makes a god of the belly; whatever is esteemed

Or loved, feared or served, delighted in or depended on, more

Than God, that (whatever it is) we do in effect make a god of. [16]

ENDNOTES

1. Virginia Ely, *I Quote* (New York: George W. Stewart Publishers, Inc., 1947), 228-229.

2. Webster's II New College Dictionary, Riverside University dictionary (New York: Houghton Mifflin Company, 1995), 712.

3. Ibid., 1216.

4. David A. Noebel, *Understanding The Times*, (Eugene, OR: Harvest House Publishers, 1991), 227.

5. Ely, 229.

6. Webster's II, 4.

7. Sinclair B. Ferguson, David F. Wright and J. I. Packer, *New Dictionary of Theology* (Downers Grove, IL: InterVarsity Press, 1988), 445.

8. Webster's II, 1050.

9. John R. Kohlenberger, *The Expanded Vine's Expository Dictionary of New Testament Words, A Special Edition* (Minneapolis, MN: Bethany House Publishers, 1984), 781.

10. Webster's II, 47.

11. Kohlenberger, 5.

12. Dr. Karl A. Barden, *The Enlightened Church Satan Who?*, (Shippensburg, PA: Destiny Image Publishers, 1994), 9.

13. Webster's II, 729.

14. James Strong, *"Greek Dictionary,"* Strong's Exhaustive Concordance of the Bible (Nashville, TN: Abingdon, 1976), #572.

15. Ibid., #573.

16. Matthew Henry's Commentary, Genesis to Deuteronomy, Volume 1 (McLean, VA: MacDonald Publishing Company), 358-359.

8

A Society Without Covetousness

And He said unto them, Take heed, and beware of covetousness: for a man's life consisteth not in the abundance of the things which he possesseth (Luke 12:15 KJV).

Judges sell verdicts to the highest bidder, priests mass-market their teaching, prophets preach for high fees, all the while posturing and pretending dependence on God (Micah 3:11 The Message).

The closing years of the 19th century were very fruitful years in the Church in England. It was a time of social outreach and bold evangelism. Renowned missionary, C.T. Studd, a man of great privilege, was one of the most endearing examples. He founded the Heart of Africa Mission and committed himself to practical holiness and sacrifice. He emphasized this in the lives of other believers much to their chagrin. Eventually, this straight-laced approach to holiness produced discontent in other missionaries. However, one powerful incident proved he was sincere in his walk and delivered from the spirit of covetousness. On his 25th birthday, Studd came into a large inheritance, which in light of Christ's teaching, he decided to give to Christian work. On January 13, 1887, he sent off four checks of £5000 each to Moody, Muller, Holland of Whitechapel, and Booth-Tucker of India. Other checks went to Barnardo, Archibald Brown, and the Misses McPherson and Smyly, plus some of the remainder to China Inland Mission.[1] He later gave the rest of his money away and chose to live by faith. His heart was to be fully yielded to the life of Christ.

In reading this story, it reminded me of some of the developmental process the Lord walked my wife and me through. Ann and I learned some of our most valuable, enduring lessons in the early days of our ministry. As I ponder them, I value much more God's grace in bringing us through all of them. One of the most important was the money lesson. Young ministers must know what it is to be freed from the love of money in order to minister effectively; and as one grows older, to continue to remain free by being watchful. Somewhere along the course of time, one will be tempted with the highest bidder for one's services (see Judg. 17:6-13). Whether one becomes a hireling or not depends upon whether one effectively learns the lessons our Master teaches. In the specific words of the apostle Paul, we must learn *"how to be abased, and...how to abound"* (Phil. 4:12). Preachers, particularly ascension gift ministers (see Eph. 4:11), must have experience in living humbly, and living in prosperity. This is not to promote that all ministers will have enormous amounts of wealth; it is simply to say that true biblical prosperity can't always be measured by dollars and cents. God's people will fall into both categories.

The particular way God dealt with us was by sending us in the early days to rural churches with scanty memberships. Our offerings consisted of a few dollars and cents. Sometimes people were doing the very best they could, and other times they weren't! We always felt our value was much higher, but endured that period with dignity. The heavenly Father instructed us to never make money an issue. There were times my flesh desired to reject those instructions, especially when the gas tank was low, and my small children were hungry. We would have terminated some valuable lessons from those assignments from the Lord prematurely if we had listened to our flesh. Thank God grace prevailed, and we proved ourselves faithful in small things, and in visions and ministries that belonged to other men.

The Father was establishing us in trustworthiness, faithfulness, loyalty, etc., and destroying any possibilities of covetousness in our hearts. Those experiences allowed us to know the wisdom behind the words of the wise sage: *"He who loves silver will not be satisfied with silver; nor he who loves abundance, with increase. This also is vanity"* (Eccl. 5:10). A prophet's motives in ministry can't be money. We were placed in those meager situations so that our motives, which are invisible, could truly test our character. As our character was proven in that crucible, God has entrusted us with greater Kingdom assignments.

Using hindsight, my experiences with covetousness were probably like most Americans; it is so common and interwoven into the culture we sometimes forget about its ugliness. I recall a phrase often repeated in my childhood and adolescent years: "Keeping up with the Joneses." Exactly where this phrase came from I don't know; however, it was very popular. In the highly competitive world of adolescence, never stumbling over an opportunity to display raw power, this could mean many things. Among them, if someone received a material blessing, something inside us made us earnestly desire the same. One had to keep up with the Joneses! Adults were often gripped by the same competitive snares, though attempting to be less obvious in their motives. Their purchases were noticeably more expensive, such as new cars, new homes, vacations (affordable or not), etc. People would often spend beyond their means just to keep up with the Joneses. This *undisciplined* type of spending and longing paved the way to many of the economic catastrophes people were swamped with in the latter part of the 20th century. Rather than tempering and curtailing desires, and living a life of sobriety, people lived bankrupted lives produced out of overtaxed selfishness. The Bible calls this type of lifestyle *covetousness*.

If there is anything deadly and destructive, causing the manifest presence of God to abate in a developing culture, it is found in the lifestyle of covetousness. In laying the foundation stones of a new morality for a newly born nation, God chose the final stone as a ban against covetousness (see Exod. 20:17). Webster's II defines covetous as "enviously and culpably desirous of another's possessions; marked by extreme desire to acquire."[2] Covetousness, as first connected with the original sin of mankind (see Gen. 3:6), is man snatching beyond the measure ordained for him as he disdains God's limited restraint for his life. God does have a plan and a time to release certain things. Initially, God gave Adam one restriction and much liberty. Adam used this liberty as an occasion to the flesh, and that was his last truly free day. He opened the floodgates for the practice of religion without having a relationship with God. Conversely, religion gives very few liberties and many restrictions.

In the first scenario of the human drama, covetous actions were a prelude to religious behavior. Provoked by the malady of discontentment, and letting his guard down, Adam was beguiled by the serpent and reached beyond his measure. Covetousness is more than greedily grabbing at the goods of others. Being a malignancy, it disrupts the harmonious order in man, the creation, and his relationship with others. The apostle Paul called covetousness idolatry (see Col. 3:5; Eph. 5:5) and judged that a covetous person had no inheritance in the Kingdom of God. Covetousness causes a man to give the worship that is due our heavenly Father only, to worldly wealth and human acquisition. It is more highly provocative to God than is commonly thought—enough to block fellowship with the Almighty.

In the Greek sphere, *covetousness* had the meaning of "having more, receiving more, and wanting more."[3] Normally, this is in reference to outdoing others, being superior, taking precedence, excelling, or forging ahead at others' expense.[4] Self-centeredness rather clearly superimposes its will in each of these attitudes. It is tightly wrapped in greed and self-enrichment; and it disembowels what rightfully belongs to others. A covetous mentality refuses to allow a fellow human being to have a shining day in the sun.

The passion of most great thinkers in antiquity was relative equality for all people rather than competition bred out of covetous hearts. Relative, in this sense, means having social applicability to all men. When Israel first came out of Egypt, and in the embryonic days of the New Testament Church, this was the practiced social order (see Exod. 16:16-18; Acts 2:44; 4:32,34; 5:2). Individual excess was considered an unnecessary impiety when it came to the best design for society. Therefore, covetousness was unacceptable, whereas moderation was highly welcomed. If society was to ever be just, covetousness had to be eradicated. It damaged the individual conscience of every person as well as the collective rights of others, especially since it seeks for more than is necessary. Consider this: There is no covetousness within the family of the Godhead. Since man is in the image of God, there should be no covetousness in his world. Checking and managing one's desires (for desire is a bottomless pit) is a wonderful remedy to reverse the devastating consequences of covetousness. Jesus, and others, taught it was better to suffer wrong than to greedily participate in covetousness. What good does it do a person anyway to practice immoderation, when in the end, everyone loses because of greed? This is why we must allow God to deal with our hearts to empower us to avoid at all cost covetousness.

Covetousness was the dominant problem in Jerusalem in the pre-captivity era. The prophet Jeremiah reveals the severity of this matter just prior to Judah's captivity in Babylon.

> *Because from the least of them even to the greatest of them, everyone is given to covetousness; and from the prophet even to the priest, everyone deals falsely* (Jeremiah 6:13).

> *Therefore I will give their wives to others, and their fields to those who will inherit them; because from the least even to the greatest everyone is given to covetousness; from the prophet even to the priest everyone deals falsely* (Jeremiah 8:10).

If we could place these verses in modern words, they could be summed up this way: "Big shots and little shots alike are seeking more than they can handle!" These improper attitudes and practices cost everyone, even to the extent of nullifying legal inheritances. Even religious leaders showed no restraint. They exemplified an unconquerable love of appropriation, a morbid lust for acquisition. Without sounding judgmental, this reminds me of many modern attitudes. Preachers and people alike are greedy, believing they deserve every natural thing that comes to mind. The question is: Will blessings bring us closer to Christ, or lead us astray? Too many blessings into the hands of the immature provoke them to seek the hand of God more than His face. There's a clear call from God for men of God to get back to the place of moderation and model its superior worth for the people. No matter how one views it, our model, Jesus Christ, lived a very simple, fulfilling life. He was never trapped by the lust for money and the natural influence it brings. Spiritual leaders are under divine mandate to model the same.

On one hand, we must remember that all natural blessings are temporal things. No matter what it is, or how wonderful, if it was manufactured, it will finally wear out! On the other hand, because we are King's children, it isn't grasping too far to expect blessings at all levels of life (see 3 John 2). God's ideal presents a balanced prosperity. Our heavenly Father was the One who identified us as kings and priests (see Rev 1:6). In doing so, He blended together two Old Covenant offices. Prior to this, it was illegal for kings to intrude into the priest's office, and priests were not kings. The two worked together in that kings were sovereignties, conquerors, and champions while priests blessed kings and distributed the spoils of great kingly victories. They needed each other! Our sphere of ruling, under the King of kings, is the earth (see Rev. 5:9-10). These descriptions help us to properly relate to our full identity.

Furthermore, there is a fine line of balance between being a king and a priest. Kingship is the right of vast personal properties which stewards and servants manage; whereas priesthood is the order of sacrifice (see 1 Pet. 2:5). As kings, we recognize we are stewards of all that our Father has (provision), simply to become priests (distribution). Priesthood affords us the privilege to give away what we own from a balanced stewardship mentality. We know much about priesthood and sacrifice, but very little about the wealth of kingly people apart from covetousness. Because most of us have cut our teeth on a culture motivated by pure greed, it has been essential for the Lord to carry us this way. God has purposed to synchronize our priesthood and kingship in the 21st-century Church.

After hearing the vehement teaching that Christians should cast off the poverty spirit, I shudder to think about the negative side of this. We sometimes, have the tendency to pursue truth at the expense of running from one imbalance to another. *The Bible has several examples of covetous kings, priests, and prophets.* This spirit is broken off people through extravagant giving—not taking. That may sound like a broad, sweeping statement, nevertheless, a true one. Position doesn't rid one of covetousness. A revelation and manifestation of our identity in Christ, however, will. Note these examples.

> *But Jezebel his wife came to him, and said to him, "Why is your spirit so sullen that you eat no food?" He said to her, "Because I spoke to Naboth the Jezreelite, and said to him, 'Give me your vineyard for money; or else, if it pleases you, I will give you another vineyard for it.' And he answered, 'I will not give you my vineyard.'" Then Jezebel his wife said to him, "You now exercise authority over Israel! Arise, eat food, and let your heart be cheerful; I will give you the vineyard of Naboth the Jezreelite"* (1 Kings 21:5-7).

> *Meanwhile he also hoped that money would be given him by Paul, that he might release him. Therefore he sent for him more often and conversed with him* (Acts 24:26).

> *They have forsaken the right way and gone astray, following the way of Balaam the son of Beor, who loved the wages of unrighteousness; but he was rebuked for his iniquity: a dumb donkey speaking with a man's voice restrained the madness of the prophet* (2 Peter 2:15-16).

> *But Gehazi, the servant of Elisha the man of God, said, "Look, my master has spared Naaman this Syrian, while not receiving from his hands what he brought; but as the Lord lives, I will run after him and take something from him"* (2 Kings 5:20).

> *Now the sons of Eli were corrupt; they did not know the Lord. And the priests' custom with the people was that any man offered a sacrifice, the priest's servant would come with a three-pronged flesh-hook in his hand while the meat was boiling. Then he would thrust it*

into the pan, or kettle, or caldron, or pot; and the priest would take
for himself all that the fleshhook brought up. So they did in Shiloh
to all the Israelites who came there (1 Samuel 2:12-14).

We must know spiritual blessings in Christ are the only permanent blessings. They go beyond the temporal corruption of
things in time (see Eph. 1:3). Henceforth, nothing is worth for-
feiting or obliterating our fellowship with Jesus Christ—nothing!
If we happen to accumulate much, I say to God be the glory! Just
remember: To whom much is given, much is required! If the
Father requires us to release all, do you suppose anything is
worth clutching? The rich young ruler who had kept the horizontal commandments didn't know he really had a problem with
covetousness until Jesus lovingly challenged him (see Luke 18:20-
22). Covetousness was such a part of ordinary life that the young
man was blind to its grips. The national fathers of that time had
cast a shadow of covetousness that shrouded and overloaded the
entire nation.

Things will come and go. Settle it! Cars, clothing, homes, etc.
wear out. Even when they don't, people get tired of them and desire
something different just for the sake of change. The dealings of the
Holy Spirit are the only ones who can produce the fruit of moderation in our lives. The apostles and early Church believers sought
the Kingdom of God at the expense of relinquishing things, thus
modeling moderation. Many modern believers seek things at the
expense of losing the Kingdom of God. Prevailing wisdom says, "If
you are hungry for God, things will not totally satisfy; seek the
Kingdom!" God is urging humanity to repossess the original
design of relationship with Him—which is one without the spirit
and practice of covetousness, but, instead, one of complete divine
enrichment.

After observing the malignity of covetousness during the captivity, predictable wisdom should have opened the eyes of Judah to her
present lot. Unfortunately, they never comprehended their misfortune
or demise.

And it came to pass in the twelfth year of our captivity, in the tenth month, on the fifth day of the month, that one who had escaped from Jerusalem came to me and said, "The city has been captured!"..."As for you, son of man, the children of your people are talking about you beside the walls and in the doors of the houses; and they speak to one another, everyone saying to his brother, 'Please come and hear what the word is that comes from the Lord.' So they come to you as people do, they sit before you as My people, and they hear your words, but they do not do them; for with their mouth they show much love, but their hearts pursue their own gain" (Ezekiel 33:21,30-31).

Covetousness was bound in the heart of Judah. Many years later Paul cited covetousness as the mother of all sinful vices (see Rom. 7:7-8). This spirit gives sin the opportunity to ambush the integrity of man's character and to drown him in illicit desires. In promoting moderation in his young disciple Timothy, Paul proclaimed that the love of money is the root of all evil (see 1 Tim. 6:10). Some of the better translations of New Testament Greek say, *"For the love of money is a root of all kinds of evil."* Loving money is the one root a man of God can least afford to be nabbed by; it opens the door to so many other spiritual and social disorders. This love stems from covetousness that destroys eager pursuers.

Both Testaments are full of people subdued by the spirit of covetousness. Jesus described covetousness as one of the evil thoughts originating in the heart of man, arising from within to defile him (see Mark 7:20-23). After telling the parable of the unjust steward (see Luke 16:1-13), Jesus exposed the Pharisees as covetous. Paul placed covetous men among the wicked and immoral of his day (see 1 Cor. 5:9-13; 6:9-11). It was the first sin in the Garden of Eden, the first sin in the Promised Land, and the first major sin in the New Testament Church.

So when the woman saw that the tree was good for food, that it was pleasant to the eyes, and a tree desirable to make one wise, she took of its fruit and ate. She also gave to her husband with her, and he ate (Genesis 3:6).

When I saw among the spoils a goodly Babylonish garment, and two hundred shekels of silver, and a wedge of gold of fifty shekels weight, then I coveted them, and took them; and, behold, they are hid in the earth in the midst of my tent, and the silver under it (Joshua 7:21 KJV).

But a certain man named Ananias, with Sapphira his wife, sold a possession. And he kept back part of the proceeds, his wife also being aware of it, and brought a certain part and laid it at the apostles' feet. But Peter said, "Ananias, why has satan filled your heart to lie to the Holy Spirit and keep back part of the price of the land for yourself?" (Acts 5:1-3).

Today, we deal with more subtle, polished forms of covetousness, such as lotteries, attending church gatherings to get rather than to give, desiring national or global ministries because someone else has one, etc., in which people often fail to discern their true motives. Sometimes I wonder if some of the religious disasters of the late 1980s weren't driven by a spirit of covetousness, especially in the Christian media field. Men often compete for dollars and influence when they have highly visible ministries. Ironically, this sometimes leads to devaluing and ridiculing of other brethren. Many large, need-driven, religious gatherings of the 1990s were secretly driven by highly skilled marketing agents rather than anointing. It doesn't take long to discern covetousness is underneath that kind of system. It seems that questionable preachers have preyed on people's need to be blessed one more time. Sorry to say, people were blessed (or thought they were) but never changed. Can you really call that being blessed?

Pulpit competition was strong. We often heard ideas floating around like, "the greatest preacher." Rather than embracing and respecting one another, we sometimes made awkward, ungodly comparisons. Competition breeds this type of environment. As a rule, all men and women of God should respect and cover one another with the fabric of love. Exposing one another's nakedness or weaknesses with vindictive spirits won't prove anything other than to expose the harshness of judgmental practices. Spiritual people are under a mandate to restore others who have fallen. It breaks my heart to see or hear of Christians following any other pattern. I have discovered that if any exposures are necessary, God will entrust those painful unveilings to the most mature apostles and prophets.

America and, probably, most of the nations of the world are full of get-rich-quick schemes. The idea is to get more of the necessary evil called money. A poem I read out of *Poems and Poets*, entitled "Money" (McGraw-Hill, Inc., New York, 1965), captures what people do with money. Pay close attention to the miser, who is in the same boat with the greedy and covetous.

Workers earn it, Spendthrifts burn it,

Bankers lend it, Women spend it,

Forgers fake it, Taxes take it,

Dying leave it, Heirs receive it,

Thrifty save it, Misers crave it,

Robbers seize it, Rich increase it,

Gamblers lose it...I could use it.

- Richard Armour[5]

Many countries have lotteries and other gambling institutions in order for people to be exposed to and teased by the idea of more money. From what I can tell, only a few people actually get more money under this system. In today's unstable economies, the truth is: Some people could use more money, and others could use what they have more wisely. Most lotteries tantalizingly draw the most underprivileged people of society into their entrapments. Some Christians even call it the Father's blessings. It may or may not be! Most studies that have followed up on lottery winners prove that it isn't. In fact, it is nothing more than an undisciplined habit for most people—a web that has no spider until one has been entrapped. The best way to improve your lot is to follow time-honored principles in the Word of God that teach us to properly sow and reap based upon God's timetable. So many of us are in such a hurry it's hard to wait on God anymore. Covetousness will breed family problems, disappointment, folly, apostasy, misery, pain, oppression, theft, disobedience, robbery, meanness, unscrupulousness, scoffing, and a host of other things. It is essentially covetousness that prompts a man to want to keep up with the Joneses. Strong desire to have what belongs to another is purchasing a ticket to ride the wings of nothing, going to a city called nowhere. In the end, it doesn't pay.

It is important to know that the principles that govern an alternate society are different from those that govern capitalistic, free enterprise systems. From an ideological standpoint, large amounts of money, goods, and services make capitalism work. A *Big God* is what makes the Kingdom work. Capitalism feeds the spirit of greed; whereas, in an alternate society, money works to further Kingdom purposes, primarily through giving, prudence, and temperance.

European adventurers during the 15th and 16th centuries demonstrated the glut of capitalism through exploration and exploitation. What they discovered by looking for new spice routes totally overwhelmed the spirit of desire within them. The Church, at that time, could have offset this image if she hadn't been muddied with the manipulative predispositions of despotism. The authoritarians of the Church were just as greedy and covetous as their secular counterparts.

Modern capitalism is an extension and a more refined, systematic practice of old-time greed. In past centuries, the Aztec Indians were virtually obliterated because of covetousness. Africa and Asia were thoroughly plundered because of European avarice. North America became the training grounds of a new breed of covetous men during the slavery era. God's idea was that North America should have become a bastion of Kingdom activities. African nations shouldn't have been encroached on repeatedly. Here's the bottom line: Imperialism, colonialism, and slavery were all based upon greed and a spirit of acquisition. The rich and powerful became richer and more powerful at a very great price.

Please remember, money is only an object to be used as a means to operate the system we live in. In itself, it is neither good or evil. It is the barter of business which helps society in general by giving work opportunities, encouraging a higher criterion of livelihood. The real issue behind covetousness is the mental and psychological pressure it places on people controlled by it. Someone may lose everything—all possessions —and still be covetous. A person may lose every dime and still be greedy, because greed is something conceptual rather than concrete. If we thump greed and covetousness, they must be replaced with something spiritual. God has a plan that will not disguise greed, extravagance, and a monstrous appetite for wealth with the clothing of hypocrisy. It is called the Kingdom of God! In the Kingdom, pretense is totally against God's nature.

GOD'S ANSWER TO COVETOUSNESS

The primary way to deal with covetousness is to first seek the Kingdom of God and His righteousness. In doing so, we are trusting God's fatherly instincts for us at all times in everything. The truth of right identity allows us to serve the purposes of God's Kingdom without illegal intentions to advance ourselves. Unwarranted affections toward wealth, without an open, cheerful hand of giving, can be very dangerous to our growth, development, and service. To focus on wealth in this manner is what the apostles meant by idolatry; regrettably, it locks us intentionally on things rather than on our God. We all must remember that we are created for God's glory rather than carnal satisfaction.

Very simply, our new nature repeals covetousness. The old nature had covetousness ingrained in it as the rational option. It filled society with its coconspirators of violent theft and envy, birthing generations that were accomplices with fraud. In America, and in all other nations, we will prevail over this malignancy by fearing God and keeping His commandment of love. God has a marvelous future and hope for us. Although we behold the old order self-absorbed and decomposing, an alternate society is coming forth out of its ruins. Our heavenly Father is birthing a son with the spirit of contentment.

The spirit of contentment produces balance and equilibrium to a culture distorted and beleaguered by covetousness. Contentment is not containment, which means enclosure. There's no opportunity for growth in this paradigm. However, contentment primarily signifies to be sufficient, to be possessed of sufficient strength, adequate, needing no assistance; hence to be satisfied. It enables believers to receive the pace by which God chooses to release things into their lives. Moreover, that tempo is never the same for all believers. The Scripture is rather clear that a son of God actually has what he's able to responsibly handle. Rather than foolishly chasing blessings at the expense of perverting righteousness, men can finally settle that their steps are truly ordered by the Lord. Our minds, affections, and energies are not consumed with trying to get ahead. Neither are we jealous and envious of other brethren, thinking they have some edge merely because they have, maybe, more material blessings. Contentment enables us to honestly walk in love, seeking to advance the cause of others without feeling cheated by God. If men would practice contentment more, we wouldn't see the wholesale disintegration of individual lives and society in general. Covetousness will always be practiced at the neglect of contentment, and to our own peril.

One of the most practical principles of contentment is found in the writings of the Book of Hebrews. It says,

> *Let your conduct be without covetousness; be content with such things as you have. For He Himself has said, "I will never leave you nor forsake you." So we may boldly say: "The Lord is my helper; I will not fear. What can man do to me?"* (Hebrews 13:5-6)

> *Don't be obsessed with getting more material things. Be relaxed with what you have. Since God assured us, "I'll never let you down, never walk off and leave you," we can boldly quote, "God is there, ready to help; I'm fearless no matter what. Who or what can get to me?"* (Hebrews 13:5-6 The Message)

First, contentment releases faith in us to always count on God to be there—it's the reality of His name Jehovah Shammah (see Ezek. 48:35). Since Hebrews is a Book of overwhelming change, it affirms the presence of God in the midst of tremendous transition, changeovers, alterations, modifications, and spiritual evolutions. This promise was necessary every time the Kingdom of God was being advanced to comfort the chosen agents of change. God promised Jacob, saying, *"For I will not leave you until I have done what I have spoken to you"* (Gen. 28:15b). When the change of command moved from Moses to Joshua, Moses encouraged the people and Joshua, declaring, *"He is the One who goes with you. He will not leave you nor forsake you"* (Deut. 31:6,8). When the Lord personally spoke to Joshua, He said: *"I will be with you. I will not leave you nor forsake you"* (Josh. 1:5b). David promised Solomon, his son, that *"the Lord God—my God—will be with you"* (1 Chron. 28:20b). Finally, just before ascending into Heaven, Jesus promised the apostles, saying, *"Go therefore and make disciples of all the nations, baptizing them in the name of the Father and of the Son and of the Holy Spirit, teaching them to observe all things that I have commanded you; and lo, I am with you always, even to the end of the age"* (Matt. 28:19-20). Each vessel could be content because of the Lord's personal assurance to them of His abiding presence.

Second, contentment releases faith to say, *"God is my Helper!"* Absolutely and unequivocally, there is now no reason to fear man when God is helping you. Jesus, our King and High Priest, is really on our side without reservation. The Word of God verifies this in the most profound way.

> *The Lord is my light and my salvation; whom shall I fear? The Lord is the strength of my life; of whom shall I be afraid?* (Psalm 27:1)

> *In God I have put my trust; I will not be afraid. What can man do to me?* (Psalm 56:11).

> *The Lord is on my side; I will not fear. What can man do to me?* (Psalm 118:6).

I, even I, am He who comforts you. Who are you that you should be afraid of a man who will die, and of the son of a man who will be made like grass? (Isaiah 51:12)

What then shall we say to these things? If God is for us, who can be against us? (Romans 8:31)

When the Holy Spirit dealt with my wife and I about leaving North Carolina and going to Florida, we had to pack up the lessons learned in contentment and bring them with us. Remember, contentment is something one learns (see Phil. 4:11). We had to rest in the fact that God was with us, and there was no reason to fear man. The early days of launching a ministry means one may do without many material things; and one may absorb much ridicule. Part of our training was to learn the art of self-denial voluntarily. For example, we learned contentment by living in a small apartment after attempting to purchase a home. After all, the American dream is to have a single-family dwelling. We figured because our income was adequate God would permit us to acquire a home. Frustrated several times, we finally concluded this may not be in accordance with God's will for us at this time. The operative idea is: *at this time.*

Enthusiastically, and rather idealistically, we came to Florida with no intentions of putting down deep roots. We had a deciduous root mentality rather than a taproot mentality. We thought we would plant a local church within a few years and move on. Our heavenly Father had other thoughts. He immediately provided us a house to live in. Wow! No more apartments! The next year, we purchased our first home. First, we were really rapt with happiness, but soon became immersed with our new responsibility and mandatory commitment it demanded. Amazingly, our income level was far less than what we had in North Carolina. It proves that if one remains in the will and timing of God, He'll withhold nothing that is right. I knew then that this current assignment wasn't a short-term song-and-dance in the park. Whether our souls desired to express displeasure or not, the spirit of contentment aided us in receiving the longevity of our assignment with joy. A man or woman of God is in a despicably dangerous position when one cannot accept what God has willed with joy and contentment. Arnold H. Glassgow said, "A real leader faces the music when he doesn't like the tune."[6]

NATIONAL LEADERS AND CONTENTMENT

National leaders must vitally demonstrate a proclivity for contentment. Because God has purposed spiritual leaders to be impact people, they're the first ones who must get this. When Korah and all his company railed against Moses' leadership, Moses was able to provide proof of the spirit of contentment working in him.

> *Then Moses was very angry, and said to the Lord, "Do not respect their offering. I have not taken one donkey from them, nor have I hurt one of them"* (Numbers 16:15).

Samuel, a man of note among all the Old Testament prophets, provides an elegant example of the spirit of contentment.

> *"Here I am. Witness against me before the Lord and before His anointed: Whose ox have I taken, or whose donkey have I taken, or whom have I cheated? Whom have I oppressed, or from whose hand have I received any bribe with which to blind my eyes? I will restore it to you." And they said, "You have not cheated us or oppressed us, nor have you taken anything from any man's hand." Then he said to them, "The Lord is witness against you, and His anointed is witness this day, that you have not found anything in my hand." And they answered, "He is witness"* (1 Samuel 12:3-5).

For all the modern apostles who have cut their spiritual teeth on the American Christian enterprise, Paul is the apostolic model of contentment.

> *I have coveted no one's silver or gold or apparel* (Acts 20:33).

> *For neither at any time did we use flattering words, as you know, nor a cloak of covetousness—God is witness. Nor did we seek glory from men, either from you or from others, when we might have made demands as apostles of Christ. But we were gentle among you just as a nursing mother cherishes her own children.*

So, affectionately longing for you, we were well pleased to impart to you not only the gospel of God, but also our own lives, because you had become dear to us (1 Thessalonians 2:5-8).

These national leaders were outstanding models of men delivered from the spirit of covetousness. They were agents of empowerment, and not self-aggrandizement. Some of the national leadership scandals of the 1990s were fueled by men snatching beyond their measures—which is covetousness mixed with pride. Father God does not call every leader to lead thousands of people; it is presumptuous to think that way. If you're called to lead one hundred, do it faithfully. A society without covetousness is a society in which the leadership has shown distaste for the culpability of covetousness. Many ancient and modern wars have been started because of men's covetous hearts. As the Old Testament prophet challenged the nation of Israel during a time of national reform, so must we consider our ways (see Hag. 1:5,7) We must examine our ways to determine if they line up with the principles of God's grace. If we will, God will help us to build a society without covetousness.

In my previous book, *The Sound That Changed Everything* (Destiny Image Publishers, 2003), I stated that the Church must learn to deal with large sums of money in an age of economic empowerment.[7] Crucial to this is the need for impact leaders to be delivered from the spirit and practice of covetousness. Followers will mimic the example leaders establish. Leaders must stand strong and ennobled in the truth of contentment, painlessly and comfortably walking in the nature of the new man. We must have no regrets that God has delivered us from something as reprehensible as covetousness. True Kingdom greatness is not measured by how deep one's pockets may be, how large portfolios are, or how lavish the bottom line of a bank balance. As one anonymous quote says, "It is not wealth or ancestry, but honorable conduct and noble disposition that make men great."[8] Great men aren't greedy men. It is very important that we heed the warnings of the Scriptures as they speak so profoundly about greed.

When Samuel got to be an old man, he set his sons up as judges in Israel. His firstborn son was named Joel, the name of his second, Abijah. They were assigned duty in Beersheba. But his sons didn't take after him; they were out for what they could get for themselves, taking bribes, corrupting justice (1 Samuel 8:1-3 The Message).

We'll load up on top-quality loot. We'll haul it home by the truck-load (Proverbs 1:13 The Message)

A greedy and grasping person destroys community; those who refuse to exploit live and let live (Proverbs 15:27 The Message).

Sinners are always wanting what they don't have; the God-loyal are always giving what they do have (Proverbs 21:26 The Message).

In closing, it takes years of basking in grace to learn how to withstand the insidious assaults of greed and covetousness. Balaam is a powerful biblical illustration of how the prophetic ministry can become compromised and commercialized. We are in trouble when ministry fringe benefits lure us more than obedience to the purposes of God. What amount constitutes enough? Some men have become so sinister in their practices that *dial-a-prophet* has become a despicable practice in modern Christianity. Alas! The way of Balaam has become the way of some who began in purity. There's no doubt about it, that Balaam was a prophet of God. However, he permitted the cunning sway of money to corrupt his ministry and lead him off track. Every apostle and prophet must be free from the subjugation of money. If we permit it, modern society will train each of us in the art of greed. This behavior is often well cloaked beneath an inward departure from God. Judas Iscariot was living proof of that! We must remember: *"For we brought nothing into this world, and it is certain we can carry nothing out. And having food and raiment let us be therewith content. But they that will be rich fall into temptation and a snare, and into many foolish and hurtful lusts, which drown men in destruction and perdition"* (1 Tim. 6:7-9 KJV). Men and women of God must live their lives diametrically opposed to nonbelievers. Unbelievers live to get, thinking that produces increase; while we live to give, knowing it shall be given back unto us (see Luke 6:38). In addition, what is given can't always be measured in dollars and cents.

I admonish every minister to truly develop a stewardship spirit. Our spiritual ancestor, King David, was a wonderful example of this for us. When he was preparing Solomon to build the Temple, he set his affection on the house of God. He accumulated much during his lifetime and gave much (see 1 Chron. 29:2-7). David didn't have "I'm going to get mine" mentality; he wasn't greedy and materialistic. He was humbled to know that God had chosen him to prepare such a legacy, stretching into future generations. David said: *"But who am I, and who are my people, that we should be able to offer so willingly as this? For all things come from You, and of Your own we have given You"* (1 Chron. 29:14). To make it simple, The Message says, *"But me—who am I, and who are these my people, that we should presume to be giving something to You? Everything comes from You; all we're doing is giving back what we've been given from Your generous hand."* In these times, which call for great courage to walk in the Word of God, I advise every servant of God to be vulnerable enough to follow David. The passion of our lives should be that God could trust us to model contentment, and to censure covetousness.

> The people of our nation and the people of the whole world need to be gripped by the moral imperatives which grow out of the nature of God, by a sense of right, by principles of truth, and by ideals of decency. Nothing is more needed by this sinful world than a revival of simple goodness and genuine uprightness.
>
> Clifton J. Allen[9]

ENDNOTES

1. Geoffrey Hanks, *70 Great Christians* (Great Britain: Christian Focus Publications, 1992), 212.

2. Webster's II New College Dictionary, Riverside University dictionary (New York: Houghton Mifflin Company, 1995), 261.

3. Geoffrey W. Bromiley, *Theological Dictionary of the New Testament* (Grand Rapids, MI: William B. Eerdmans Publishing Company, 1985), 864.

4. Ibid., 864-865.

5. David Aloian, *Poems and Poets* (St. Louis, MO: McGraw-Hill Book Company, 1965), 254.

6. Vern McLellan, *Wise Words and Quotes* (Wheaton, IL: Tyndale House Publishers, Inc., 1998), 158.

7. Stephen Everett, *The Sound That Changed Everything* (Shippensburg, PA: Destiny Image Publishers, Inc., 2003), 141.

8. Virginia Ely, *I Quote* (New York: George W. Stewart Publishers, Inc., 1947), 149.

9. Ibid., 229.

9

Death to Disenfranchisement

Now these are the judgments which you shall set before them
(Exodus 21:1).

The judgments of the Lord are true and righteous altogether
(Psalm 19:9b).

The decisions of God are accurate down to the nth degree (Psalm
19:9b The Message).

*The entirety of Your word is truth, and every one of Your righteous
judgments endures forever* (Psalm 119:160).

*Your words all add up to the sum total: Truth. Your righteous deci-
sions are eternal* (Psalm 119:160 The Message).

In the last decade, two events, among many, reminded me that my
life had once been affected by the unrighteousness of disenfranchisement. First, I joined Dr. Kelley Varner for a short mission's trip to
South Africa in February 1999. Without sensationalizing the trip's
significance, just touching the soil of the African continent became
very important and endearing to me. Although I live in the Western
world and enjoy its current privileges and wealth, I realize some of
our nation's historical dealings have been rather shady. What I mean
by this is: Our national government didn't necessarily acquire all of

its land and labor with impeccable integrity. History bears this out with many infallible proofs.

I thought that this trip would be therapeutic internally without all the meaningless externals of American toys and Western cultural benefits. My desire was to have a simple, scaled-down trip. Before I boarded the flight, I said, "I'm going to one of the wealthiest continents in the world—rich mineral resources, rich cultures, and rich histories, yet needing to be released from the death-grip of modern barbarism, AIDS, superstitions, exploitation, and poverty." The only remorse I felt was that my family wasn't with me. When the flight landed in Johannesburg, something very emotional occurred in my soul just as it did when I returned to America. It was as if I had made a pilgrimage back to see from whence some of my ancestors came. Of course, I acknowledge that most African-Americans have ancestral links to mostly West African nations. However, it was important for me just to physically and spiritually reconnect with the continent known as the cradle of civilization.

Some of the young flight attendants engaged me in conversation during the flight across the Atlantic Ocean. Unless my discernment was incorrect, they anxiously awaited to speak with African-Americans of the African Diaspora. As we spoke eye-to-eye for a few minutes, something connected in each of us. We knew we were brothers from the same bloodline and shared a rich heritage. They had some knowledge of the struggles of African-Americans; and I certainly was aware of the anti-civilization history of the apartheid regime, and the suffering associated with that unjust system. While we spoke, my mind wandered, remembering the many ancestors whose suffering and deaths had gone unnoted, unappreciated, and unmentioned. As the conversation was ending, I was thankful we, by the grace of God, had survived. That fact was more important than any act of reparation, more redemptive than anything other than the cross of Jesus Christ was. We still have a thriving spirit, though much healing is needed in both South Africa and the United States. Economically and in every other way we are challenged, nevertheless we're here! The gospel of grace and the Kingdom of God will become an effectual tool in our full liberation. As the 16-hour flight finally ended, the young men said: "Welcome to the motherland!" I said, "Yes! I'm here! This is a great day! Let's see what God has in mind!"

The other event was less moving emotionally, though not less important. Our leadership team made some very important decisions in the earlier years of our local church's ministry. After pondering the pros and cons, we decided to conduct home-cell meetings. Somewhat frustrated, we realized Sunday's celebrations weren't fulfilling certain needs relationally. My background as a public school teacher afforded me the luxury of appreciating small groups, although I was well aware of the horror stories that could accompany them if rebellion arose. It always gave me heart-to-heart time with people that otherwise I couldn't have had. In one of those meetings, a senior member of our congregation reminded me of a mind-set all too familiar. While just chatting, she said with a voice of genuine honesty, one concerned for my success: "You know that if you were White, with your anointing and knowledge, your ministry would fare better in Cape Coral!" She wasn't playing the race card because she was a member of the majority race in America. I was stunned she had the courage to say it, but had to admit, she was probably stating a fact. Immediately, I remembered that something might be factual and not have a bit of relevance to the truth. For instance, the fact is that my skin color is what it is; the truth is: Only God can rightly give increase to a ministry, no matter the skin pigment of its leader.

Cape Coral was notoriously one of the most segregated cities in Southwest Florida in the mid 1980s. There were a number of reasons for this. Acknowledged or not, unspoken social, religious, and political strongholds were keeping it that way. Most of America was reasonably desegregated by the 1980s. Not Cape Coral! When I first moved, the population was just under 33,000 people, with less than five percent being non-White. Although the tenor and tone of blatant, dissenting voices of prejudice were gone, they had mutated into stares that said: *How did you get here?* Historically, humans can be unkind to others who are different. Crude, overt racism had given way to silence and avoidance. Please understand I'm not saying 32,500 people were racists. (Some religious people objected to our presence because of differing assumptions about our doctrines.) The Lord had used certain brethren to get us to our assignment who judged us on the content of our character rather than the color of our skin. If not for them, I'm not quite sure how my family would have responded to our initial unwelcome. We ran headlong into the carefully coded message and spirit of disenfranchisement. The question was: How do we deal with this without becoming defensive, insolvent spiritually and attitudinally, and yet, manifest the love of Christ?

JUST WHAT IS DISENFRANCHISEMENT?

Disenfranchisement is a hideous system that denies people the right of privileges that others may benefit from, especially economic benefits. It is a watershed between the powerful and the impoverished, something every minority group has been forced to tolerate, taking the rough with the smooth. *Minority* may be defined as "a racial, religious, political, national, or other group thought to be different from the larger group of which it is a part."[1] That's a very broad definition. Because Israel and the Church are alternate societies in the midst of every ancient and modern culture, both would fall into this category. There are very few places in which Judeo-Christian culture has been or is the dominant culture within the cultural spread. For example, we call America a Christian nation, but frankly, it isn't. Some Americans display Christ-like traits, and many also display many heathen traits. Our republic has endorsed and supported a system with many imbalances of power. Enduring imbalances of power, such as racial oppression, social exploitation, economic disempowerment, has been the scourge of disenfranchised people. Any type of oppression includes a set of strategies to feed the spirit of exploitation. We have been very good at developing these in America, and are in great need of repentance.

When you look at various surveys in America alone, non-White Americans own about one dime of wealth for every dollar of wealth owned by White Americans. In this paradigm, even if poor people have constructive ideas very relevant to community issues, their economic conditions won't allow them to be heard (see Eccl. 9:14-16). Very simply, poor people have very little voice in democracies. What if we dealt with subgroups within these larger groups, such as male versus female wealth? Do males possess more accumulative wealth than females because they're more brilliant, savvier? Alternatively, is there something about the existing system that favors male dominance, no matter the size of the cranium? I wonder if this holds true in the Christian community as well.

Ten to one is a large gap from anyone's perspective. How can one justify such a wealth disparity that seems to grow larger with each succeeding year, thus producing more wealth, more income, more representation that is political and access, more status, and reinforcement to self-worth and decorum? The answer is more complicated than the lingering effects of laziness, poor attitudes, and historical slavery, which still contribute attitudinally in a very surreptitious manner. I submit these imbalances will never be dismantled until the spirit of disenfranchisement is destroyed in every nation by the power and coming of the Kingdom of God. Membership in the privileged majority will always produce benefits the economically disadvantaged minority knows nothing about. The balance of power is found in the judgments of God's Word and how He intends society to function. He has a verdict that will undo the long-standing, unrestricted, even generational harm of disenfranchisement.

I have stated in earlier chapters that Israel and the Church are parallel stories. This has held consistently true as we have sketchily studied each of them in this book. Both have been minorities in their communities in contrast to other groups. Each has been under God's mandate to maintain its independence from the world's culture in order to properly affect it. Both are called to be holy, with a resolute commitment to the Kingdom of God in order to firmly represent God in the earth. This would be done by modeling Kingdom values, and second, becoming a Kingdom envoy to the culture. The Lord established a set of righteous judgments to prevent both from abusing the privileges of this power, strictly the power of productivity and fruitful influence. Often, human nature causes oppressed people to become oppressors once they are empowered. Let's discover how 21st-century Kingdom advancement depends upon the Church's ability to apply these principles in a practical way. We must not become complicit and absorbed by the current culture.

THE COMING OF THE JUST ONE

Which of the prophets did your fathers not persecute? And they killed those who foretold the coming of the Just One, of whom you now have become the betrayers and murderers (Acts 7:52).

The coming of the Lord is a multilayered concept not fully understood by most people. It requires various words and ideas to convey the full import of this wonderful thought. One of them is *parousia.* It indicates Christ's coming and presence.[2] Once Christ is present, there's a reason for His arrival. Within the context of Acts 7:52, Jesus Christ is the arrival and subsequent stay of the projected Just One. The Greek word used for this is *eleusis.*[3] Rarely used outside of the Bible, it occurs for the coming of the Righteous One proclaimed by the prophets, probably with a reference to the coming judgment.[4] A new structure of justice must be preceded by a just person. A just person is equitable in character and behavior. Pertaining to Christ, it designates the perfect agreement between His nature and His acts (in which He is the standard for all men).[5] Webster defines *equitable* as "impartially just, fair, and reasonable."[6]

Jesus Christ, as a just man, released the impartial judgments of Father God. He is the pattern of judgment that doesn't disenfranchise anyone; doesn't condemn from the premise of humanistic viewpoints. Christ said, *"I can of Myself do nothing. As I hear, I judge; and My judgment is righteous, because I do not seek My own will but the will of the Father who sent Me"* (Jn. 5:30). The first key to righteous judgment is hearing with accuracy (see Mk. 4:24) and finely tuned discernment (see Lk. 8:18). By the time Jesus arrived, the various ruling religious groups had clouded lenses and certainly weren't judging in this manner. When you have nothing to gain, or no hidden agendas, it is easy to rule impartially. Father God set this as the standard even in the Old Covenant. Listen to these words:

You shall appoint judges and officers in all your gates, which the Lord your God gives you, according to your tribes, and they shall judge the people with just judgment. You shall not pervert justice; you shall not show partiality, nor take a bribe, for a bribe blinds the eyes of the wise and twists the words of the righteous. You shall follow what is altogether just, that you may live and inherit the land which the Lord your God is giving you (Deuteronomy 16:18-20).

It is hard to miss the unadulterated standard God was establishing as they entered the kingdom. Many years later, when Jehoshaphat, a godly king of Judah, reformed the land, he gave some very specific instructions to the men established in judgment. It is almost a repeat of Moses' words to the first generation heirs of the land.

Then he set judges in the land throughout all the fortified cities of Judah, city by city, and said to the judges, "Take heed to what you are doing, for you do not judge for man but for the Lord, who is with you in the judgment. Now therefore, let the fear of the Lord be upon you; take care and do it, for there is no iniquity with the Lord our God, no partiality, nor taking of bribes (2 Chronicles 19:5-7).

A clear pattern of judgment emerges in each passage of Scripture. God demands total uprightness when judgments are executed. Frankly, this was impossible until the Just and Holy One arrived. His integrity allowed Him to see humanity out of the eyes of our loving heavenly Father. His message to the entire creation, after four thousand years of miserable failure, was: *You're forgiven!* Humanity was at a low point, and this was the only justifiable sentence Father God could issue. What no dispensation could do, grace did instantly. Through Jesus Christ, grace answered wisely every legal claim of the law. People and groups who were once disenfranchised are no longer alienated outcasts. Jesus is indeed the great equalizer, the administrator of God's justice. The apostle Paul captures and summarizes this thought with these words:

But don't take any of this for granted. It was only yesterday that you outsiders to God's ways had no idea of any of this, didn't know the first thing about the way God works, hadn't the faintest idea of Christ. You knew nothing of that rich history of God's covenants and promises in Israel, hadn't a clue about what God was doing in the world at large. Now because of Christ—dying that death, shedding that blood—you who were once out of it altogether are in on everything (Ephesians 2:11-13 The Message).

231

A consummate illustration of this point is when Jesus crossed over and ministered to people on the "other side" (see Mt. 8:18-34). The character of those cities was primarily Gentile, but many Jews lived there and in surrounding territories. The people on the other side are different. They are other! Bigotry and discrimination become habitual and convenient when people are other. Jesus Christ first identified His mission as being to the lost sheep of the house of Israel (see Mt. 15:24). When He crossed over and touched others, it became a statement against the spirit of disenfranchisement. The Just One temporarily moved into the bigger picture, widening the spectrum of those whom He ministered to. The Bible says, *"For even the Son of Man did not come to be served, but to serve, and to give His life a ransom for many"* (Mk. 10:45). I suggest "many" is not one color, one culture, or one kind—it's exactly what it says, *"many!"* Jesus was anointed with the Holy Spirit and power, and He went about doing good and healing *all*. Other leaders were prejudiced, but He didn't allow their cultural negativism to distort His mission. Jesus was truly the coming of the Just One. If all Christians would follow His lead, and touch that person called *other*, no one would ever suffer under the spirit of disenfranchisement.

The Church, as a Kingdom envoy, must determine how far to the other side we are willing to go. Do we choose just to sneak across the borders, or penetrate deeply into the infrastructure of the other side? Either way, be prepared for some humungous challenges! When Jesus first came to the other side, He was greeted by a powerful welcoming committee: two criminally insane demoniacs. Jesus compassionately delivered both of them. The citizens of that district knew He wasn't one of them, and didn't know how to appreciate what had happened. However, this great deliverance proved to be useful for His next trip to the other side. When the men of the city recognized it was Jesus, they gathered all the sick of the surrounding region to be touched (see Mt. 14:34-36). What produced the change of heart? It's difficult to reject a man who has lovingly delivered two people who had no hope other than to be institutionalized. When the Church makes a difference in some of the hard cases on the other side, think about the kind of welcome we will receive in the postmodern world.

AN ADMINISTRATION OF JUSTICE

For the Lord your God is God of gods and Lord of lords, the great God, mighty and awesome, who shows no partiality nor takes a bribe. He administers justice for the fatherless and the widow, and loves the stranger, giving him food and clothing. Therefore love the stranger, for you were strangers in the land of Egypt (Deuteronomy 10:17-19)

Central to breaking the spirit of disenfranchisement is an understanding of God's system of justice. Father God doesn't take bribes and cares mightily about the have-nots. Nationally, America survives because the Church is mission-minded and typically shows great interest for the disenfranchised of the world. However, our national government tends to cater more easily to the affluent nations and disregard the poorer ones. When this is so, in the end, we hurt ourselves. Leaders of the free world aren't expected to have vacant mercy accounts, which have insufficient funds when it comes to expressing multilateral concern for all people. Leaders of the free world are expected to be equal opportunity distributors in their charity.

Father God commanded Israel to love the stranger, and He commanded the Church to be hospitable; which means *"loving strangers!"* (see Rom. 12:13; Heb. 13:2) This would require a radical, revolutionary mind-set, something different from anything either Israel or the Church had ever practiced. The Father always discloses a sincere concern for the disenfranchised when the order of civilization is being established. Improper care of them fosters resentment—it's the breeding ground of extremism, fanaticism, and philosophies that produce countercultural movements. All major revolutions of the last 300 years have spun out of the turmoil associated with disenfranchised people: the American, French, Russian, Chinese, and Cuban Revolutions, just to name a few. Some of the Japanese brass, which led them in World War II, had felt the sting of American racism while studying at some of our finest universities. Who knows! Proper hospitality may have averted some of the carnage and cruelty of World War II. Disenfranchisement, year in and year out, leads to potential violence.

I'm reminded, at this point, of how much I deplore violence—period. Our country has seen its fair share of violence, from presidential assassinations to violent deaths to other great historical leaders. The Middle East is ablaze with violence and disenfranchised people. How will the international community come together and solve a seemingly endless dilemma? The options are minimal. There should be no substitute for stability and control, which should help everyone build a sense of security. Terrorism isn't the way to free you from colonial dependency when the other nation has shown a penchant for retaliation. Wouldn't it be feasible just to establish a peaceful and cooperative relationship based on mutual interests for the region? Could it not benefit everyone to forgive and reconcile with each other? It's neither an illusion nor naivety to think this is possible. The road map to peace can come only through one administration: the Kingdom of God. Many Christians have prayed earnestly for the Kingdom of God to transform this geopolitical region. Every other arrangement is temporary, and can only be on an interim basis.

In order to maintain the principles of civilized society, violence must be snuffed out, particularly violence against the most vulnerable in society—the unborn, the young, the old, and the poor. A just society has great concerns for proper relationships between its citizenry. A powerful illustration of this is management and labor (masters and servants in the Old Testament). If detailed research was conducted, I am almost positive labor unions evolved out of the lack of true concern by upper management for workers. Even workers deserve to be respected and treated fairly if they're productive.

In addition, animal control becomes an essential issue in modern society, all of which speaks to the sanctity of life. Culturally violent people often do not show that concern, therefore provoking laws against animal cruelty. I must admit, however, that it concerns me that the modern Western world has shown greater concern for the lives of their pets than for the lives of fellow human beings. Something is out of balance. There's not one single pet created in the image of God as every human is!

Today we must also consider such things as global equalization in the knowledge of God, social reforms, deforestation, and redistribution of wealth. Society can't function fluidly with any sense of civility without a recognized system of justice for all. When judgment is perverted, it opens the floodgates for every foul opportunity for disenfranchisement. Remember, the entire creation is waiting to experience the glorious liberty of the children of God. Our full freedom and nature's freedom is the same (see Rom. 8:19-22).

BUILD FRESH ALTARS

The place in which we begin to correct some of these dilemmas and receive fresh solutions is the altar. In the Old Covenant, Israel was commanded to build altars. Every place Abraham would go, he would pitch his tent and build an altar. If Father God doesn't have our lives and our homes, He doesn't have us! The altar is a neutralizer of human strengths, an ego-wrecker, a prejudice-incinerator, a place of commonality for rich and poor alike, and a place of vision. We have no titles other than children of God when we go to the altar. It reminds us we're not in charge of our lives. It's a speed bump that compels us to bow to the One who gives us breath and being. The altar gave God continual accessibility to the people; and they could express continual reverence for the Lord. Their God-connection would fuel their hearts with love for everyone. As the nation stayed in a sacrificial position, humbling itself, it would be difficult to pervert judgment.

There is a supernatural unction in the earth once again to repair altars. We are commanded *"to present your bodies a living sacrifice, holy, acceptable to God, which is your reasonable service"* (Rom. 12:1). The Message says, *"Take your everyday, ordinary life—your sleeping, eating, going-to-work, and walking-around life—and place it before God as an offering."* The Father desires to release a fresh supernatural manifestation of His presence, thus settling all issues other methods can't. All altars built today are simply extensions of the greatest altar ever raised: *Calvary!* It was the highest ideal of God's heart and remains a point of connection for all people. Calvary was the center of divine justice and became the focal point of human adjudication. Our identification with the altar of Calvary is to become a living sacrifice that recognizes that the killing of Jesus was indeed our killing as well. His death ended humanity's abject poverty and disenfranchisement from divine things, and one another.

THE NEW COVENANT AND THE SERMON ON THE MOUNT

Jesus' death inaugurated the New Covenant, which provides a new kind of justice. His baptism by John was a precursory statement ending the Old Covenant, preempting the New. Most of what we see in the Gospels, although positioned in the New Testament, is the ending of the Old Covenant. The prelude to New Covenant theology begins with Jesus teaching what has been called the Sermon on the Mount. The setting is a multitudinous gathering, with people expecting something from this amazing teacher. He reveals the heart of the heavenly Father and sets the stage to train His pupils who will serve as the next-generation movers and shakers.

We must understand that this message isn't some legalistic manifesto, improving upon what the Sinai law could not do. Also, it isn't particularly a new kind of morality that requires greater exertion of physical and mental efforts. It's the influx of glad tidings declaring a blessed state of Kingdom bliss built upon the foundation of God's grace. Jesus made it clear that the first requirement to experience this was an association with poverty, an emptiness in the soul that has absolutely nothing to flaunt. The recipient of Kingdom life is acquainted with grief—one knows suffering which produces a hunger and thirst for God. Despised and maligned, these ones are candidates for an experience with outrageous grace.

As I have read and reread Matthew 5–7, I'm still amazed at the characteristics of this new justice and its administration. It isn't a system of shortcuts, exploitation, retribution, and bashing your enemies; instead, it is one of taking the initiative to love unconditionally and sacrificially. Everything about it rebukes the spirits of injustice and disenfranchisement. Humanly speaking, it is impossible to keep, unless Jesus removes one from the throne of his or her heart! This justice doesn't exist within the framework of human decency; it is very dependent upon a sovereign work of grace.

When God appeared in Jesus Christ, the earth was presented with the prototype of God's justice and justice Man. Jesus mingled with many disenfranchised people of His day: lepers, adulteresses, and tax collectors to name a few. He acquainted Himself with their emotional and physical pain, their shame, and society's disdain. Basically, Christ was everything to them the religious mind thought He shouldn't be. Christ didn't walk around with some halo shrouding Him, attracting the affluent, the admired, or the academic. No, in fact, most of that crowd tried to disenfranchise Him. They falsely accused Him of functioning by the spirit of Beelzebub, and being the son of fornication (see Mk. 3:22; Jn. 8:41). He was a marvelous illustration of what it means to be salt and light. Jesus lives today, by the Holy Spirit, in His Body—the Church. The Creator's justice actively works in us because of that. We now stand within the framework of a justice that has no human pedigree, no human rights, and no reason to oppose anyone. Our reason for existence is to be living manifestations of God's love embodied.

Let me tell you why you are here. You're here to be salt-seasoning that brings out the God-flavors of this earth. If you lose your saltiness, how will people taste godliness? You've lost your usefulness and will end up in the garbage. Here's another way to put it: You're here to be light, bringing out the God-colors in the world. God is not a secret to be kept. We're going public with this, as public as a city on a hill. If I make you light-bearers, you don't think I'm going to hide you under a bucket, do you? I'm putting you on a light stand. Now that I've put you there on a hilltop, on a light stand—shine! Keep open house; be generous with your lives. By opening up to others, you'll prompt people to open up with God, this generous Father in heaven (Matthew 5:13-16 The Message).

As stated, when Jesus was in the world, He was the salt and light of the world. As salt, He kept and preserved those whom the Father had given Him (see Jn. 17:12). As light, He dispelled darkness and revealed the glorious life of the Father (see Jn 9:5). Just as the heavenly Father identified Israel as a kingdom of priests, a holy nation, and a peculiar people, Jesus identified Kingdom citizens as salt, light, and a city. These aren't metaphors the Church chose; they're declarations of the Master helping His disciples to visualize their new mission. Each of these words speaks to an aspect of the Church's ministry to society, particularly when it comes to breaking the spirit of disenfranchisement.

Our life of love allows us to light all men, flavor all men, and incorporate all men into the culture of a Kingdom society without prejudice. We build community, flowing from the Spirit of God, independent of human strength. Our labors are congruous with the spirit of life rather than the law of sin and death. Our heavenly Father accomplishes through us what we cannot accomplish in our own strength. Perhaps because salt is less noticeable in human experience today than in the past, people fail to understand this illustration fully. Growing up in a fishing community, I watched my parents salt fish to preserve them. The salt accomplished its purpose by consuming itself. As salt, we give our lives for the Kingdom of God with great joy, knowing we are spending ourselves as a drink offering for King Jesus. We're commanded to shine as lights in the midst of a crooked and perverse generation (see Phil. 2:15). Selfless devotion given in love is the proliferation and essence of the Kingdom of God. Such love is the preservation, flavor, and coloration of society.

The Sermon on the Mount is grasped only where people heartily declare Jesus Christ as Lord. Its message is planted as seed into the hearts of Kingdom citizens. It isn't a message of fantasy or madness; it's a message of death to the spirit and operations of death itself. Because it is a message authenticated by the resurrection of Jesus Christ from the dead, it is a clarion of victory over every human weakness. Seeds, or principles of the Kingdom, enter the heart. When the condition of the soil (heart) is right, they must by law reproduce themselves into good fruit—fruit that remains. Immediately, one discovers the principles Jesus taught are the mortal enemies to things like hatred, murder, lust, adultery, hypocrisy, anxiety, and false judgments. For example, He wanted men to know the heart can be corrupted by lust even quicker than the body. Legalism could no longer mask and hibernate heart failures. The Sermon on the Mount was God's grace provision for maturation.

> *In a word, what I'm saying is, Grow up. You're kingdom subjects. Now live like it. Live out your God-created identity. Live generously and graciously toward others, the way God lives toward you* (Matthew 5:48 The Message).

The Sermon on the Mount helps us to understand that this world isn't a stage, a place for commanding attention and applauding spiritual theatrics. This world is our domain to live our God-created lives. The Message says, *"A pretentious, showy life is an empty life; a plain and simple life is a full life"* (Prov. 13:7). Our lives are full when we can show love tempered with tenderness or toughness when necessary. Demonstrating compassion and mercy have nothing to do with whether someone notices. Prayer and fasting have even less to do with formulas, specific techniques, platforms, and programs. When we read the simple instructions Jesus gave, we realize many Christians would fit into a category that lacks specific Kingdom intelligence. I challenge all adults to listen to the tender heart of your child or grandchild when he or she prays. Believe me! You will hear the beautiful heart of how to properly approach God. I'll never forget the time Father God challenged me to listen to my son pray. In his wonderful, simplistic way, he said: "Lord, it's me again, Stevie!" This moment left such a profound impression on me because immediately the Father spoke into my spirit, "This is how you should pray!"

I had to admit that I had been praying religiously for years, thinking my efforts and high-powered language pleased my heavenly Father. The Father is never impressed with all the adjectives we place before His name—highfalutin and high-powered words, which many times do not reflect our broken hearts. There is something excessively rich and wholesome about saying, *"Our Father,"* knowing you have the undivided attention of Father God. I call this the Father and His child sharing private moments. The history of God is that He creates quietly and unobtrusively, whether in the hearts of humans or in the world. Hoping for stardom may be a politically correct desire in the postmodern world; however, it has no place in the Kingdom of God. Because God expresses genuine love for His children, we may simply and honestly manage our lives without role-playing. Kingdom justice dismisses that which is loud and conspicuous.

The Sermon on the Mount births a new attitude of trust. These words from Proverbs appropriately capture the overview of that trust: *"Trust God from the bottom of your heart; don't try to figure out everything on your own. Listen for God's voice in everything you do, everywhere you go; He's the one who will keep you on track"* (Proverbs 3:5-6 The Message). Webster's II defines trust as "total confidence in the integrity, ability, and good character of another."[8] It may be a shocker to people, but God can be trusted: It is impossible for Him to deceive! We question things because we don't see everything from God's perspective. The foundation of all trust is truth. Jesus Christ said, *"I am the way, the truth, and the life"* (Jn. 14:6). He doesn't just speak truth—He is truth! If we accept that Jesus is God, then it is inconceivable or impossible for Him to lie; and He can be trusted. One lie would totally disintegrate His person; it would abolish the existence of God.

Trust allows one to never give up on God or the promises of God. It keeps us running toward Him at all times. We become focused on the unseen—the eternal rather than the temporal. Many great thinkers understood how important truth was in providing a firm basis for trust. Listen to their powerful convictions as they provide fresh insights for us today:

"Truth is always the strongest argument."

- Sophocles[9]

"Truth is the highest thing that man can keep."

- Geoffrey Chaucer[10]

"No pleasure is comparable to standing upon the vantage ground of truth."

- Francis Bacon[11]

"There is nothing so powerful as truth—and often nothing so strange."

- Daniel Webster[12]

"Keep one thing forever in view—the truth; and if you do this, though it may seem to lead you away from the opinion of men, it will assuredly conduct you to the throne of God."

- Horace Mann[13]

Jesus made it clear that we must trust the reliability of the Father when it comes to our future. The truth is: God holds every person's future! God has no desire to abort His own expectation in our lives, which has a future dynamic. Expectation is the umbilical cord that keeps us attached to God when the natural mind begins to chip away at hope through the means of reason. The place in which this thought is most dramatic, particularly in aged men, is in the area of wealth. Accumulating wealth isn't the final answer; it's just a tool to get Kingdom business accomplished. Many Christians have bought into the myth that the more money or net worth one possesses, the more secure one is. That is only a myth because wealth can be lost instantaneously due to any number of reasons. We must not sacrifice treasure in Heaven just to build a treasure chest on earth. The size of our bank account, stock portfolio, or retirement fund in no way determines whether or not we trust our Father either.

Unfortunately, many servants of God have spent lifetimes planning and investing only to leave their small fortunes to someone else. Jesus commanded us to consider the birds and flowers if we dared contemplate total trust. The message in this Sermon will transform our fears into courage, our doubts into liberating faith. Trusting God turns man from a predator, attempting to make a way for himself, while wholeheartedly disenfranchising others. After exhausting many failed, independent methods, the burden of wasted creativity usually breaks people down, creating a cesspool of remorse and vulnerability.

If we choose to do things in our own strength, the best we'll ever reap is a heap of ruins. Father God has promised us deliverance, protection, and enlargement. Seeking the Kingdom first is like walking through an open door, from a garden of herbs to a vast, unlimited Promised Land.

Jesus concluded the Sermon on the Mount by talking about how we build our lives. Do we build with a lamb-like nature, or a wolf nature? Are we going to be childlike in our disposition, or grabbing, grasping, and gluttonous in will and desire? One constitutes a wise, intelligent builder versus a foolish or uninformed builder. The Spirit of God provides new building materials (principles of the Kingdom) in order to transform our unredeemed predatory natures into Kingdom building materials. God is building a new justice order in the earth. The foundation of this order is being carefully laid into the lives of His children. The superstructure, the full formation of the Kingdom, cannot be built until the foundation is laid, appraised, and approved.

I worked in construction during my early adult years. It gave me an appreciation for building things correctly, following plans carefully. Inspectors insisted that all shoddy work be reworked. One would lose precious time and money by doing this. When a Kingdom house is in the preparatory stages to be built, wisdom says, "Read the plans!" We must first dig deeply and remove all field dirt between the Rock and ourselves. Jesus Christ is the Rock—and a confession of Him based on the revelation of His true identity is essential. The heavenly Father must give us this revelation. Flesh and blood, which equates to natural understanding, cannot. It is after we have masterfully laid the foundation that the Father issues a building permit. Otherwise, He will red-flag the foundation and require it to be redone.

Since it is God's justice system, only He can honor His plans. This plan is held in trust by the builders the Father gives to the Church. It is very important that the Church convene from time to time to listen to God's commissioned team of architects who possess spiritual intelligence in Kingdom building. They are the ministries of Ephesians 4:11, supervising and overseeing the new order. Convocations are reprieves, reconnecting seasons. Their purpose is to provide a truth continuum throughout the generations of God's children. The house being built is in the name of our King. If it doesn't reflect Him, He'll burn it with a fiery word of loving correction.

The Sermon on the Mount sets a clear criterion to the degree that after reading and studying it, one cannot come away with haphazard conclusions. Our humanity desperately needs an inoculation of God's grace. The carnal tree produces mixed fruit—sometimes good, and other times evil. As we repent and receive grace to stand, we start to eat from another tree—the tree of life. The fruit on this tree is love—the same fruit of the Spirit (see Gal. 5:22). Love is a wonderful treasure. Out of it evolves a life of health, productivity, and longevity. We emerge a culture of freewill givers, releasing the abiding presence of the Lord, triggering the revelation of His glory. The Message says, *"Give away your life; you'll find life given back, but not merely given back—given back with bonus and blessing. Giving, not getting, is the way. Generosity begets generosity"* (Lk. 6:38). What more can an alternate society become? Disenfranchisement will receive its death when God's children responsibly walk the high road of love nurtured by grace. Remember, the entire creation is waiting. Global warming, deforestation, acid rain, nuclear proliferation, terrorism, substance abuse and drug addiction, disease, domestic violence, and hurting human beings in general are all symptomatic of a waiting creation. We all are waiting for the glorious liberty of the children of God (see Rom. 8:19-21).

Jesus raised the bar in the Sermon on the Mount; the Kingdom water level was elevated. In Christ, the Father finally exposed the criterion to make righteous judgments to the nth degree. Jesus judged death, disease, poverty, and the principle of sin, the sin nature, the world system, and everything that evolved out of Adam's mistake. He contrasted what He said to what was said in previous generations (see Mt. 5:21-22). What Jesus said superseded anything spoken before; it spanned every human dispensation. Whether you're speaking first century or postmodern, the words of Jesus covered all eras. Father God had enough foresight to see the plenitude of lingering human problems. Therefore, the Sermon on the Mount tackles every major relational issue.

What most people haven't understood is that Kingdom culture isn't the same as the cultures created by carnal human beings. There is one message Father God has for all subjects, regardless of where they reside: "Come out from among her, My people!" When nations are brought into the Kingdom, "nations" is not referring to churchy Americanism, Europeanism, or Asianism. Each continent consists of diversified cultures that must be absorbed into the Kingdom of God. Democracy isn't Kingdom: it's a human government form for and by the people. Though it's the best of most human systems, it still pales in comparison to Kingdom government. Total victory over disenfranchisement is only in the Kingdom of God. The final issue is: Will the Church everywhere release the Kingdom as God's final solution? The Sermon on the Mount is the ammo that arms us with God's grace message to make a difference. Let us arise and become the gallant new world of the Kingdom we are!

ENDNOTES

1. Webster's II New College Dictionary, Riverside University dictionary (New York: Houghton Mifflin Company, 1995), 698.

2. Geoffrey W. Bromiley, *Theological Dictionary of the New Testament* (Grand Rapids, MI: William B. Eerdmans Publishing Company, 1985), 791.

3. Ibid., 259.

4. Ibid.

5. John R. Kohlenberger, *The Expanded Vine's Expository Dictionary of New Testament Words, A Special Edition* (Minneapolis, MN: Bethany House Publishers, 1984), 613.

6. Webster's II, 381.

7. Kohlenberger, 565.

8. Webster's II, 1184.

9. Virginia Ely, I Quote (New York: George W. Stewart Publishers, Inc., 1947), 339.

10. Ibid.

11. Ibid.

12. Ibid, 340.

13. Ibid, 341.

THE SOUND THAT CHANGED EVERYTHING

There are many sounds in the Body of Christ—some resonate well and others create discord. The Sound that Changed Everything describes the sound created by a "united, corporate people" ministering out of passion for Jesus. It is a clear trumpet call urging the Church to return to the simplicity of Jesus.

ISBN 0-7684-3011-9

Pantumplas   Pijamas: sock: x large
Dial or no dial ← Melanie
Gurming mama:

D gaone ← Indiana Jones
    2 nены

Loma Señida # 62
Fracc. Bonanza: 58090

   hur

Luz Nabarro y camino 103

Inf Los Girales: